NEITHER JEW NOR GREEK?

NEITHER JEW NOR GREEK?

Constructing Early Christianity

JUDITH LIEU

t&t clark

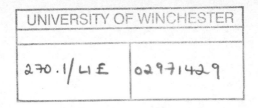
Published by T&T Clark International
A Continuum imprint
The Tower Building, 11 York Road, London SE1 7NX
15 East 26th Street, Suite 1703, New York, NY 10010

www.tandtclark.com

Copyright © T&T Clark Ltd, 2002
First published 2002 in the Studies of the New Testament and Its World series
This impression printed 2005

British Library Cataloguing-in-Publication Data
A catalogue record for this book is available from the British Library

ISBN 0567083268 (paperback)

Typeset by Waverley Typesetters, Galashiels
Printed on acid-free paper in Great Britain by The Bath Press, Bath

Contents

Part IV
The Shaping of Early 'Christian' Identity

Preface

These essays, written over the last twelve years, trace a number of journeys in dialogue. First of all, they trace my own journey of exploration in a subject of growing interest in scholarly debate, the origins of early Christianity, particularly within and out of its Jewish matrix. That journey has taken me through the texts of Judaism, of Christianity, and of the Graeco-Roman world, but also through modern scholarship on the issue, and, more recently, scholarship on the 'construction' of identity. Yet there is also the dialogue that I am convinced continued between 'Judaism' and 'Christianity' as they emerged as identifiable traditions; a dialogue, perhaps sometimes more visible as conflict and repudiation, that was conducted both in social experience, sometimes called 'real life', and through texts. Yet, endeavouring to listen to the past must also be the seed of continuing dialogue as we come to understand ourselves and 'the other' more clearly, particularly as we reflect on centuries of negation of dialogue, and their tragic consequences.

I am grateful for the opportunity to bring these essays together, and particularly grateful to John Barclay, as one of the editors of *Studies in the New Testament and Its World*, for the initial suggestion to do so, as well as to his fellow editors, John Riches and Joel Marcus, for their encouragement and advice. Once again, I would also like to thank Dr Geoffrey Green of T&T Clark for his support. Through the years I have had many dialogue partners, whether or not they always realized it, particularly colleagues and students at King's College London and at Macquarie University, as well as the audiences of some of these papers; some are visible in the footnotes of these papers, others perhaps less so, but I am indebted to them all. The initial footnote to each paper acknowledges its first appearance in print, and in several cases, in oral presentation. Those acknowledgements must serve to express my deep gratitude. In particular, while none of them directly addresses contemporary Jewish–Christian dialogue, they are offered as a contribution to it, and are an opportunity to acknowledge what I have learned from many dialogue partners in lay as well as in academic settings.

Abbreviations

AJA	*American Journal of Archaeology*
AJSR	*Association for Jewish Studies Review*
ANRW	*Aufstieg und Niedergang der römischen Welt*
BETL	Bibliotheca ephemeridum theologicarum lovaniensium
BHTh	Beiträge zur historischen Theologie
BIS	Biblical Interpretation Series
BJRL	*Bulletin of the John Rylands University Library of Manchester*
BJS	Brown Judaic Studies
BNTC	Black's New Testament Commentaries
BZAW	Beiheft zur Zeitschrift für die alttestamentliche Wissenschaft
BZNW	Beiheft zur Zeitschrift für die neutestamentliche Wissenschaft
CB.NTSer	Coniectanea Biblica New Testament Series
CBQ	*Catholic Biblical Quarterly*
CBQ.MS	*Catholic Biblical Quarterly* Monograph Series
ET	English translation
GNB	Good News Bible
HTR	*Harvard Theological Review*
HUCA	*Hebrew Union College Annual*
JbAC	*Jahrbuch für Antike und Christentum*
JBL	*Journal of Biblical Literature*
JBTh	*Jahrbuch für biblische Theologie*
JECS	*Journal of Early Christian Studies*
JFSR	*Journal for Feminist Research in Religion*
JJS	*Journal of Jewish Studies*

JQR	*Jewish Quarterly Review*
JRS	*Journal of Roman Studies*
JSJ	*Journal for the Study of Judaism in the Persian, Hellenistic and Roman Period*
JSNT	*Journal for the Study of the New Testament*
JSNT.SS	JSNT Supplement Series
JSOT.SS	Journal for the Study of the Old Testament Supplement Series
JSS.M	*Journal of Semitic Studies* Monograph
JSSR	*Journal for the Scientific Study of Religion*
JTS	*Journal of Theological Studies*
MBTh	Münsterische Beiträge zur Theologie
NCB	New Century Bible
NIV	New International Version
NRSV	New Revised Standard Version
NT.S	*Novum Testamentum* Supplement
NTS	*New Testament Studies*
OECT	Oxford Early Christian Texts
OTL	Old Testament Library
PL	Patrologia Latina
PMS	Patristic Monograph Series
PTS	Patristische Texte und Studien
RAC	*Reallexikon für Antike und Christentum*
REB	Revised English Bible
Rech.Aug	*Récherches Augustiniennes*
RevBib	*Revue Biblique*
RSR	*Revue des sciences religeuses*
SBL	Society of Biblical Literature
SC	Sources Chrétiennes
SJOT	*Scandinavian Journal of the Old Testament*
SNTS.MS	Society for New Testament Studies Monograph Series
SPB	Studia Post-Biblica
SR	*Studies in religion / Sciences religeuses*
TAPA	*Transactions of the American Philological Association*
TDNT	*Theological Dictionary of the New Testament*, ed. G. Kittel (ET ed. G. W. Bromiley)

ThQ	*Theologische Quartalschrift*
TRE	*Theologische Realenzyklopädie*
TSAJ	Texte und Studien zum Antiken Judentum
TU	*Texte und Untersuchungen*
VC	*Vigiliae Christianae*
WUNT	Wissenschaftliche Untersuchungen zum Neuen Testament
ZDMG	*Zeitschrift für die deutsche morgenlandische Gesellschaft*
ZKG	*Zeitschrift für Kirchengeschichte*
ZNW	*Zeitschrift für die neutestamentliche Wissenschaft*
ZPE	*Zeitschrift für Papyrologie und Epigraphik*

Introduction: Neither Jew nor Greek? Constructing Early Christianity

When did 'Christianity' first appear? A simple enough question, but one that will permit no simple answer. The words of Paul echoed in the title of this volume, 'Neither Jew nor Greek' (Gal. 3.28; cf. Col. 3.11), might suggest that a sense of distinctiveness, something without analogy or precedent, was already there, in if not before his preaching. Of course, Paul does not use the term 'Christianity' or 'Christian', and his words invite considerably more reflection and interpretation than a first-time reader may have supposed. Here two further questions will help refine the one with which we started. Was early Christianity really a 'new creation', without precedent, its relationship with its wider world characterized only negatively, by what it was not? Did Paul and those who received his letters really think of themselves as neither Jews nor Greeks, and would they have been right to do so? Sometimes in the past those seeking to write the story of early Christianity have, implicitly if not explicitly, answered all these questions affirmatively. In recent study it has become ever more impossible to do so. Paul wrote in Greek, and for long after him the majority of those whom we might label Christians and about whom we know something, would have used Greek. So too would many Jews, certainly the majority of those living outside the Land of Israel, who, numerically, represented the overall majority of Jews in this period. This is not just an observation about language, for it would be easy to object that 'Greek' means much more than 'Greek-speaking'; it also points to the continuities of culture and world-view in what will here often be labelled 'the Graeco-Roman world', continuities within which undoubted differences were also experienced and expressed. In recent study, debates about 'Judaism and Hellenism' have come to be expressed not in terms of opposition and negation so much as in terms of trying to plot continuities and discontinuities. The same must be true as we try to understand how early Christianity also emerges as a recognizable way of interpreting the world and life.

The continuities and discontinuities with what we label 'Judaism' are no less complex. Again, some of the most important insights into the nature of 'early Christianity' in recent study have arisen out of a recognition of its Jewishness; continuities provide the framework within which discontinuity can be explored. Growing awareness of the rich variety of 'Judaism' at the end of the Second Temple period, an awareness fuelled by discoveries such as that of the Dead Sea Scrolls but also by renewed interest in literature other than that of developing rabbinic Judaism, has made it possible to locate the early 'Christians' within that diversity. Yet a consequence has been that it becomes more difficult to understand why, how, and when, 'Christians' could no longer be located there, in their own self-understanding or in that of others, or – and this is an important distinction – in that of the scholars who describe them. Christianity, as it came to be called, was born out of Judaism, and has always seen itself, rightly, as in continuity with its Jewish past, and yet the on-going history of the two faiths frequently has been one of suspicion and conflict.

Awareness, particularly by scholars from the Christian tradition, of the long legacy of that suspicion, of what, for all the debates it provokes, may be labelled Christian anti-Semitism, has impelled new attempts to understand not just how and why Christianity emerged as a separate religious tradition from Judaism, but why that separation was accompanied by such negative, even vitriolic, and often caricaturing, language and images. For this reason, several of these essays will suggest that the historian's task is not neutral: we have a responsibility to the present and to the future as well as to the past.

The questions we have been asking have been about people, and the way they have viewed themselves and others. In some cases we are able to answer those questions from epigraphic or archaeological sources, or from anecdotal evidence; several of these essays do appeal to such sources, particularly where they may suggest a picture different from that of literary sources. Yet, it is of the nature of both traditions, Judaism and Christianity, that we encounter them for the most part through literary texts. It is not simply that these texts are the sources for accessing the people behind them: often they may be seeking to represent a position that would not have been visible or persuasive to all those concerned; sometimes, as recent study has increasingly emphasized, they may be masking or silencing other voices, which we now may want to recover. Moreover, the texts do not simply reflect a 'history' going on independently of them, they are themselves part of the process by which Judaism or Christianity came into being. For it was through literature that the ideas were formulated, a self-understanding shaped and articulated, and then mediated to and appropriated by others, and through literature that people and ideas were included or excluded. What the texts were doing is sometimes as, if not more, important than what they were saying. In this way, the second part of the title, 'constructing early Christianity', refers not only to the historian's task in trying to understand the past, but also to the process by which, particularly through literary texts, early Christianity acquired its identity.

Although these essays cluster around a common theme, they were conceived independently and not as part of a consistent argument: a collection of essays inevitably will reflect the idiosyncrasies of the author and her research more than does a monograph. For this reason they have not been updated substantially, for to do so might involve writing something quite different. However, the opportunity has been taken for the correction of minor errors, for indicating cross-references between them, and for some acknowledgement of subsequent work in the form of Bibliographical notes, or supplements to the footnotes. They are not printed in order of publication, for I have not changed my mind so substantially as to leave some behind, nor is it necessary for the reader to know their sequence in order to understand them. Neither is there a separate conclusion: the essays raise questions and offer reflections on methods as well as on the reading of the 'evidence'; frequently they are more concerned to suggest that things may not have been so straightforward as ancient or modern writers imply. If they lead to more questions rather than to certain conclusions, they have served their purpose.

Rather than following any chronological sequence the essays are grouped thematically, while also reflecting a development from a more historical set of questions to a greater emphasis on literary representation – although both historical questions and a sense of rhetorical construction in the sources are present throughout. The first part, 'Disappearing Boundaries', focuses particularly on models in the historical reconstruction of early 'Jewish' and 'Christian' separation and interaction. The model which has become dominant in recent discussion is one of a parting of two 'ways' which shared a common origin. Reflecting broader developments in scholarship, this model emphasizes the multiformity of 'Judaism' at the end of the Second Temple period; it is out of this variety that there emerge two separate paths, one of which eventuates in rabbinic Judaism and the other which leads to 'Christianity'. Expressed in terms of particular historical details, this model also gives a significant place to those potentials within late Second Temple Judaism which would flower in Christianity: prominent here are those Gentiles who were already attracted to 'the Synagogue' by the Jewish Scriptures and ethos, the so-called 'God-fearers'; they, it is commonly argued, would have provided a ready audience for the Christian law-free Gospel, and constituted a bridge for its spread into the 'pagan' world. The first essay explores, and to some extent questions, this model of a 'parting of the ways', demonstrating that as a model it, as much as any other, including the more triumphalist one it superseded, is not 'value-free' theologically; it embodies a particular agenda for the interpreter, and, moreover, may imply a precision which obscures the complexity of the data it seeks to interpret. The following two essays on 'the God-fearers', first, show how our sources do not substantially support the common current picture, and, secondly, that the epithet which has been hijacked for this hypothetical group played a very important rhetorical role within the self-presentation of both Jews and Christians within the Graeco-Roman world, and so points to their continuing interaction. The final essay, which was presented as a paper to a wider audience and so lacks extensive footnoting, returns to listen again to the Christian texts, asking why it is that they would hardly recognize the parting ways or the shared market-places which are assumed by modern reconstructions. Therefore, this section points to the continuing 'fuzziness' of boundaries between the different groups in the emergence of early Christianity out of its 'Jewish' past; at the same time it shows how both the early texts and modern 'historical' reconstructions which draw on them are indebted, consciously or not, to ideological or 'theological' frameworks, and serve similar ideological or theological ends; they are 'rhetorical' – in a non-technical sense – constructions.

Alongside the 'God-fearers', and sometimes included among them, women have attracted particular attention in reconstructions, both modern and ancient, of the spread of Christianity. On the one hand, there is a significant number of inscriptional texts which refer to women who converted to Judaism. On the other, for some interpreters, women are the paradigm of the marginalized who found in 'the Christian Gospel' acceptance and recognition of their equal standing (at least before God), and, it is often assumed, who therefore joined the new movement in significant numbers. So understood, such women have been presented as demonstrating the superiority of Christianity over the exclusivism supposedly inherent in Judaism: this is the attraction of their attraction in the double-meaning of the title of the first essay in Part II. The paper explores the evidence cited in such reconstructions, in the light of attitudes to 'women and religion' in the ancient world. In doing this it offers a reminder of something that has become familiar more generally in recent gender analysis, that what we read in the ancient texts – as well, often, as in their more recent expositors – is men talking about women, or men 'using women to think'; a reminder, therefore, that we cannot take ancient (or modern) claims about the presence and role of women as impartial data, but have to ask the agenda or 'politics' of the discourse. The second essay in this Part addresses this problem of gendered discourse from a different angle: a key expression of the revolutionary Christian 'inclusion' of women has often been found in the rejection of the male-specific rite of circumcision, and in the (potential) egalitarianism of Gal. 3.28, a verse which has become something of a *shibboleth* in feminist analysis of early Christianity. Yet as both these essays, and any historical analysis, has to recognize, 'Christianity', no less than 'Judaism', has been very ambivalent for women. So how, or how far, does each tradition, in its historical context, consider women as 'included', and how far can contemporary and ancient agenda intersect?

The essays in the first two parts have been engaged in listening to the texts and in discerning their agenda while seeking to be able to use them to answer historical questions. Certainly, recognition of their own agenda warns against simply reading the social or historical 'realia' off the sources. Moreover, since the extensive rabbinic corpus has little interest in directly addressing or countering Christianity, the available sources are for the most part 'Christian'. As has been increasingly demonstrated in recent discussion, Christian authors also 'use Jews to think with'; polemic against or about the Jews in Christian texts regularly in practice addresses a range of issues, pastoral as well as theological, more often internal than external. Yet the older view that in the majority of cases, at least after the first century, Christian authors had little contact with 'real' Jews has given way in much recent study to one envisaging continuing contact and interaction on a range of levels, both conceptual and personal. Starting with an exploration of this phenomenon, the essays in Part III focus on early Christian sources and issues, both to listen to their agenda, and to read between the lines or to counter-read, in order to understand what might have been going on and how the Jews figured in the real as well as in the thought world of these texts. What emerges particularly strongly is the formative effect of Scripture in shaping their perceptions of the Jews; sometimes this may make the actual events almost irretrievable, as in Christian claims that Jews were involved in the persecution they suffered. The final essay in this section centres on a particularly influential text in developing Christian ideas about themselves and about 'Judaism', Deuteronomy 21.23. It shows how such later ideas have then been read back into the text, even in modern translations and interpretation, and argues for the importance not only of being aware of this, but also of recognizing and of listening to other readings. Just as the shared Scriptures became a source of differentiation, so, perhaps, they may now become a basis for dialogue.

The final three essays turn explicitly to a theme which has been implicit from the start. Christianity, or the sense of being a Christian, is something that we, as modern interpreters, read back into the past, sometimes to very early in the period covered by the New Testament. Yet Christian 'identity' is not something which appears clearly as such at a given moment; in one sense it emerges through the centuries in ways which are difficult to plot clearly; in another sense, we impose it on a range of texts and ideas, creating some idea of unity out of their rich diversity. How did early Christian writers, like their Jewish peers, find ways of inscribing their sense of who they were as part of and yet also as separate within the complexities of the Graeco-Roman world? How were they perceived by others as similar and as different, from each other and from others? In using the label 'Christian' where it does not appear in the sources, how far are we imposing a false sense of unity and of difference? These are pertinent questions, for debates about the nature and construction of identity in the ancient as well as in the modern world are now pervasive in scholarly discourse.

These essays can only begin to explore some of the complexities both in the texts and in the ways we talk about them as sources of the sense of Christian identity. Three themes emerge particularly clearly from these explorations. First, the strong lines of continuity with Jewish experience in Christian self-understanding, even when there appears to be discontinuity. Secondly, that for the developing self-understanding of both Jews and Christians there are also continuities as well as discontinuities with the surrounding Graeco-Roman 'pagan' world: it is not just that we cannot understand Christianity or Judaism apart from that world, but that we must see that world, of which they were a part, as a dynamic whole. The third theme is, once again, the primacy of literature in the formation of both Christian and Jewish identity, not merely as constituting our major sources but also as making both traditions what they were. Each essay approaches the topic from a different angle, just as each was given originally in a different, specific, context. The first, which was my first move into the area, uses a specific text, the *Letter to Diognetus*, as a window through which to view some of the issues, asking how far the assertion of Christian distinctiveness could be sustained. The second, given as an inaugural lecture upon taking up the Chair of New Testament Studies in the University of London, explores the shifting boundaries that we encounter even when we are seeking to understand the apparent facticity of 'the New Testament' (the title of the chair), which is often seen as the foundation of Christian identity. Yet, as the final essay acknowledges, it is through a readiness to die for it that identity is particularly clearly affirmed; this has become a characteristic element in Christian self-understanding, and the manifold ways it was achieved through textual accounts of martyrdom once again remind us both of how literary representation impresses itself as experience, but here also of the clear patterns of similarity with as well as of difference from Jewish experience, once again within the broader context of Graeco-Roman values and society.

The rich complexity of what we call 'early Christianity', and the fluidity of the boundaries which separate it from what it was not, mean that these essays do not give a single account of its birth. They, rather, demonstrate its elusiveness, and so seek also to demonstrate the fragility of confident descriptions of what made 'early Christianity' 'Christian'. As already noted, they offer historical questions, if not answers, at the same time as reminding us that our texts, ancient and modern, are engaged in persuading as much as in informing. Yet, in different ways, one theme keeps re-emerging: certainly it becomes clear that we cannot speak of early Christianity without speaking of 'early Judaism'; yet, equally clearly, 'identity' derives from a sense of givenness and immutability, and too frequently leads to the demonizing of the excluded 'Other' – as has so often happened in the history of Christian attitudes to 'the Jews'. If this is so, then the discovery of actual instability and conditionality may engender more creative dialogue: we are recalled to the multiple responsibilities of our interpretative, historical or theological, task.

Part I

Disappearing Boundaries

2

'The Parting of the Ways':
Theological Construct or Historical Reality?*

There is no need to interpret the image of 'the parting of the ways'; in recent years the metaphor has become a convenient shorthand for speaking of the separation between Judaism and Christianity understood not as a T-junction but as a Y-junction – two channels separating from a common source. University course units are so titled; J. D. G. Dunn beat his rivals to the winning post by publishing a book under that title, and, judging by the footnotes, even hoped to gain the authority of two witnesses with a second volume of which he was editor with the same title, a volume which in fact appeared under the title *Jews and Christians*.[1] It is not clear when this metaphor first began to be used in modern study, although an anticipation of it is to be found in the title of Foakes-Jackson's collection of essays *The Parting of the Roads*;[2] it does not, as far as I can see, appear in Marcel Simon's seminal *Verus Israel*, first published in 1948, which prefers to speak more neutrally of separation, and even talks of the church 'having seceded from Judaism with the object of supplanting it'.[3] By now the model appears to have become a truism which needs no justification.

However, that the image is by no means self-evident quickly becomes clear; indeed to speak of the separation between the two religious systems

* First published in *JSNT* 56 (1994) 101–19. Reprinted by permission of Sheffield Academic Press.

---

1 J. D. G. Dunn, *The Partings of the Ways* (SCM Press: London/ Trinity Press International: Philadelphia, 1991); idem, ed., *Jews and Christians: The Parting of the Ways AD 70 to 135* (WUNT 66, Mohr: Tübingen, 1992).
2 F. J. Foakes Jackson, ed., *The Parting of the Roads: Studies in the Development of Judaism and Early Christianity* (Arnold: London, 1912). I am grateful to Professor G. N. Stanton for this reference. However, the essays do not seriously tackle our question, while the Introduction by W. R. Inge echoes the denigration of Judaism typical of the period.
3 M. Simon, *Verus Israel* (ET Littman Library, Oxford University Press: Oxford, 1986) xiii.

in these terms is a very modern perception. To quote Adolf Harnack is not to suggest that the battles against his model still need refuting – to successfully achieve that was the major contribution of Simon; rather, Harnack illustrates well the possibility of an entirely different perception. In his 'historical' study of the *Expansion of Early Christianity* he writes:

> Such an injustice as that inflicted by the Gentile Church on Judaism is almost unprecedented in the annals of history. The Gentile Church stripped it of everything; she took away its sacred book; herself but a transformation of Judaism, she cut off all connection with the parent religion. The daughter first robbed her mother and then repudiated her! But, one may ask, is this view really correct? Undoubtedly it is, to some extent, and it is perhaps impossible to force anyone to give it up. But viewed from a higher stand-point, the facts acquire a different complexion. By their rejection of Jesus, the Jewish people disowned their calling and dealt the death blow to their own existence.[4]

One wonders on what level Harnack really believed, despite surely much evidence to the contrary, that Judaism had received a self-inflicted mortal blow eighteen hundred years earlier? Again:

> the place of the Jews was taken by the Christians as the new People, who appropriated the whole tradition of Judaism, giving a fresh interpretation to any unserviceable materials in it, or else allowing them to drop . . . Christians established themselves in the strongholds hitherto occupied by Jewish propaganda and Jewish proselytes. Japhet occupied the tents of Shem, and Shem had to retire.[5]

Neither is such a perception a peculiarity of early twentieth-century Germany, as may be illustrated from W. H. C. Frend's magisterial *Rise of Christianity* : 'what direction Judaism would have taken without the coming of Jesus is anyone's guess' (p. 43) and again, 'the sub-apostolic era saw Judaism's last great effort to proselytize the Graeco-Roman world and its collapse amid the trammels of the law'.[6] If we are inclined to dismiss these perceptions, which could be readily multiplied, with a

---

[4] A. von Harnack, *The Expansion of Christianity in the First Three Centuries* (ET Williams & Norgate: London, 1904–5) I, 81.
[5] Harnack, *Expansion of Christianity*, I, 82–3.
[6] W. H. C. Frend, *The Rise of Christianity* (Darton, Longman & Todd: London, 1984) 126.

superior knowingness, it might be worth considering whether many recent church statements on Judaism and on the relation between the two faiths, and, even more, many of those who fill the pulpits and the pews would not find themselves considerably closer to Harnack than to Dunn. For them it was not a parting of the ways but a take over, a replacement leaving the rejected branch to wither and die.

It is, however, not just the modern church spokesperson who might find themself ill at ease with the current model. If we go back to the period that the metaphor is held to describe, we will find few if any who would speak of 'the parting of the ways'. Not surprisingly, voices from the Christian camp are in broad sympathy with Harnack, which tells us rather more about Harnack than it does about them! A much quoted example is Melito of Sardis in the second half of the second century in his homily *On the Pascha*, the Christian Passover. Melito explores the Christian redemption through a broadly typological understanding of the Exodus and Passover redemption. Exodus and Passover are, for him, rather like the architect's plan or model, or the artist's mental image – necessary and of value in its own time, but, once the reality which gave it its *raison d'être* is executed, redundant:

> The people was precious before the church arose and the law was marvellous before the Gospel was illuminated. But when the church arose and the Gospel came to the fore the model was made void giving its power to the truth and the law was fulfilled giving its power to the Gospel . . . So too the law was fulfilled when the Gospel was illuminated and the people made void when the church arose. (*Peri Pascha* 42–3)

The homily was discovered after the time of Harnack, but it would have suited him well. More violently Melito holds Israel responsible for the death of Jesus, and, because within his Christology Jesus is God, for the death of God: this invites the retort, 'in recompense for that you had to die' (90), and the triumphant declaration, 'you forsook the Lord so you were not found by him; you did not accept the Lord and so you were not pitied by him; you dashed down the Lord, you were dashed to the ground. And so you lie dead' (99). It has been said often enough – and with some reason – that the Israel whom Melito castigates is not the community down the road whom we would like to imagine comfortably revelling in their magnificent synagogue now exposed by the archaeologists – were it not two centuries too late – but the Israel of the Scriptures. Yet when he declares 'you lie dead' that is not only a

13

theological judgement (to which we shall return) but also, we must suspect, a historical or pseudo-historical one; it looks back on and interprets the failure and the consequences of the revolts against Rome in 66–70 and 132–4 CE.[7]

If we feel uncomfortable with Melito's passion we may prefer to turn to Justin Martyr. At the very beginning of his *Dialogue with Trypho* he sets out his agenda as being to establish that 'we are the true Israelite race, the spiritual one, that of Judah and Jacob and Abraham' (11.5). By the end, when Trypho incredulously grasps the full extent of Justin's assertion and asks, 'Are you Israel, and are all these (Scriptures) said about you?', Justin replies, 'We are both called and are in reality Jacob and Israel and Judah and Joseph and David and true children of God' (123.7, 9). In clever irony he takes the promise to Abraham of children as numerous as the sand on the beach, and applies it to the unbelieving Jews: they are like sand 'though vast and extensive, barren and fruitless' (120.2).[8]

All this is very familiar, and Justin and Melito are not quoted here to justify Harnack; rather the theological compulsion which drives them in the face of all evidence to the contrary – the vast and extensive diaspora, the Sardis synagogue – reveals Harnack equally not to be writing history but dogmatics. That has been pointed out enough times, and needs no more demonstration, although I shall want to return to it.

However, if Justin would not have spoken of a 'parting of the ways' neither would his opponent, the Jew Trypho. Here, we are going to listen not to his voice but to that of the Jew extensively quoted in the second century by Celsus in the *True Word*, assuming that Origen fulfils his promise to give a fair account of this. 'What was wrong with you, citizens, that you left the law of your fathers, and, being deluded by that man whom we were speaking of just now, were quite ludicrously deceived and have deserted us for another name and another life?' (Origen, *c. Celsum* II.1). The same insight is repeated in other words a little later: 'Why did you take your origin from our religion, and then, as if you are progressing in knowledge, despise these things, although you cannot name any other origin for your doctrine than our law?' (II.4). This then is not a 'parting of the ways' but apostasy

---

[7] On this see now J. M. Lieu, *Image and Reality: The Jews in the World of the Christians in the Second Century* (T&T Clark: Edinburgh, 1996) 199–240.
[8] See Lieu, *Image and Reality*, 103–53, esp., 136–7.

or desertion, a deliberate rejection and turning the back on truths inherited. It is a perception which is not difficult to defend, even now, and we should not be surprised that Celsus himself seemed convinced by it. He too accuses the Christians of deserting the practices of the Jews, which at least had antiquity and national custom in their favour (V.25):

> I will ask them where they have come from, or who is the author of their traditional laws. Nobody, they will say. In fact they themselves originated from Judaism, and they cannot name any other source for their teacher and chorus leader. Nevertheless they rebelled against the Jews. (V.33; cf. III.5, 'a revolt against the community led to the introduction of new ideas')

Celsus was not alone in seeing things in this light: 'the Christians are those who have deserted their ancestral ways and adopted the myths of the Jews, the enemies of humankind; at the same time they have deserted the God honoured by the Jews and his precepts.' That, in the third century, is the complaint of the great polemicist against the Christians, Porphyry, reported by Eusebius (*Praep.Ev.* I.2.3–4), this time targeting Christians from a pagan background. The Emperor Julian, perhaps not surprisingly, made the same complaint: 'they preferred the belief of the Jews to ours, and in addition they have not even remained firm to those but having abandoned them have turned to a way of their own' (*c.Galil.* 43A).

These views underline two fairly obvious points. The 'parting of the ways' is a model and only one among a number of possible models of the changing relationship between Judaism and Christianity in the first two centuries CE. It is not a model which would have made much sense to any of the participants or observers of the drama itself. That does not of course rule it out of court, although presumably we should always at least listen to the perceptions of the actors in a historical drama; it does invite the question, in what ways is it better than its predecessors? That it is more conciliatory than either the supersessionism of Melito or the apostasy charge of Celsus' Jew goes without saying, but is it more appropriate; does it help us understand the evidence better?

We may start by recalling that Harnack's model of supersession, like that of Melito and Justin before him, had a clear theological base; in Harnack it was perhaps the more dangerous because it was not articulated and so could be taken on by others who would have had little interest in theological issues, and thus enter the history books: Christianity took over from Judaism its finest insights and flourished, while Judaism collapsed into increasing sterility.[9] Behind the historical façade is the early Christian conviction that they were the heirs to the promises of the Scriptures, that in them and them alone God's covenant was now fulfilled.

On the surface, the 'parting of the ways' may appear to be free of this theological pleading, and to present a more historically sensitive analysis. It recognizes the continuing vitality of rabbinic Judaism as another way and not, presumably, a cul-de-sac. It is also 'historical' in that it gives full weight to the variety within first-century Judaism without the loaded judgements, 'orthodox' or 'sectarian'. Thus both rabbinic Judaism and Christianity can be seen to have their roots within the open-ended potential of that variety, a variety which has been one of the insights of post-World War 2 study. More particularly, it recognizes a continuity within Christian history, affirming 'Jesus the Jew' as one who did not differ so fundamentally from his contemporaries, and acknowledging no subsequent radical break even in the person of Paul.

However, it is at this point that we may begin to question just how free from theological apologetic it is. The affirmation of continuity is precisely the issue which divides Justin or Melito from their Jewish or pagan opponents; it is problematic rather than given. That, of course, has been true in theological terms since the time of Marcion and before, and the church has had to find ways of answering the problem and reaffirming the continuity. The early church met this need for continuity by a largely typological exegesis of the past; it is our greater historical consciousness which demands a continuity that can be expressed in historical terms.

There is here a, perhaps surprising, parallel with Biblical Theology in its 1980s' and 1990s' dress, one which is both instructive and salutary. Biblical Theology in this form, particularly as stemming from Germany, also lays great store by the discovery of 'intertestamental Judaism' and sees here the clue to the essential continuity in the biblical revelation; thus for Helmut Gese there is an unbroken complex of 'biblical tradition' which leads from an 'Old Testament' which is not yet a fixed canon, through the on-going process of growth visible in the intertestamental

⁹ See J. Lieu, J. North and T. Rajak, *The Jews among Pagans and Christians* (Routledge: London, 1992) 1–8.

literature and into the New Testament.[10] In that this Biblical Theology sees the New Testament as the proper completion of the Old it is considerably less dialogue-friendly than the 'parting of the ways' model. However, its weakness lies not only in its difficulties in giving an adequate account of contemporary Judaism but also in its reliance on certain historical assertions whose validity lies outside its sphere of control, for example that the theological outlook represented by 'sectarian' literature such as the Dead Sea Scrolls is not to be assigned to a esoteric sidewater, that the Hebrew Canon was not yet fixed in the time of the first apostles but that, again in Gese's words, 'it was the Judaism which rejected the Christ event [which] remarkably enough terminated the Old Testament tradition'.[11] Indeed, what is remarkable is how what one might consider the 'historical' question of the development of the Hebrew Canon has become a sparring ground for those committed to Biblical Theology.

Some of these, or at least similar, problems are shared by the 'parting of the ways' model: a good example is the question of the existence of the God-fearers. What is remarkable in this case is the passion with which the apparent support for their existence afforded by the possibly third-century inscription from Aphrodisias has been seized by New Testament scholars, a breed who are otherwise notoriously blind to the social and political realities of their period and rightly cautious about reading back evidence from nearly two centuries later to illuminate it. They need the God-fearers both to establish continuities leading into the Christian church – it was from this group of synagogue adherents that the earliest Christians were drawn – and to demonstrate the fuzziness of first-century ideas of being a Jew – thus Christian redefinition falls within this internal debate. They are persuaded, therefore, by evidence whose sparsity and ambiguity far outweighs anything in the quest for the historical Jesus![12]

Equally important for our purposes is the charge that has been laid against the version of Biblical Theology here described, namely that it never seems completely clear whether it is presenting a theological account or a historical one or perhaps a history of religions. The same question must be asked of the 'parting of the ways', except in reverse.

[10] H. Gese, *Essays on Biblical Theology* (ET Augsburg: Minneapolis, 1981); see H. G. Reventlow, *Problems of Biblical Theology in the Twentieth Century* (ET SCM Press: London, 1986) 148–54.

[11] Gese, *Essays*, 13.

[12] On the question of the God-fearers see now below, pp. 31–47, 49–68.

How far are theological assertions being couched in the form of a historical or history of religions account?

This may be explored further: first, despite its adoption by Jewish scholars – notably Alan Segal in his *Rebecca's Children* which works with the related idea of sibling rivalry[13] – the 'parting of the ways' is essentially a Christian model. Its concern is to maintain the Christian apologetic of continuity in the face of questions about that continuity from a historical or theological angle. Secondly, although it appears as a historical model, it actually works best with a theological agenda. This too needs a little more exploration. The question that the model seeks to answer is how to understand an early first century in which we find Judaism and, within it, a charismatic preacher with a band of followers, and a later period (at least, let us agree, by the time of Constantine) in which Judaism and Christianity are recognizable as two separate and independent systems: a historical datum. Yet as soon as one asks the questions of time and place appropriate to a historical account, the model becomes increasingly vague – hence Dunn's book is in fact titled *Partings*; there seems little to decide between those who, when asked for a date, speak of the 50s of the first century, and those who would put it a century later. Both can appeal to good evidence on their side in the terms in which they define the question. The problem is exacerbated when we find that geography equally resists the scheme and we are forced to speak of considerable variation in time and place. There is, without a doubt, good cause for all this: both Christianity and Judaism in the period in which we are interested and later were diverse phenomena, and we cannot expect a coherent and uniform development within or between them. The problem with the model of 'the parting of the ways' is that, no less than its predecessors on the pages of Harnack or Origen, even while fully acknowledging that variety, it operates essentially with the abstract or universal conception of each religion, Judaism and Christianity, when what we know about is the specific and local. I would suggest that the abstract or universal is, certainly for our period, problematic. What we need is a more nuanced analysis of the local and specific before we seek to develop models which will set them within a more comprehensive overview.

[13] A. Segal, *Rebecca's Children: Judaism and Christianity in the Roman World* (Harvard University Press: Cambridge, Mass., 1986).

The model also works best with a theological agenda in the sense that particular theological affirmations can be taken, explored within the two systems, and traced back to earlier roots within the first-century variety: for example, the unity of God, ideas of covenant or of eschatology. Both religions are being defined in terms of their beliefs or affirmations. To some extent this must be right, yet it has long been recognized in the study of first-century Judaism that a purely doctrinal definition is far from obvious or adequate; hence the debate here has been not only about variety over against normative but also orthopraxy over against orthodoxy. Perhaps we also need to remember that to explain theological data with historical categories is never straightforward, and that theological boundaries and social boundaries are not necessarily coterminous. People do continue to live and worship with those with whom, theologically, they ought not be able to, and separate from those with whom they believe most things in common!

I used the word 'problematic' above of the abstract or universal. This is not to imply that the 'universal' is non-existent. Certainly Bauer taught us in his *Orthodoxy and Heresy* to recognize the inchoate character of earliest Christianity;[14] yet it remains broadly true that even from the New Testament period there is a consciousness of being a single body, *the* church. It is an awareness which is recognized from outside not much later. Martin Goodman has sought to argue recently that it is only after the time of Nerva, when the *fiscus iudaicus* was limited (or extended) to those practising the Jewish religion, that pagan writers become aware of the Christians as separate from the Jews.[15] Even if true, what his theory does not explain – and I shall return to this – is why they recognize them as a single and definable body. Pliny's dilemma in the second decade of the second century as to whether Christians were to be punished for the name alone, a policy he started by taking for granted and which Trajan does not question, reflects such a recognition. We may say the same of Judaism; for all our awareness of the varieties of it in its first-century existence, talk of Judaisms has failed for the most part to win overall support. Whatever the fuzziness at the edges, the use of the term Ἰουδαῖοι without apology both in pagan literature and in Jewish inscriptions implies a coherent perception from outside

---

[14] W. Bauer, *Orthodoxy and Heresy in Earliest Christianity* (ET Fortress Press: Philadelphia, 1971).
[15] M. Goodman, 'Nerva, the *Fiscus Iudaicus* and Jewish Identity', *JRS* 79 (1989) 40–4.

and from within. If the relationship between unity and diversity is a contentious one for those who study the theology of the New Testament, it is equally, perhaps more so, for those who seek to understand the structures and life of the early church; and it is this dilemma which lies at the heart of the caution expressed in this paper.[16]

However, it would seem best to give flesh to this analysis by a number of case studies. This is not to reject the validity of adopting a Christian perspective and speaking of a 'parting of the ways', in full recognition that to do so is a theological judgement. It is, however, but one perspective, and as we look at the relationship between Jews and Christians from other, different perspectives we are presented with a variety of patterns which need to be brought together to discover a more comprehensive map. More particularly, in what follows I shall focus not only on other views but also on the social realia that must have occupied most people most of the time far more than the theological debates, and which suggest that apparently neat theological patterns may hide much messier social experience.

First we should consider the validity of the perspectives of the actors in the drama itself. We may leave aside for the moment the Christian perspective because it has been well enough represented, although it would have to remain part of the total map. The pagan perspective clearly has to be seen within the framework of Judaism as already well established on the stage by the first century CE. Pagan attitudes to Judaism are, of course, well-documented and much discussed. They have the virtue for our purposes of directing our attention to the Diaspora when the weight of surviving Jewish literature has tended to lead us to think of 'the other way' only in terms of rabbinic Judaism. The *fiscus iudaicus* mentioned earlier, and probably already earlier measures, witness to the readiness by outsiders to see the Jews wherever they were to be found as a single group. Even a casual reading of the sources demonstrates how pagan characterization of the Jews points to a predominantly phenomenological perception, that is particular patterns of behaviour and practices: Sabbath observance, male circumcision, food laws, ambivalence towards city life, a strong cohesiveness expressed socially both in an avoidance of intermarriage and in communal structures. This is confirmed by Josephus's description of the masses

---

[16] I would now probably be more cautious about the extent of the sense of unity in the first century outside certain texts; see below, pp. 176–8.

who want to adopt 'our piety' as manifested by the spread to every city of Sabbath observances, fasts, lighting of lamps, and food prohibitions (*c.Apion.* II.38 [282]).

Pagan perceptions of Christians in relation to Jews vary considerably but we should expect a similar starting-point. Here we may be disappointed: surely pagans knew that Christians did not circumcise their male children or converts, did not avoid pork – or did they in practice if most meat for sale in the city was that 'sacrificed to idols'[17] – and did not maintain a tight community existence on the sabbath – or was that outweighed by an equivalent focus on Sunday? In practice, however attractive these innovations might have been as missionary strategies or however significant on the theological level, they pass unnoticed in the literature. Rather it seems to have been the political front which prompted changed perceptions. Whatever Luke's own theological agenda, for Gallio in Acts 18 and for the Ephesian crowd in Acts 19.33–34, Christians are still Jews; the same may be true for Suetonius in his account of the expulsion of Jews disturbances in Rome in 49 CE(?) 'impulsore Chresto' (*Claud.* 25.4), although it remains uncertain whether this is a covert reference to Christian provocation.

Things are different when we move on to Tacitus's account of the fire under Nero: he knows well that the Christians, on whom the blame was laid, had their origin in Judaea, were a pernicious superstition and justifiably loathed by the masses for their 'hatred for the human race' (*Annal.* XV.44.2–5), charges regularly laid against the Jews. For Martin Goodman, Tacitus, writing after the redefinition of the *fiscus iudaicus* under Nerva, is witness to the new awareness of the Christians as a separate religious grouping. But Nero's actions themselves, and Suetonius's account of the same event with its even blander description of the Christians as a new and dangerous superstition (*Nero.* 16.2), suggest that the Christians were already being viewed as a self-standing group open to the suspicion of disloyalty that 'superstition' implies, a suspicion not previously unique to the Jews. The novelty in Tacitus's account on this reading would be to rediscover and capitalize on their Jewish origins, perhaps especially, as Syme suggests, in the light of the recent (when he wrote) and bloody revolt of the Jews against Trajan.[18] In so doing Tacitus

---

[17] There is good evidence that Paul's more liberal position (1 Cor. 8–10) was not universally adopted.

[18] On Tacitus's loathing of the Jews see R. Syme, *Tacitus* (Clarendon Press: Oxford, 1958) II, 467–8 and, on his attitude to the Christians, 530–3.

prepares the ground for those with whom we started, those who see Christians as an apostate movement – a negative judgement in a world which valued antiquity and loyalty to the traditions of one's forbears – sharing the vices but not the virtues of their origins among the Jews. If we were looking for reasons for the split, all this might suggest that a prime factor in differentiation was the potential of those involved to provoke social unrest; perhaps Christians, in their different demands on those who joined them, rejected the *modus vivendi* achieved by the Jewish community, and quickly suffered the consequences. This may be why Pliny does not see the Christian groups in anything like Jewish terms despite the fact that his good friend Tacitus was proconsul of the neighbouring province of Asia at much the same time. They are a group associated with certain unspecified crimes and responsible for the lamentable collapse in the sacrificial meat trade (Pliny, *Epist.* X.96). Steve Benko's argument that Pliny devised the unprecedented test of invoking the gods and offering incense and wine to Trajan's statue on the analogy of what would have been recognized as impossible for the Jews remains intriguing but unproven.[19] It is true that Josephus does report the use of such measures in the disturbances in Antioch which were provoked by a Jewish apostate (*B.J.* VII.2.3 [50–51]), yet it is more important that Pliny's language may be closer to that used of action taken against other alien groups.[20] So too, when Fl. Domitilla was swept up in the action taken against those charged with lapsing into 'Jewish ways', her misfortune was as much to be related to Flavius Clemens who fell under the suspicion of Domitian, as to be the victim of the confusion between the two religions (Eusebius, *H.E.* III.18.4; Cassius Dio, *Hist.Rom.* LXVII.14.1–2).[21] Here then it is not apostasy

---

[19] S. Benko, 'Pagan Criticism of Christianity during the First Two Centuries AD', *ANRW* II.23.2, 1055–1188, 1075. However in *Pagan Rome and the Early Christians* (Batsford: London, 1985) 23 he overstates the case in suggesting that in Pliny's eyes the Jewish origin of Christianity counted even more against it than for Tacitus.

[20] A. N. Sherwin-White, *The Letters of Pliny: A Historical and Social Commentary* (Clarendon Press: Oxford, 1966) 692, 705 rejects the suggestion made by R. Grant that Pliny's language is coloured by Livy's account of the measures taken against the Bacchanalia in 186 BCE and suggests that he is influenced more generally by measures taken against other cults.

[21] See P. Lampe, *Die stadtrömischen Christen in den ersten beiden Jahrhunderten* (WUNT 2.18, Mohr: Tübingen, 1989) 66–71, who argues that Domitilla but not Flavius Clemens was a Christian, while remaining agnostic on the true cause of the arraignment of the latter.

which determines the model of relationships but social and political characteristics.

In non-political contexts Christians might appear to be rather more like Jews, although the evidence is inevitably ambiguous: when Epictetus speaks of the true Jew as being the one who makes his choice and is baptized – not circumcised (*Diss.* II.9.19–21) – the scholarly uncertainty as to whether he means Jew or Christian may be as much a reflection of our desire to find as many early references to the Christians as possible as an understandable phenomenological harmonization. Similarly, what are we to make of Lucian of Samosata's description of the undoubtedly Christian community duped by Proteus Peregrinus in surprisingly Jewish terms? Peregrinus is converted to Christianity, admittedly in Palestine, by associating with 'their priests and scribes'; he rises to great prominence and becomes prophet, cult leader (θιασάρχης) and synagogue head (συναγωγεύς) as well as interpreting and explaining their books (*Peregrinus* 11).

Yet, for the outsider, doctrinal issues must have seemed to put the two groups close together, depending perhaps on one's sensitivity to the significance of abstruse doctrinal debate. Galen, the medical doctor born in Pergamum in Asia Minor, who rose to fame and spent the second part of his life in Rome, wrote voluminously on philosophy, on philology and also on medical matters. He may well have had contact with Jews at Rome, but his period there (in the late second century) also saw the increasing influence of the Christians.[22] It is therefore surprising to find him speaking in a comprehensive way of 'the followers of Moses and Christ' as if they were a single group, a group of almost proverbial resistance to being weaned away from their present convictions: one might more easily teach novelties to the followers of Moses and Christ than to the physicians and philosophers (*de Puls. Diff.* 3.3); elsewhere he treats them as a single philosophical school, but one which hardly abides by the proper rules of philosophy, for they take things on trust and do not subject them to analysis, 'as if one had come into the school of Moses and Christ (and) might hear about laws that have not been demonstrated' (*de Puls. Diff.* 2.4). These are but passing references to illustrate his real concern with analysis and argument; they show that from some perspectives Jews and Christians were but variants of

---

[22] On this see R. Walzer, *Galen on Jews and Christians* (Oxford University Press: London, 1948) 8–9.

the same commitment to blind faith, a unity more significant than any divisions between them.

Such confusion on the phenomenological level might explain the reactions of those Christians, widely discussed, who took refuge in synagogues in times of persecution or who were happy to attend synagogue and church:[23] to speak of Judaizing here is to adopt the viewpoint of the purist who rejects such confusion, and is hardly a value-free judgement; it implies that what was happening was a conscious theological symbiosis rather than pragmatism. Ignatius witnesses to the problem in reverse. In two much-quoted passages in his letters to the Magnesians (8.1; 10.3) and to the Philadelphians (6.1) he reaffirms the impossibility of combining Judaism and Christianity; he is the first to coin and use this word 'Christianism', modelling it on 'Judaism', a term which, since the time of the Maccabean literature, already indicated not a belief system but a total pattern of practice and adherence. When he wants to explain what distinguishes the two he does not enter into any theological argument; for him Judaism is circumcision and Sabbath. Christianity is the absence of these. He is reaffirming a phenomenological separation which we would expect would be immediately self-evident for his non-Jewish readers; but his anxiety betrays that it may not have been.[24]

When we turn to Jewish views we encounter a number of problems, not least because of the vexed questions of the sources. In this context the starting-point is usually rabbinic references to the *minim*, usually advocating their avoidance or exclusion, even when it is recognized, as usually nowadays, that these are unlikely to have been exclusively Christians.[25] For our purposes it is equally important that they *were* Jews, that a *min* is an insider even when being treated as an outsider: 'we do not sell to them, nor do we buy from them, we do not take from them, neither do we give to them' (*t. Hull.* 2.20–21). As Philip Alexander has argued, whoever is talking here is putting into effect a social parting of the ways; but at the same time we may wonder how widely observed that division was in practice and may even suspect that what 'we do not

---

[23] See J. Lieu, 'History and Theology in Christian Views of Judaism', in Lieu, North and Rajak, eds., *Jews among Pagans and Christians*, 79–96, 89–94 = pp. 127–33 below.

[24] Lieu, 'History and Theology', 92–4 = pp. 131–3 below; also now eadem, *Image and Reality*, 23–56.

[25] P. Alexander, '"The Parting of the Ways" from the Perspective of Rabbinic Judaism', in Dunn, ed., *Jews and Christians*, 1–25, 15–16.

do' is in fact precisely what some, if not most, are doing. When the same text declares a little earlier, 'their fruits are untithed and their books are the books of diviners', we may assume that neither of these assertions was obvious to the outward eye. All this is evidence not only of continuing interaction on a number of levels balanced by official distancing, but of irritation with nonconformists who defy any unitary description – hardly a parting of the ways.

Discussion of the *minim* usually leads to or is focused in discussion of the *birkat-ha-minim*. We need not retread the ground to show how uncertain it is when this prayer was introduced, how widely it was used and precisely what effect it would have had.[26] Yet it is usually discussed alongside the celebrated ἀποσυνάγωγος of John 9.22 and in the light of 'they shall put you out of the synagogues' as a translation of ἀποσυναγώγους ποιήσουσιν ὑμᾶς in John 16.2. Once this is done it is all too easy to think of Jewish–Christian relations in institutional terms, to slip into the language of 'the synagogue down the road'; it is language which is encouraged by patristic authors' tendency to speak themselves about ἡ ἐκκλησία and ἡ συναγωγή. As a Methodist I cannot help thinking of the many villages and towns where until recently there still stood a humble Primitive Methodist Chapel and just down the road the grander Wesleyan edifice. This may well fit well with the surprisingly close physical relationship between the synagogue and Church of St Peter at Capernaum, or even fire our imagination as we gaze at the magnificent synagogue at Sardis and picture the contrast with the struggling Christian community in the time of Melito, but these are fourth-century structures and they may give us little insight into first- and second-century conditions. The synagogue was not the only focal institution for the Jewish community, nor need it always have been a physical structure. Prayer could take place in many other contexts, not least the home, and it was of course the home which became the major locus of the Passover celebration.[27] It is open to question whether we have any clear idea how frequently even the highly

---

[26] This is widely discussed with a general consensus on the impossibility of relating the benediction directly or exclusively to the rupture between Jews and Christians: see among others, R. Kimelman, '*Birkat Ha Minim* and the Lack of Evidence for an Anti-Christian Jewish Prayer in Late Antiquity', in E. P. Sanders, A. L. Baumgarten and A. Mendelson, eds., *Jewish and Christian Self-definition, II, Aspects of Judaism in the Graeco-Roman Period* (SCM Press: London, 1981) 226–44.

[27] See B. Bokser, *The Origins of the Seder* (University of California Press: Berkeley, 1984).

observant felt under obligation to attend what was still in some ways the new and developing institution of the synagogue.[28] Shaye Cohen has drawn attention to the scarcity of literary references to the synagogue in second- and third-century sources and to the parallel scarcity of archaeological remains from this period, even suggesting that this may point to the synagogue's failure yet to achieve 'institutional prominence'.[29] Equally, the synagogue is not to be defined purely in terms of worship even as the modern participant might experience it. As S. Reif in his study of Jewish prayer says, 'the apparently long-standing tradition of assembly on the sabbath was also related as much, if not more, to study than to prayer'.[30] Study might well lead to the sharp exchange of conflicting opinions but it might be less exclusive than are prayer, worship or liturgy, which often do have the function of defining the identity and boundaries of those who participate. To sharpen the significance of this: alongside 'the parting of the ways' the opposition *intra muros* versus *extra muros* is often used to decide whether the conflict envisaged in, for example, Matthew or John, was internal or external – whether the ways had parted. It is only a metaphor, but suppose there were no *muri*, no walls. Once we 'de-institutionalize' our understanding of Jewish communities, once we remove *the* synagogue, understood much as some Christians speak of *the* church, from the centre of our perception of their essential identity, with what are we left?

It is particularly important that in looking at Jewish views we have perforce been focusing on the Land of Israel, although what has been said about the synagogue goes beyond it. Despite our initial caution, it may be that here alone can we in any real sense ask about the 'parting of the ways', for here alone can we assume with confidence a Christianity which had its origins in the Jewish community, and a Judaism which developed into the rabbinic Judaism which most adherents of the model presuppose as 'the other way'. Even here there are major problems in determining the numbers of and the relations between Christians of Jewish or of Gentile background. However, it is significant that both Philip Alexander and Stefan Reif independently speak of the separation

---

[28] On this see S. Reif, *Judaism and Hebrew Prayer* (Cambridge University Press: Cambridge, 1993) 67, 71.

[29] S. Cohen, 'Pagan and Christian Evidence on the Ancient Synagogue', in L. Levine, ed., *The Synagogue in Late Antiquity* (ASOR: Philadelphia, 1987) 159–81, 161.

[30] Reif, *Prayer*, 47.

of the two ways as only really established by the fourth century: both are essentially drawing on Jewish sources and are talking about the Land of Israel.[31] Yet such a timescale makes the model even more problematic in its usefulness, and leaves unanswered the question why it must be 'parting' that we are seeing.

In a perverse sense this view is confirmed by Jacob Neusner in his *Judaism and Christianity in the Age of Constantine*,[32] where he sees the fourth century as the first point at which Jews and Christians began to talk about the same things to the same people, even to each other. The Christianization of the Empire under Constantine and the insecurities occasioned by the reign of Julian forced both sides to address common questions: the status of 'Israel', the coming of the messiah. Before then they were talking about different things to different people. In his words 'Judaism and Christianity as they would live together in the West met for the first time in the fourth century' (p. ix). Again, his representative texts are first from the land of Israel and Syria, Eusebius, Chrysostom, and Aphraat – over against *Genesis Rabbah*, *Leviticus Rabbah*, and the Palestinian Talmud. Yet how are we to relate this distinctive experience to the wider experience of the Christian church outside those borders?[33]

What was the experience of, for example, the Christians of Rome or of Asia Minor? Here, even more on the social level, we can in different contexts speak of both separate identity and development, and of close interaction in combinations which defy any simple model. In apparent contradiction to what was said earlier about the separation of Jews and Christians in the eyes of the political commentators in the first and second centuries, there is evidence of Jews and Christians not only living in the same areas but even being buried in the same cemeteries, if not the same catacombs.[34] This last prompts Leonard Rutgers to suggest that for the Jews of the period 'their daily lives were hardly effected by the sterile patristic discussions as to which faith really constituted the *Verus Israel*'.[35]

---

[31] See nn. 25 and 28.
[32] J. Neusner, *Judaism and Christianity in the Age of Constantine* (University of Chicago Press: Chicago, 1987).
[33] See also W. Kinzig, '"Non-Separatists": Closeness and Co-operation between Jews and Christians in the Fourth Century', *VC* 45 (1991) 27–53.
[34] L. Rutgers, 'Archaeological Evidence for the Interaction of Jews and non-Jews in Late Antiquity', *AJA* 96 (1992) 101–18, 110–15.
[35] Rutgers, 'Archaeological Evidence', 115.

This picture is confirmed by a range of studies of the cultural interaction between religious groups in the period elsewhere. The archaeological studies by Louis Robert, Anthony Sheppard and Stephen Mitchell of religious groups in Phrygia are a case in point.[36] Here we have inscriptions to 'Hosion (kai) Dikaion' which are of undoubted pagan provenance, possibly showing Jewish influence and perhaps part of what has been described as a 'predilection for innovative forms of paganism . . . and an attraction towards the abstract, almost mono-theistic';[37] we find Christians apparently borrowing from Jews formulae threatening divine punishment for disturbance of the grave well into the third century; we find reverence for angels perhaps adopted by pagans from Jews, and later by Christians; we find all three addressing God as the most high, θεός ὕψιστος, often leaving twentieth-century com-mentators at a loss as to which group to assign the monuments. It would be wrong to assign all this to syncretizing or Judaizing tendencies, tendencies which in the 'parting of the ways' model occupy the muddy ground between the two more clearly marked and well trodden paths. To locate them there is to interpret social phenomena by theological categories, and also to adopt unquestioningly the perspective of those who like Chrysostom in Antioch saw Judaism as a threat.[38] Yet in the present case it is not clear that the 'parting of the ways' is at all relevant for understanding the attitudes of those involved or the history of the area. We know little about the origins of Christian communities in the area and nothing to suggest that it was not from very early on a predominantly Gentile phenomenon. In a series of famous inscriptions from northern Phrygia the dedicators unashamedly declare 'Christians for Christians'; these, if they are earlier than Constantine, point to a clear separate self-identity.[39] Yet there is much to suggest that this probably coexisted with the confluence of religious language, symbolism

---

[36] L. Robert, *Hellenica* XI–XII (1960) 381–439; A. R. R. Sheppard, 'Jews, Christians and Heretics in Acmonia and Eumeneia', *Anatolian Studies* 29 (1979) 169–80; idem, 'Pagan Cults of Angels in Roman Asia Minor', *Talanta* 12–13 (1980–1) 77–101. S. Mitchell, *Anatolia: Land, Men and Gods in Asia Minor* (Oxford University Press: Oxford, 1993) is fundamental for future discussion.

[37] E. Gibson, *The 'Christians for Christians' Inscriptions of Phrygia* (Harvard Theological Studies 32, Scholars Press: Missoula, 1978) 2.

[38] There is a sub-text here or a provocation for another essay: over-reliance on the 'parting of the ways' model prejudges any historical and theological assessment of that diverse range of phenomena commonly herded under a single umbrella of Judaizing.

[39] See Gibson, '*Christians for Christians*'.

and values just described, whether in the same or in adjacent groups, a confluence which must have had expression in a fluidity of social patterns.[40]

These brief case-studies or sketches could be multiplied. It would be interesting to examine the social interaction implied by the Christian reception and editing of originally Jewish non-biblical texts, or by the possible influence of Jewish prayer forms on developing Christian liturgy. These and other examples need to be set alongside the rhetoric that each side engaged in, not least that of separation or appropriation with which we are familiar from Christian sources. The 'parting of the ways' may continue to be useful to explore theological development or to defend a theological interpretation; in trying to make sense of the uncertainties of the early history of Christianity it may prove to be theologically less satisfying but sociologically more persuasive to picture a criss-crossing of muddy tracks which only the expert tracker, or poacher, can decipher.

BIBLIOGRAPHICAL NOTE

The Bibliography on the general topic has continued to grow since the first publication of this essay, and is too rich to be enumerated here. For a thorough study of the texts and of different groups and issues see S. G. Wilson, *Related Strangers: Jews and Christians 70–170 C.E.* (Fortress Press: Minneapolis, 1995), which recognizes the complexity of issues and the broad time-span, which militate against a simple model. This complexity is now inspiring detailed studies of particular texts, situations, or issues. As indicated in the revised footnotes, in *Image and Reality: Jews and Christians in the Second Century* (T&T Clark: Edinburgh, 1996), I have tried to explore the perceptions and strategies of texts from Asia Minor, and their varying relationship with the actual social situation. D. Boyarin, *Dying for God: Martyrdom and the Making of Christianity and Judaism* (Stanford University Press: Stanford, 1999) has also argued for a much later emergence of 'Christianity' and 'Judaism' as separate systems. Although this essay has not addressed the theological questions implied, they continue, rightly, to demand attention.

---

[40] For further discussion of the situation in Asia Minor through the texts and in relation to non-literary evidence, see now Lieu, *Image and Reality*.

3

Do God-fearers make Good Christians?*

The question posed by the title makes two assumptions, assumptions which, however, seem to be becoming accepted truths in much current New Testament scholarship. First, that there were those whom we, and also their contemporaries, Jews, Christians or even pagans, would recognize as and even name 'God-fearers': people who hovered on the fringe of 'the synagogue', sufficiently interested to remain there yet unwilling to jump the final hurdle, *male* circumcision. Secondly, that a significant number of this group became Christians, at least in the early decades; indeed, they provided a vital bridge for the spread of early Christianity into the non-Jewish world. It is not the task of this essay either to question or to prove the first of these assumptions but to accept it as such – although we may contribute to an analysis of its rationale. The wording of the title, however, allows an intentional ambiguity when we come to the second of these assumptions. We are not asking '*Did* God-fearers become Christians?', a historical question which can only be answered tentatively once we leave the pages of Acts. Instead '*Do* they become good Christians?', a question intended to examine why certain people might be expected to have made certain moves, and, more particularly, 'Do they become *good* Christians?'. The common assumption has been, of course, that it was good – at least for Christianity – that they did become Christians, and indeed, as we shall see, that they were very pleased to become Christians, and so presumably would have been good ones. The provocation to wonder whether this would indeed be the case has been provided by a series of recent articles by Michael Goulder in which he appears to be moving towards a picture (or perhaps back to a picture, for it raises the spectre of earlier reconstructions of

* First published in S. E. Porter, P. Joyce and D. E. Orton, eds., *Crossing the Boundaries. Essays in Biblical Interpretation in Honour of Michael D. Goulder* (BIS 8, Brill: Leiden, 1994) 329–45. Reprinted by permission of Brill.

early Christianity) of a widespread offensive against Pauline Christianity by Jewish Christianity which has shaped much of the New Testament.[1] Three elements of his reconstruction deserve our attention here; first – and in this case he is thinking specifically of Thessalonica – many of the Gentile Christians were former 'God-fearers', and hence partly assimilated to Jewish norms; as we shall see, Goulder is not alone in this as a general assumption, although it appears more regularly to have been used to explain the failure of the acceptance of Gentiles without circumcision to become an immediate source of conflict in the early church.[2]

Secondly, that in failing to make an insistence on circumcision their first priority, the Jewish–Christian mission, which Goulder finds behind the troubles in Thessalonica, Corinth and elsewhere, was following the norms already adopted by the synagogue's acceptance of uncircumcised male God-fearers.[3]

Thirdly, if I understand him rightly, it is precisely these Gentile Christians who are vulnerable to the seductive persuasion of the Jewish–Christian mission: 'Nevertheless, any church which has come to birth from the womb of the synagogue has a hidden irritant in its system. There will always be, in all its members in varying degrees, a sense of the authority of the Law, and guilt at its neglect.'[4] Here God-fearers have not made *good* Christians, at least not from a Pauline (or even New Testament) point of view! However, Goulder is not totally alone in his interpretation of the Pauline problem. A similar background has also been posited for some of the few references to gentile Judaizers in the early church: when Ignatius says it is better to hear Christianity from a circumcised man than Judaism from the uncircumcised some have seen lurking behind the latter a former God-fearer.[5]

---

[1] M. Goulder, 'The Visionaries of Laodicaea', *JSNT* 43 (1991) 15–39; idem, 'Silas in Thessalonica', *JSNT* 48 (1992) 87–106; idem, 'Σοφία' in Corinthians', *NTS* 37 (1991) 516–34; in 'Σοφία', 516, 527 he explicitly recalls the reconstruction by J. C. Schmidt and F. C. Baur. See now M. D. Goulder, *A Tale of Two Missions* (SCM Press: London, 1994).

[2] Goulder, 'Silas', 95. See J. D. G. Dunn, *The Partings of the Ways* (SCM Press: London/ Trinity Press International: Philadelphia, 1991) 125–6.

[3] Goulder, 'Visionaries', 25; 'Σοφία', 528.

[4] Goulder, 'Silas', 95–6.

[5] E.g. S. G. Wilson, 'Gentile Judaisers', *NTS* 38 (1992) 605–16; others have seen this as evidence of uncircumcised Gentile converts to Judaism. For the argument that Ignatius is caught in his own rhetoric see J. M. Lieu, 'History and Theology in Christian Views of Judaism', in J. Lieu, J. North and T. Rajak, eds., *Jews among Pagans and Christians in the Roman Empire* (Routledge: London, 1992) 79–96, 92–3 = pp. 131–3 below.

At this point we should note that the question could also usefully be reversed: do Christians, or 'bad' Christians, make God-fearers, even good God-fearers? Of course, it would be arguable that before the so-called 'Parting of the Ways', while Christianity is still best described as a Jewish 'sect', all Gentile adherents would appear to outsiders as 'God-fearers', particularly if we are to give any credence at all to Acts 15's account of the conditions under which Gentile and Jewish Christians could co-exist. If this seems to be muddying the already murky waters too much we might at least ask whether Gentiles converted by Jewish Christians and persuaded to adopt some practices of the law, such as Justin includes in his account of attitudes to law observance (*Dial.* 47), do not merit the epithet. More usefully, at least from a later period, it would be relatively easy to martial evidence of Christians who, in the eyes of their detractors, were 'bad' Christians', lingering hopefully on the fringes of 'the synagogue', impressed by its sanctity, by the pull of its festivities, the authority of its leaders, or the logic of its attitude to the Law. The most obvious and most-quoted example here would be the erstwhile members of the church at Antioch castigated by John Chrysostom in his *Against the Jews* (I.5). Conventionally, of course, such people have been labelled 'Judaizers', a term which has generally had a negative nuance in scholarship, as indeed it does in early Christian polemic. Yet, just as Josephus can speak of known sympathizers in the cities of Syria as ἰουδαΐζοντες (*B.J.* II.18.2 [463]), conversely these waverers of Gentile origin might be included among the God-fearers as widely defined – an epithet which carries a higher measure of approval. Indeed, Louis Feldman does include them in his long list of reasons why Judaism was successful in attracting 'sympathizers' in the third century and later.[6] However, it is surely a proper question to ask how much there is in common between such people, accessible to us only through the eyes and pen of Chrysostom at the end of the fourth century, and those pagan Greeks who, in the same city but some three hundred years earlier, had been incorporated by the Jews 'in some measure' (Josephus, *B.J.* VII.3.3 [45]). Indeed, merely to ask this is to ask an important question which shall occupy us at length, why do (did) people convert, or, if not convert, move towards another religion?

---

[6] L. Feldman, *Jew and Gentile in the Ancient World* (Princeton University Press: Princeton, 1993) 375–8.

Before taking up this important, and oft-neglected, issue we shall return to our initial questions. One, perhaps the only certain, result of the recent renewed flurry of activity on the question of the God-fearers has been the recognition that the evidence to be discussed is diverse, and that the conclusions drawn often depend on the relative weight given to this diversity or to the different components within it. Thus those concerned to find explicit references to labelled 'God-fearers' (θεοσεβεῖς) are likely to draw rather more minimalist conclusions than those who focus instead on the more widespread evidence of Gentile interest in Judaism.[7] A corollary of this recognition, but one which has yet to be taken fully seriously, is the recognition that there is no single definition of *the God-fearer*, no single set of criteria by which either we or contemporary society might classify them.[8] In the light of this termi-nological and categorical confusion this present discussion will not start by rehearsing once again the sources. Since clear historical evidence of God-fearers becoming Christians, at least outside Acts, is, as I have suggested, lacking, and since that they became '*bad*' Christians is equally without certain evidence, we shall start from inference and probablility, much as Michael Goulder does in his theory of residual guilt.

God-fearers as Christian converts: a profile

Once the tendentious elements in Acts' picture of the role of 'those who fear God' (13.16, 26, etc.) in the spread of Christianity is recognized, the most frequent argument in favour of that role nevertheless being historically probable is its historical credibility. The argument goes something like this: the rapid spread of Christianity as a strange and highly distinctive religion becomes much less problematic if we assume that the ground had been prepared for it not simply by the existence of Judaism but by the possibility of partial assimilation to it. Early Christian preachers did not find themselves having to preach, at least initially, to the totally 'unchurched' pagans but to those with an existing sympathy for the monotheistic and ethical assumptions already to be found within Judaism. In the undifferentiated confusion of the Graeco-Roman city

---

[7] Contrast the well-known article of A. T. Kraabel, 'The Disappearance of the God-fearers', *Numen* 23 (1981) 113–26, with J. A. Overman, 'The God-fearers: Some Neglected Features', *JSNT* 32 (1988) 17–26.

[8] See especially S. Cohen, 'Crossing the Boundary and becoming a Jew', *HTR* 82 (1989) 13–33.

these groups would be found, with their open and enquiring minds, already in physical association with the Jewish community or synagogue. More specifically, Christian self-understanding as standing in continuity with the revelation of God in the past history and experience of the Jewish people could only be affirmed in this Gentile mission without radical reconstruction of the Christian message because their audience were familiar with and in part integrated into that past. This is most vividly illustrated by Paul's letters; his tight theological arguments often based on appeals to Scripture and on specific exegetical techniques presuppose an audience already well familiar with the Greek Scriptures and with their elucidation.

This basic argument, that the New Testament writings, and behind them the early Christian proclamation, presuppose that the soil has at least been weeded and ploughed invites wider extension. If Luke–Acts' own style is specifically 'septuagintal' this reflects the synagogue background of its author and audience.[9] W. C. van Unnik finds behind the Exodus framework of 1 Peter 2, the imagery of new birth, and the idea of being brought to God (2.24), the language of proselytism and concludes that the 'exiles of the Diaspora' (1.1) are drawn from among the God-fearers.[10] A moment of cautious reflection, if a critique be allowed at this stage, might suggest that the more extended the demand for the presence of Christian ex-God-fearers, the more suspect the argument becomes. Is it inconceivable that Gentile converts either failed to follow Paul's detailed argument or had a quick crash-course in what they needed to know? Indeed, to push the problem a stage further back, how did the God-fearers, hovering on the fringe of the synagogue and not fully integrated into its tradition of study, themselves acquire their understanding of the Greek Scriptures and of the interpretation of them? How long and how faithful a membership would be required for such familiarity? Neither can we ignore the fact that 1 Peter assumes that his audience have typically left behind them a life of 'doing what the Gentiles like to do, licentiousness, passions, drunkeness, revels, carousing and lawless idolatry' (4.3), while Paul himself, who notoriously fails to mention the synagogue in his letters, seems to assume that his Gentile audience are just that, Gentile.

[9] So P. Esler, *Community and Gospel in Luke–Acts* (SNTS.MS 57, Cambridge University Press: Cambridge, 1987) 45.

[10] W. C. van Unnik, 'The Redemption in 1 Peter 1 18 – 19 and the Problem of the First Epistle of Peter', in *Sparsa Collecta* II (NT.S 30, Brill: Leiden, 1980) 1–82, 71–5.

To return, however, to the standard picture. What profile of the God-fearer emerges from the traditional picture of their place in the spread of Christianity? They are to be found, as has been said more than once so far, on the fringes of the synagogue, 'the synagogue' being here understood as a gathered community and as a worshipping community. One feels that 'the synagogue' is often also being understood as a physical structure, although this need not be so. They are attracted by and probably persuaded by Jewish monotheism, even if practical necessity meant some sort of continued involvement in pagan, and hence idolatrous, religious life. Jewish ethical values play a similar role in their relationship with Judaism. Through attendance at the synagogue they have become familiar with the Septuagint or other Greek versions of the Scriptures and find patterns of Scriptural interpretation persuasive. Thus, in the words of T. Finn, 'Gentiles deeply attracted to Judaism who appear to have had some sort of relationship with the Jews of the Diaspora synagogues, which they appear to have frequented and in which they may have been enrolled.'[11] However, for many their relationship with 'the synagogue' is touched by ambivalence. Viewed as anomolous by 'full members' they would like to resolve that by becoming themselves full members. However, not only are there considerable social disadvantages in so doing, but the crucial step of circumcision, for males at least, would be aesthetically and morally abhorrent as well as painful if not life-threatening.[12] For such God-fearers Christianity offers an alternative resolution, granting them full membership and affirming the values they found positive, while making none of the less comfortable demands – or at least not the same ones! They would make good Christians; unlike converts from 'pure' paganism whose full understanding of the new faith was questionable, and who might too easily bring into their new life remnants of their old ways, these God-fearers had found and indeed represented the best of all possible worlds.

However, if we are to follow Michael Goulder's reconstruction we need to add some further details to this profile. His erstwhile God-fearers, it seems, had also followed laws regarding sabbath and dietary observance, and thus ensured for themselves a measure of acceptance in

---

[11] T. Finn, 'The Godfearers Reconsidered', *CBQ* 47 (1985) 75–84, 83.
[12] Women are in a rather different anomalous position: it is not immediately clear what the practical and outward distinction between a female God-fearer and a female proselyte would be; see J. M. Lieu, 'Circumcision, Women and Salvation', *NTS* 40 (1994) 358–70 = pp. 101–14 below.

'the synagogue'.[13] Yet this means they can never be *good* Christians: while Christianity confirms their impulse towards monotheism and ethical values, the loss of law observance leaves unresolved tensions which make them easy victim for a Jewish–Christian mission; they know the Law *too* well and know that the requirements of food and calendar are not so easily disregarded. They may not yet have always realized that the same applies to male circumcision, but that no doubt will come!

Matching the profile

How does this profile appear when set against the diverse material usually cited to establish the existence of the God-fearers? We must start by returning to the elusive 'fringes of the synagogue'. An underlying assumption throughout this picture has been that the God-fearers and their choices are to be defined in essentially 'religious' and to some extent intellectual terms; underlying this assumption in its turn is the further one that paganism was religiously unsatisfying or unconvincing, at least compared with Judaism, while Christianity offered a further improvement on Judaism. Working from the opposite end, the supposedly known reasons for Gentiles becoming Christian, reasons which themselves are defined in terms of religious needs, are then retrojected onto the unattested reasons for their earlier attraction to Judaism. Yet the evidence for the God-fearers fails to support these assumptions.

A. T. Kraabel has sought to remind us that Jewish Diaspora communities, and this means 'the synagogue' which is used so often as a shorthand for these, cannot be defined in exclusively religious terms.[14] It seems clear that the same is true for the God-fearers. Indeed the term θεοσεβής itself, despite its resonances for the English mind, cannot be understood as exclusively or even primarily a religious term. Its use by Jews in dedications in the Sardis synagogue reflects its ambivalence;[15] they are indeed pious in as much as their benefactions are in fulfilment

---

[13] Goulder, 'Visionaries', 25 and n. 1.
[14] A. T. Kraabel, 'The Roman Diaspora: Six Questionable Assumptions', *JJS* 33 (1982) 445–64.
[15] Assuming that these are Jews as argued by L. Robert, *Nouvelles Inscriptions de Sardes* I (Librairie d'Amérique: Paris, 1964) 43–4, but see below, p. 40 n. 24 and the discussion at that point.

of a vow, a motivation they share with their pagan peers, but they are also benefactors and it is as benefactors that they can be proclaimed to later generations as God-fearing. It is perhaps equally likely that the God-fearers at Aphrodisias, who in this case do appear to be Gentiles, also merit the title 'God-fearing' because of their financial support for the organization memorialized by the inscription. Benefaction in the Graeco-Roman city is not necessarily a sign of religious commitment; it is a political and social act. It equally does not imply exclusive commitment – the benefactor might distribute his or her largesse as seemed most expedient. 'Expedient' reminds us that patronage does not so obviously reflect psychological needs as the possibilities of mutual benefit.[16]

The Aphrodisias inscription merits a little more attention here. There is, of course, nothing in the inscription itself to tie it specifically to 'the synagogue', understood either as a physical structure or as 'the worshipping community'. If there was a synagogue building at Aphrodisias it has been lost; none of those on the initial list of members of the 'decany' are identified by any synagogue office or title.[17] While the group is described as 'those who love study and praise unreservedly', it seems to take the form of a charitable association or benefit society, of which there were many examples in the Graeco-Roman city to which people might offer support for a variety of reasons. The nature of the institution itself recorded by the inscription is, due to the state of the stone, a matter of reconstruction, but it is not necessarily to be understood in primarily religious terms. The editors' suggestion of a soup kitchen after a rabbinic model and possibly under rabbinic influence is one of the least certain parts of their reading of the text and various other possibilities have been offered.[18] However, even their

---

[16] This understanding of 'crossing the boundaries' is well emphasized by T. Rajak, 'The Jewish Community and its Boundaries', in Lieu, North and Rajak, eds., *Jews among Pagans and Christians*, 9–28, 24.

[17] See J. Reynolds and R. Tannenbaum, *Jews and Godfearers at Aphrodisias* (Cambridge Philological Society Suppl. 12: Cambridge, 1987). The only exceptions to this may be 'Samuel presbyter priest' who, on epigraphic and internal grounds, may be a later addition to the list or the only (?) non-Aphrodisian Jew present, and Benjamin the 'Psalm-singer'. Joshua is 'archon', perhaps as son of the 'Patron' Jael, and therefore within the 'decany' but not necessarily as a *synagogue* office.

[18] See M. H. Williams, 'The Jews and Godfearers Inscription from Aphrodisias – A Case of Patriarchal Interference in Early 3rd Century Caria?', *Historia* 41 (1992) 297–310, who argues the decany is a burial society and the building a *triclinum*; L. M. White, *Building God's House in the Roman World* (Johns Hopkins: Baltimore, 1990) 88–90, while accepting

definition of the institution need not lead to a religious interest on the part of the 'God-fearers': Murphy O'Connor suggests, tongue in cheek, that those on the God-fearers list who are described as councillors may have been interested in the poor vote.[19] The 'religious' definition both of the inscription and of the God-fearers has necessitated discussion of the compatibility of the professions of some of those listed with any degree of Jewish allegiance – so, for example, Adolios the dealer in mincemeat, or Paramonos, the sculptor or painter of pictures with images.[20] This is to create unnecessary problems, for the definition itself is unwarranted.

Thus attachment to the Jewish community, in its varying degrees, is to be understood in social terms. A well-known inscription from Acmonia acknowledges Julia Severa as having erected the building which she then apparently donated to the Jewish community and which was subsequently used as a synagogue (*CIJ* 766). Since she is known as a highpriestess of the Imperial cult in the time of Nero, it is usually recognized that Julia Severa cannot be a God-fearer as traditionally understood, namely with any degree of religious commitment. Yet, while the synagogue probably saw value in terms of status and perhaps future patronage in naming her original donation, this publicly acknowledged association with the synagogue no doubt also offered her certain social and political advantages. It seems probable that at least one of the synagogue officials, whose donations towards the refurbishment of the building are celebrated by the inscription, belongs to her circle of dependents and that we are seeing here something of the significance of networks of allegiance and power.[21] Thus 'attachment to the synagogue' has to be interpreted not in terms of personal religious needs and commitment but in a wider framework of social allegiance and status. We would then also have to consider other patrons and donors such as Marcus Tittius whose benefactions earned him regular crowning with

---

the 'soup kitchen', emphasizes that this is a separate form of organization from the 'synagogue'.

[19] J. Murphy O'Connor, 'Lots of God-fearers: Theosebeis in the Aphrodisias Inscription', *RevBib* 99 (1992) 418–24, 422.

[20] See Reynolds and Tannenbaum, *Jews and Godfearers*, 57f.

[21] I.e. P. Tyrronius Cladus; see L. M. White, 'Finding the Ties that Bind: Issues from Social Description', in L. M. White, ed., *Social Networks in the Early Christian Environment: Issues and Methods for Social History* (Semeia 56, Scholars Press: Atlanta, 1992) 3–22, 18–20. See also n. 16 above.

an olive wreath by the Jewish community at Berenice (*CIG* III. 5361).[22] It is true that neither Julia Severa nor he are labelled God-fearing, but then the epithet is not current in their period, which at least is contemporary with the New Testament, nor apparently in north Africa at all, and Marcus Tittius is credited with being 'good and noble'. The much discussed inscription from the theatre at Miletus perhaps also belongs here.[23] If indeed the text should be read as 'place of the Jews and God-fearers', which in any case seems unnecessary, the setting of the inscription remains significant. Whether or not the theatre seats were ever occupied, and whether or not presence at the theatre invites criticism of their faithfulness to rabbinic norms, the political dimensions of visibility in the theatre can not be ignored. Association of these two groups at the theatre, and I repeat that this is not a necessary reading of the inscription, says nothing about any other aspects or contexts of their joint association.

Where some sort of positive relationship with the Jewish community – and there seems no neater way of saying this – is expressed in social or political terms and, perhaps predominantly or even exclusively, motivated by social and political considerations of this nature, it seems unlikely that there would have been fertile ground for attraction to the Christian community, at least in the early decades. *Prima facie* the God-fearers of Aphrodisias, if they had been around one hundred and fifty years earlier, are unlikely to have made good Christians, for the latter could not offer the same social advantages found in liaison with the Jewish community. This is not to say that Christian communities did not also depend on patronage; indeed, recognition of the importance of social networks in the spread and continuity of Graeco-Roman cults,[24] suggests that the recruitment of a member of this type would give significant access to a much wider network of mutually obligated and inter-dependent people.

---

[22] See G. Lüderitz, *Corpus Jüdischer Zeugnisse aus der Cyrenaika* (L. Reichert: Weisbaden, 1983) no. 71. The similar inscription honouring D. Valerius Dionysius for his decorating of the amphitheatre may illustrate obligations the Jewish community could incur towards the city and the assumption of those obligations by an individual, here probably a Jew (?); see G. Horsley, *New Documents Illustrating Early Christianity* 4 (1979) (Macquarie University: Sydney, 1987) 202–9.

[23] *CIJ* II. 748; see below, pp. 63–4.

[24] See, for example, the Agrippinilla inscription set up by an association of more than four hundred members centred on a single *familia*: B. McLean, 'The Agrippinilla Inscription: Religious Associations and Early Church Formation', in B. McLean, ed., *Origins and Method: Towards a New Understanding of Judaism and Christianity: Essays in Honour of John C. Hurd* (JSNT.SS 86, JSOT: Sheffield, 1993) 238–70.

Nonetheless, there is no reason for the Jewish community in particular to have been the loser in the process. Understood in these terms, and in particular in the light not of individual needs but of social patterns, these God-fearers betray no hint of frustration at the impossibility of further integration; it is true that the God-fearers on the Aphrodisias inscription are separated from the Jewish donors but this might not always be the case. It is possible that one of the 'synagogue officials' responsible for the refurbishment of the οἶκος donated by Julia Severa, and honoured with the title ἀρχισυνάγωγος, was himself a Gentile, and while the θεοσεβεῖς of the Sardis synagogue have been interpreted above as Jews there is nothing in the inscriptions to prove this and so to distinguish Jews from non-Jews.[25] It may at this point properly be objected that the argument is proceeding from silence – but this is no less true with the contrary argument which defines God-fearers primarily in religious terms, and the texts used are those often appealed to by proponents of the alternative definition. A more pertinent objection would be that epigraphic texts are inherently more likely to reflect social issues than religious commitment.

Both this problem and also the general argument so far can be illustrated from other texts. Shaye Cohen has shown that in the *Jewish War* Josephus presents adherence far more in social and political terms, even when he is referring to the Jewish sympathizers (ἰουδαΐζοντες) whose uncertain loyalty exacerbated the conflict in the cities of Syria during the Jewish revolt (*B.J.* II.18.2 [463]), to the large number (in fact a majority) of women in Damascus 'who had gone over to the Jewish *religion* (θρησκεία)' (*B.J.* II.20.2 [560]), or even to the large number of Greeks in Antioch who had been attracted 'to their religion' and been made a part of themselves 'to a certain degree' (*B.J.* VII.3.3 [45]).[26] However, in the *Antiquities* adherence manifests itself less politically, as support of the Temple or as honouring of the Jewish God or of Jewish customs, but with no suggestion that adherence might lead to conversion, while in the *Against Apion* it is devotion to and imitation of

---

[25] Whether Tyrronius Cladus was necessarily Jewish has been asked by T. Rajak and D. Noy, 'How to be an *ARCHISYNAGOGOS*', *JRS* 83 (1993) 75–93, 88. On the God-fearers at Sardis see Robert, n. 15 above and the criticism by J. Gager, 'Jews, Gentiles and Synagogues in the Book of Acts', *HTR* 79 (1986) 91–9.

[26] S. Cohen, 'Respect for Judaism by Gentiles according to Josephus', *HTR* 80 (1987) 409–30, 423. Cohen sees the Greeks of *B.J.* VII.3.3 as converts; yet the context here stresses the high status accorded the Jewish community through royal patronage.

the Laws of Moses that comes to the fore in adherence.²⁷ Quite apart from the fact that the social context of Christianity in these cities would have little in common with that of Judaism and that attraction to the latter would be unlikely to result in attraction for the Christian version, this imposed interpretative framework makes it difficult to redefine adherence in religious terms, or to find a common rationale for it in ways which might suit our model pre-Christian God-fearers. An exception to Cohen's pattern, and one often quoted as just such a model is Izates of Adiabene, who comes close to following the women of the court and his mother by converting to Judaism but is dissuaded from going so far as to be circumcised for fear of the political consequences (*Ant.* XX.2.3–4 [34–48]);²⁸ without circumcision he remains a 'God-fearer' and his allegiance is seen in religious terms; yet even here we are only told in general terms of the royal household's adoption of 'the ancestral customs of the Jews' (τὰ πάτρια τῶν Ιουδαίων) – a term which has definite socio-political connotations as evidenced by its use in the decrees cited by Josephus in the *Antiquities*, and also in the context of martyrdom in Maccabean literature.²⁹ Moreover, modern scholarship has also stressed the considerable political attraction for Izates of an allegiance to the Jewish community,³⁰ while Josephus himself says that Izates's brother, Monobazus, decides to convert when he sees 'that the king because of his pious worship of God had gained the admiration of all men', which in the context means his political success (*Ant.* XX.4.1 [75]).³¹ We need not deny entirely the religious component in these 'God-fearers'' commitment; yet equally clearly we cannot speak only in terms of a religious attraction which might be replaced by an even more persuasive one.

A very different social and religious context is presented by Juvenal's much quoted passage about the son who takes his father's flirtation with Jewish scruples one fatal step further (*Sat.* 14.96–106). If the son is the convert, the father is, as conventionally understood, the God-fearer.

---

²⁷ Cohen, 'Respect', 427.
²⁸ Cohen, 'Respect', 424, 427.
²⁹ See J. W. van Henten, B. Dehandschutter and H. J. W. van der Klaauw, eds., *Die Enstehung der jüdischen Martyrologie* (SPB 38, Brill: Leiden, 1989) 222.
³⁰ L. Schiffman, 'The Conversion of the Royal House of Adiabene in Josephus and Rabbinic Sources', in L. Feldman and G. Hata, eds., *Josephus, Judaism and Christianity* (Brill: Leiden, 1987) 293–312.
³¹ See M. H. Williams', 'θεοσεβής γὰρ ἦν: The Jewish Tendencies of Poppaea Sabina', *JTS* 39 (1988) 97–111, 103.

However, in Juvenal's eyes – and how much credence can we give the satirist? – what has attracted him about Judaism is not its more obvious intellectual and ethical virtues but sabbath observance and dietary laws, or at least avoidance of pork. This, of course, coheres with other pagan responses to Judaism which seem to pay more attention to its phenomenological characteristics than to its ethics or monotheism, although the convert son does worship nothing but 'the clouds of heaven'. The son, by his antisocial behaviour, identifies himself with the Jewish community; that the father had been on its fringes is hardly necessary – what upsets pagan detractors of Judaism, including Juvenal, is the spread of foreign customs into society, something which can happen without any conscious adherence to the parent body. That the Jewish community would have honoured the father as a God-fearer is unlikely; that he would have been attracted by Christianity even more so – although if he were he may well have missed his sabbath and food observances and have been easy prey to those who promulgated them. The attraction of Jewish customs is more widely attested; Josephus himself boasts that 'there is not one city where our practice of the seventh day on which we abstain from work, and the fasts and lighting of lamps and many of our prohibitions regarding food have not spread' (*c.Apion* II.40 [282]),[32] but again such imitation could well be independent of any relationship with the Jewish community, and offers no obvious basis for a Torah-free Christian mission. A similar attraction, of course, was still felt by the objects of Chrysostom's sermons mentioned earlier – not 'good' Christians – who this time did find in the synagogue the mystique and religious pattern that they missed within the church.

Since we have returned to Chrysostom we may also point to the evidence of the attraction of the Jewish reputation for magic and exorcism; the Christians both decried competition voiced in these terms and shared in it, even excelled in it. We should not dismiss too readily the power of the supernatural as a factor in conversion: it is clearly at work in the establishment and success of other new cults such as that founded by Alexander of Abonoteichus whom Lucian denounces as 'the false prophet' but whose popularity is archaeologically attested long

---

[32] For other references see E. Schürer, *The History of the Jewish People in the Age of Jesus Christ*, new edn. G. Vermes, F. Millar et al., eds. (T&T Clark: Edinburgh, 1973–87) III, 161, n. 50.

after his death (*Alexander*). Ramsay MacMullen has pointed out that conversion as a response to the miraculous proof of divinity makes much the best sense of the spread of Christianity among the masses within the context of the pagan world:[33] he describes the sequence of thoughts or feelings leading to conversion as 'first, the operation of a desire for blessings, least attested; second, and much more often attested, a fear of physical pain . . . ; third, and most frequent, credence in miracles'. Yet if we envisage the market now swayed by Judaism now swayed by Christianity in these terms we are a far cry from the God-fearers of our Pauline/Lukan reconstruction.

It is the incoherence of the material discussed so far that gives some credence to Folker Siegert's distinction between God-fearers and sympathizers, even if his imposition of this distinction on the different types of texts offers too rigid a schema.[34] It would seem far too icono-clastic to deny that there were any Gentiles who were attracted by the monotheism, the ethical teaching, and the antiquity and awesomeness of the Law. There is some force in the argument that Jewish Hellenistic writings which give far more if not exclusive emphasis to these aspects of the Jewish way of life presuppose such a respect even if they cannot have hoped to reach that audience directly;[35] and we do know of at least one first-century pagan who has read the Septuagint, Ps. Longinus, *On the Sublime* (9). Moreover, it would be wrong to dismiss out of hand the evidence of Acts, although both the terminology and the location of those involved is far less consistent than is always recognized. There is also substantial evidence of a trend towards monotheism, particularly in Asia Minor, which may owe something to Jewish influence and which manifests itself in dedications to a single deity with Jewish-type epithets.[36] Neither can we totally deny the argument that the reasons which attracted Gentiles to Christianity, which lacked the 'virtues' highlighted so far, may, where held in common, have also attracted them to Judaism – although this does not mean it is the same people who are being

---

[33] See R. MacMullen, *Christianizing the Roman Empire AD 100 – 400* (Yale University Press: New Haven, 1984) 108.

[34] F. Siegert, 'Gottesfürchtigen und Sympathisanten', *JSJ* 4 (1973) 107–64.

[35] See J. J. Collins, *Between Athens and Jerusalem: Jewish Identity in the Hellenistic Diaspora* (Crossroad: New York, 1983) 163–8.

[36] See P. W. van der Horst, 'A New Altar of a Godfearer?', *JJS* 43 (1992) 32–7; also the debate surrounding dedications to 'the most High God', see above, p. 28 and n. 36, and below, p. 48 n. 40.

attracted or that the traffic from one to the other would go in one direction only.[37]

From the material studied so far – material usually cited in the discussion – it can not be said that the God-fearers self-evidently would have made good Christians; it is hardly obvious that they would have become Christian at all, or at least not with any regularity or uniformity. They are not necessarily anomolous nor dissatisfied, neither are they as a whole longing for a closer membership of the group. That some observed Sabbath and Kosher laws is clear, but that this had brought them a measure of acceptance as suggested by Goulder is nowhere hinted, although observance of the latter, *if felt to be reliable*, might have been socially advantageous where social contact was desired. Knowledge of the Septuagint and of Jewish styles of exegesis can not be taken for granted. Finally, there is little trace that these God-fearers were to be found in groups hanging around the doors of the synagogue listening to the debates or preaching going on within. The synagogue at Sardis was indeed centrally situated and so placed that casual passers by and even those who came to draw water from the public fountain in its forecourt could observe the activities within, but this is a fourth-century structure; the lack of attestation to the character of earlier synagogues forbids us from extrapolating back to the first century. If Paul envisages a stranger finding his or her way into the Christian meeting and being awestruck by the *charismatic* power displayed (1 Cor. 14.22–25), similar casual access may have been possible to the Jewish meeting, which also developed frequently from a house base,[38] but the sense gained of what was happening might have been equally impressionistic.

This conclusion is not purely a negative one. Despite the negative thrust of this essay, at several points patterns of pagan relationship with the Jewish synagogue have offered possible models for exploring relationships with the Christian community; here the similarities as well as the differences between the social position and the religious perception of the two communities demand more analysis. Moreover, as stated at the outset, the range of evidence reflects a range of awareness among outsiders of Jewish practice, belief or community, however that

---

[37] See A. Segal, *Paul the Convert* (Yale University Press: New Haven, 1990) 106 for evidence of conversion to Christianity as evidence for Judaism.
[38] See L. M. White, *Building God's House*, 60–101.

awareness was inspired and encouraged.[39] It is reasonable to assume that some with that awareness would have a natural interest in Christianity; although, in the same way, one must add, some with a philosophical interest, such as Justin, might also develop a natural interest in Christianity and even come to argue from the Greek Scriptures without a mediating education in the synagogue. The reverse would also be true: some whose first contact with the 'Jewish tradition' was with the more proselytizing Christian version might develop a natural interest in the more full-blooded synagogue version. Justin speaks of Gentiles persuaded by Christians of Jewish descent to adopt a life under the law alongside their Christian confession; he also speaks of those who give up that confession and convert to life under the law 'for whatever reason' (*Dial.* 47.4), and their reasons may have been many and various, and not all due to the subtleties of intellectual persuasion or induced guilt.

Older descriptions of Diaspora Judaism as syncretistic and corrupt fortunately have been recognized for the tendentious distortions they were. Yet the evidence to which they appealed still requires some explanation. These include in particular the cults of Zeus Hypsistos or of Theos Hypsistos, cult groups which use names apparently related to the Sabbath such as the Sabbatistai at Elaeusa in Cilicia, and angel cults in Anatolia.[40] Each of these represents a major research problem in its own right, but it seems impossible to exclude any Jewish influence from them at all, even if we should think of pagan imitation of Jewish concepts rather than of a movement outwards on the Jewish side. This, then, is another aspect of the God-fearers; a world of fuzzy boundaries where exclusive commitment was an anomaly. If some groups, such as Jews and Christians, from within demanded sharp boundaries and exclusive commitment, that would never stop those who preferred to live on the boundary doing so. We are discovering a world not where there is a fixed class of intellectually and religiously prepared God-fearers ready to be targeted by the liberation of the Christian message, and then to be seduced back to their old convictions, but a world of

---

[39] That it was not by conscious proselytizing has been repeatedly argued by M. Goodman; see idem, 'Jewish proselytizing in the first century' in Lieu, North and Rajak, eds., *Jews among Pagans and Christians*, 53–78.

[40] Vermes, Millar et al., eds., [Schürer], *History* III, 161, n. 50; 169; S. Mitchell, *Anatolia: Land, Men and Gods* (Oxford University Press: Oxford, 1993) II, 43–51; A. Sheppard, 'Pagan Cults of Angels in Roman Asia Minor', *Talanta* xii–xiii (1980–1) 77–101.

increasing religious choice and variety where Christian claims and interpretations of life can win a hearing; a world, then, where the possibility of not being a *good* Christian was not limited to any one group, and where the decision to move from one to another form of adherence, 'across the boundary', might not only be motivated by – or inhibited by – theological arguments.

4

The Race of the God-fearers*

The 'God-fearers' have been so regularly appraised, eliminated and re-appraised that it may seem tedious to devote yet another essay to asking 'Who are the "God-fearers"?' Yet the question when asked by modern scholarship is not that asked by the texts themselves – therein, no doubt, lies part of the problem. While modern scholarship seeks to identify the bearers of the epithet and to fill out their profile and historical role, in the primary texts it belongs to a rhetoric of claims and counter-claims, betraying an implicit if not explicit competition between religious groups. Although the main concern of this essay is to trace the rhetoric of 'the God-fearers', it may be helpful first to summarize the main elements which constitute the modern debate and so shape the modern definition of the God-fearers.

Here the focus has been the existence of the 'God-fearers' as a class of Gentile sympathizers with a close relationship to the Jewish synagogue which was, however, less than full conversion.[1] The starting-point has often been the distinctive references in Acts to 'those who fear God' (οἱ φοβούμενοι τὸν θεόν: Acts 10.2, 22, (35); 13.16, 26) or 'those who revere God' (οἱ σεβόμενοι τὸν θεόν: Acts 13. (43), 50; 16.14; 17.4, 17; 18.7). These formulae, despite the enigmatic switch between them half way through Acts (between 13.26 and 13.43 or 50), appear to be used in a near technical sense, especially when put alongside 'the Jews', as in 17.17 (τοῖς Ἰουδαίοις καὶ τοῖς σεβομένοις).[2] In the context of

---

* First published in *JTS* 46 (1995) 483–501. Reprinted by permission of Oxford University Press.

[1] The bibliography is extensive and growing; see J. Reynolds and R. Tannenbaum, *Jews and Godfearers at Aphrodisias* (Cambridge Philological Society Suppl. 12, Cambridge, 1987) 48–66, and the articles cited in the footnotes there, as well as those referred to below. See also above, pp. 31–47.

[2] M. Wilcox, 'The "Godfearers" in Acts. A Reconsideration', *JSNT* 13 (1981) 102–22 denies that the Acts references need be taken consistently in this sense.

Luke–Acts' own ideology this group plays a significant role as a bridge between Jews and Gentiles in the wider extension of Christianity, and it is this theological *raison d'être* which has given room for doubt as to the historical reliability of Luke's picture when taken on its own.[3]

However, this putative group of 'sympathizers' have gained their name not only from the Lukan material but also from the use of the term θεοσεβής (pl. θεοσεβεῖς) in inscriptions from Jewish contexts where it is applied to people who *in some cases* appear to be adherents rather than full members of the synagogue. It is this term which is the main concern of this essay. The most notable and most compelling – perhaps only certain – example of this use is the recently discovered early third-century(?) inscription from Aphrodisias which lists some fifty-two male names under the heading 'such as are God-fearers', clearly differentiating them from the earlier list(s) of apparently full-members of what is probably a Jewish association of some sort.[4] The fact that the two participial phrases from Acts as well as this adjective can alike be translated as 'God-fearing' has sometimes made it possible to hide both the difference between the terms and the significant failure of Acts to use the inscriptional term or of its term to be witnessed epigraphically; equally important is the chronolgical distance between the attestation of the different terms – Acts belongs to the first century, the inscriptions to the third or fourth centuries – which makes it hazardous to interpret one by the other when there may be more pertinent parallels.

That 'Gentile sympathizers' did exist is clear and can be illustrated by such diverse examples as the father of Juvenal's satire whose reverence for the seventh day and avoidance of pork is the first step down a slippery slope which ends with the son's full conversion (*Sat.* 14. 96–106), or Josephus's reference to the 'masses' who have long 'joined themselves to

---

[3] So A. T. Kraabel, 'Synagoga Caeca: Systematic Distortion in Gentile Interpretations of the Evidence for Judaism in the Early Christian Period', in J. Neusner and E. S. Frerichs, eds., *'To See Ourselves as Others See Us': Christians, Jews, 'Others' in Late Antiquity* (Scholars Press: Chico, 1985) 219–46, 224–30; idem, 'Greeks, Jews and Lutherans in the Middle Half of Acts', in G. Nickelsburg and G. MacRae, eds., *Christians Among Jews and Gentiles: Essays in Honor of Krister Stendahl* (Fortress Press: Philadelphia, 1986) 147–57. Kraabel also notes the lack of reference to such a background in the Pauline letters, although some would argue that the assumption that Gentile readers will follow the complex use of the 'Old Testament' suggests that they have come to Christianity via the synagogue.

[4] Reynolds and Tannenbaum, *Jews and Godfearers at Aphrodisias*, 48–66; prior to this it could be questioned whether the term ever conclusively referred to a Gentile: so A. Kraabel, 'The Disappearance of the "God-fearers"', *Numen* 28 (1981) 113–26; L. Robert, *Nouvelles Inscriptions de Sardes* I (Librairie d'Amérique: Paris, 1964) 43–5.

us in some measure' (*B.J.* VII.3.3 [45]; cf. *c.Apion.* II. 10 [123]),[5] or the implied audience of some Hellenistic Jewish literature. Yet it is equally significant that these sympathizers are given no regular profile or epithet and are never called 'God-fearing'.[6] We may also put to one side the limited references in rabbinic sources to שמים יראי, 'those who fear heaven', apparently of Gentiles who show some loyalty to the Jewish people, since it is impossible to demonstrate a link between the admittedly similar terminology.[7]

While modern scholarship has focused on the possibility of drawing these diverse bodies of evidence together in pursuit of a single historical referent, the texts themselves are motivated by different concerns and by arguing separate causes. It is this which we shall be exploring here with specific reference to the use of 'God-fearing', θεοσεβής. However, while the epigraphic evidence has been analysed frequently, the use of this same term in literary sources has not received similar systematic attention.

The race of God-fearers

The general history of θεοσεβής or of the noun θεοσέβεια, fear of God, can be traced from its occasional use by Aristophanes and Euripides, through to its adoption by Hellenistic Judaism and then by Christianity, where it finally becomes a technical term and even an ecclesiastical title. In his survey of this history G. Bertram commented, 'On the whole, the history of the term θεοσέβεια displays the penetration into the biblical sphere of a word group alien to the biblical revelation';[8] although criticizing its anthropocentric spiritual attitude, he nonetheless did recognize its significance in denoting 'the true worship of God in contrast to pagan superstition and idolatry'.

---

[5] On these and more widely on the question of Josephus's presentation of 'friendly Gentiles' see S. Cohen, 'Respect for Judaism by Gentiles according to Josephus', *HTR* 80 (1987) 409–30.

[6] J. A. Overman, 'The God-Fearers: Some Neglected Features', *JSNT* 32 (1988) 17–26 criticizes Kraabel for failing to deal adequately with this evidence, but in doing so he confuses two separate issues, the existence of sympathizers, and their inclusion in a designated group.

[7] See F. Siegert, 'Gottesfürchtige und Sympathisanten', *JSJ* 4 (1973) 107–64, 110–19 for a full discussion; for L. Feldman, 'Jewish "Sympathisers" in Classical Literature and Inscriptions', *TAPA* 81 (1950) 200–208 it is only the rabbinic term which is at all technical.

[8] 'θεοσεβής, θεοσέβεια', *TDNT* III, 123–8, 128.

It is indeed this which provides the setting when the term first emerges clearly in the Christian tradition in the second century. A good starting-point is afforded by the *Martyrdom of Polycarp*. Although it has been argued that in its present form the *Martyrdom* shows evidence of late redaction, the passages with which we are here concerned fit well in a second-century context and for our present purposes we may accept a date in the third quarter of the second century and also put to one side the question of the historical accuracy of the reporting.[9]

In the form of a letter from the Church at Smyrna, which had experienced the brunt of persecution, to the Church at Philomelium 'and all the sojouring [churches] of the holy and catholic Church in every place', the *Martyrdom* is no mere historical record nor an ephemeral missive. It is both a testimony and a summons to imitation; imbued with echoes of the account of Jesus' own Passion, Polycarp's trial and death, supported by that of his fellow martyrs, becomes a display which compels 'the whole crowd to marvel that there was such a difference between the unbelievers and the elect' (16.1). Despite its apparent apologetic tone, that motif of contrast was probably directed not to a pagan audience but to the beleagured church forced into an interpretation of the suffering they were enduring; opposition and persecution encourage tighter self-definition, a self-definition which is often expressed in terms which reverse the judgement made by the oppressors. Avoiding any overt apologetics – when invited by the governor 'to persuade the people', Polycarp considers the crowd not worthy of any (10.2) – a covert apologetic has voices from every side contributing to the key terms of that self-definition.

Thus for the narrator, the Evil One, whose hand lies behind the worst moments of the story, is the one 'who opposes *the race of the righteous*' (17.1 το γένος τῶν δικαίων). Polycarp, with the authority of the hero soon to be martyred, confirms this designation of the Christians: as he dedicates himself as a sacrifice he prays 'O Lord God Almighty, Father of . . . Jesus Christ . . . God of angels and powers and all creation and of *the whole race of the righteous* who live before you'

---

[9] The considerable debate as to whether the traditional date of Polycarp's death as 156/7 CE can be sustained does not seriously effect the present argument; on the development of the text and the relation with Eusebius's 'excerpts' see B. Dehandschutter, *Martyrium Polycarpi. Een literair-kritische Studie* (BETL 52, University of Leuven: Leuven, 1979). On this and what follows see now J. M. Lieu, *Image and Reality: The Jews in the World of the Christians in the Second Century* (T&T Clark: Edinburgh, 1996) 57–102.

(14.1).[10] Earlier, the mob, who later will observe with amazement that distinction between unbelievers and the elect, add another testimony; a young man Germanicus resolutely rejects any inducement to apostasize and instead entices the wild beast to help him leave 'this unjust and lawless life', this time compelling the watching crowd 'to marvel at the nobility of *the God-loving and God-fearing race of Christians*' (3.2 τὴν γενναιότητα τοῦ θεοφιλοῦς καὶ θεοσεβοῦς γένους τῶν χριστιανῶν). The bold apologetic force of the epithets is underlined by the crowd's responding cry, 'Away with the god-less [atheists]'.

This assertion that Christians form a 'race' or γένος of their own is also expressed in other ways – they imitate and so offer an alternative to the life of the city. It is Polycarp's life-long faithful 'citizenship', πολιτεία, which so provokes the jealousy of the Evil One but which is equally valued by the Christian community (13.2; 17.1); clearly this citizenship was not exercised in Smyrna itself but within the Christian community.[11] The 'whole crowd of pagans and Jews who live in Smyrna' add further testimony when they call him 'the father of the Christians' and 'the destroyer of our gods' (12.2); the first of these labels clearly echoes the regular epithet with which the Emperor was celebrated in decrees and inscriptions at Smyrna and elsewhere in this period, 'father of the fatherland'.[12] Together, the two titles place Polycarp in an alternative and antithetical system.

Brought before the proconsul, Polycarp is urged to swear by the Fortune of the Emperor; this he refuses to do with the proud claim 'I am a Christian (χριστιανός εἰμι)'. He even offers, if the proconsul so wills, to teach him 'the message of Christianity (χριστιανισμός)' (10.1). In the context of his refusal to swear by the Emperor's 'fortune', 'Christianity' clearly indicates a total pattern of belief and practice and is that for which Polycarp will die. The use of a single term to express

[10] An important parallel appears in Judith's prayer (9.12, 14) where God is described as 'master of heaven and earth, creator of the waters, king of all creation . . . God of all power and might, there is none other than you who shields the race of Israel'; see below, p. 58.
[11] This terminology of citizenship was by now a regular part of Christian discourse, coming frequently in *1 Clem.* and also in Justin.
[12] E.g. *CIG* 3176 = G. Petzl, *Die Inschriften von Smyrna* (Habelt: Bonn, 1982–7) no. 600 in a letter dated to the same period (157/8) where Marcus Aurelius is the son of 'the father of the fatherland'; see also *CIG* 3187 = Petzl no. 591 where a decree of the Commune of Asia speaks of the divinized emperor as 'father of the fatherland and saviour of the whole human race' (? time of Nero). See also M. d'Angelou, '*Abba* and "Father": Imperial Theology and the Jesus Traditions', *JBL* III (1992) 611–30, 623–4.

53

this is distinctive; the *Martyrdom* is only the second text to use χριστιανισμός, which first appears in Ignatius in the early second century. For Ignatius, who may have coined it himself, the term has a double point of reference. In his letter to the *Romans* 3.3, 'but χριστιανισμός is not the work of persuasiveness but of greatness when it is hated by the world', it belongs in the context of anticipated suffering and martyrdom, as it does in the *Martyrdom of Polycarp*. In two letters (*Magn.* 10.1, 3; *Philad.* 6.1), however, it appears in explicit contrast with 'Judaism', ἰουδαισμός, a term that is already to be found in earlier Jewish tradition and which may have provided Ignatius with a model for his own coinage of 'Christianism':[13] 'If anyone interpret *Judaism* to you, do not listen to him. For it is better to hear *Christianism* from a man who is circumcised than *Judaism* from the uncircumcised' (*Philad.* 6.1). The name 'Christian' belongs to the same contexts: in contrast to the other Apostolic Fathers (where it otherwise comes only in *Didache* 12.4 and the apologetic *Epistle to Diognetus*), it is important for Ignatius,[14] as well as for *Mart.Poly.*; it is equally important for the other Martyr Acts, and for the Apologists who both claim it as a self-designation and defend it against outsiders' use of it as a basis for attack.

Each of these terms plays a role in the developing self-consciousness of separate identity of the early Christians, and invites further analysis. Here, however, it is 'the race of the God-fearers' which is of particular interest. Both the idea of Christians as a race, γένος, and an emphasis on their 'fear of God' (θεοσέβεια) are not peculiar to the *Martyrdom of Polycarp* but seem to have been emerging more widely in the middle of the second century. Although these terms are foreign to the New Testament and earlier Apostolic Fathers,[15] the *Epistle to Diognetus* takes as its starting-point the pagan recipient's, Diognetus's, enthusiasm to learn more about the 'fear of God of the Christians' (1.1. θεοσέβεια τῶν χριστιανῶν); this is defined as both 'who is the God in whom they have put their trust and how they worship him so that they all disregard the world and despise death'. The theme of the *Epistle* is that by their rejection of those who are considered gods by the Greeks and

---

[13] For ἰουδαισμός see below n. 29; there is nothing to confirm whether or not the term came directly to Ignatius from Jewish sources.

[14] See K. Bommes, *Weizen Gottes* (Theophaneia, 27, P. Hanstein: Köln, 1976) 32 n. 35.

[15] See only 1 Tim. 2.10; John 9.31; *1 Clem.* 17.3 (quoting Job 1.1); *2 Clem.* 20.4. The more common Greek term 'piety', etc. (εὐσεβ-) is used more frequently by *1 Clem.* (eight times), by *2 Clem.* (three times), but by Tatian not at all and by Athenagoras as frequently as 'God-fearing' (five times).

of the superstition (δεισιδαιμονία) of the Jews, Christians are constituted a new race (γένος) or practice (ἐπιτήδευμα). The author goes on to demonstrate both the folly of Greek worship of images made of wood, stone or metal, and the self-deception of Jewish claims to worship the one God. Jewish sacrificial worship and attention to the calendar is folly and not the fear of God (θεοσέβεια) they assume it to be (3.3; 4.5), while sabbath observance is simply impious (ἀσεβές, 4.3). It is only the Christians who can validly claim a θεοσέβεια (4.6; 6.4).[16] Furthermore, although they do live in the midst of Greeks and barbarians and have none of the institutions of a separate people, Christians do have their own distinctive citizenship (πολιτεία, 6.4), and yet they are hated and persecuted by all.

The differentiating use of γένος and the polemical defence of Christianity over against the worship or fear-of-God of Greeks and Jews are also to be found in other contemporary Christian texts. In the *Kerygma Petri*, which survives only in a few quotations and which may have been a source for the *ad Diognet.*,[17] Christians are those 'who worship (fear) God (θεὸν σέβειν) in a new way and third type' or 'as a third race' (οἱ καινῶς αὐτὸν τρίτῳ γένει σεβόμενοι χριστιανοί: Clement, *Strom.* VI.5.41), to be contrasted with the old ways of both Greeks and Jews.

It is, however, in the *Apology of Aristides* that the sense of γένος as a subdivision of the human race with genealogy and extended characteristics is most developed.[18] Writing in the time of either Hadrian or Antoninus Pius, Aristides divided the world, according to the Greek recension, into three races, γένη – those who worship the so-called gods, Jews, and Christians (2.1); the Syriac recension here speaks of four races, replacing the worshippers of the so-called gods with the barbarians and the Greeks, which brings the Jews and Christians closer together but ignores the fact that for many ancient authors the Jews

---

[16] In the context 'religion' is an inadequate translation here; 'piety' would capture the contrast with ἀσεβές but loses the connection with the noun 'God-fearers'.

[17] See H. G. Meecham, *The Epistle to Diognetus* (Manchester University Press: Manchester, 1949) 58–9.

[18] On the relation between *Aristides* and *Diognetus* see Meecham, *Diognetus*, 59–61 who notes points at which *Aristides* and the *Kerygma Petri* agree against *Diognetus* and points at which the last two agree against *Aristides*. There are undoubted links between all three documents but it is difficult to establish that these reflect literary dependence. 'Race' is also used of Christians in Hermas, *Sim.* IX.17.5; 30.3 in describing apostates as losing their place in the 'race of the righteous'. On this and what follows see now Lieu, *Image and Reality*, 164–77.

were barbarians.[19] Again it is their understanding and worship of God which, as the author demonstrates at length, differentiates the 'races' from each other; the Jews, it is true, are given a special place, particularly in the more eirenic Syriac version which acknowledges the links between the Christians and the Jews through Jesus Christ who was born of a Hebrew. Yet for all this the Christians are a 'new race' and blessed more than all other people (16.4; 17.5).[20] Needless to say, a paramount concern of the *Apology* is the necessity of worshipping (σέβεσθαι) only the unseen and all-seeing God (θεόν) (13.8). Although the specific terms 'fear of God' or 'God-fearing' are not used in the extant text, the original title may have been 'concerning the fear of God (θεοσέβεια)'. This is implied by the Syriac version which alone preserves a title ('on the fear of God') and by Eusebius's reference to the Apology in the *Chronicle*,[21] although 'piety', εὐσέβεια, would be another possibility (cf. Eusebius's description of Aristides as 'faithful and devoted to our εὐσέβεια' (*H.E.* IV.1.3).

The importance of θεοσέβεια in an Apologetic setting is confirmed by Quadratus who, probably under Hadrian, also penned an Apology. According to Eusebius (*H.E.* IV.3.1) this was 'concerning our fear of God' (ὑπὲρ τῆς καθ' ἡμᾶς θεοσεβείας) and was provoked by those who sought to 'cause us trouble'.[22] Unfortunately, nearly all traces of this Apology are lost, despite Eusebius's assertion that it was still extant in his own time and testified to its author's insight and apostolic correctness. Later, Melito of Sardis addressed an Apology or appeal to the Emperor Marcus Aurelius; in this he complained of the unprecedented persecution being suffered by 'the race of the God-fearers' (τὸ τῶν θεοσεβῶν γένος) as a result of new decrees throughout Asia (Eusebius, *H.E.* IV.26.5). Precisely what these decrees were remains

---

[19] The Armenian recension also speaks of four: barbarians, Greeks, Hebrews and Christians.

[20] These are supplied from the Syriac.

[21] The original heading of the Greek was lost when the *Apology* was incorporated into the later romance of Barlaam and Josaphat. Eusebius *Chron.* 199 implies a common title for the Apologies of Aristides and Quadratus, *pro religione nostra*, probably representing θεοσέβεια. So J. R. Harris, *The Apology of Aristides* (Texts and Studies 1.1, Cambridge University Press: Cambridge, 1891) 10; R. Seeberg, *Die Apologie des Aristides* in T. Zahn, *Forschungen zur Geschichte des neutestamentlichen Kanons* V (Deichert: Erlangen, 1893) 161–411, 264–5 argues for θεοσέβεια on the grounds that borrowing from Aristides explains its use in *Diognetus*.

[22] Jerome reports the Apology as being *pro [christiana] religione [nostra]* while in George Syncellus it becomes ὑπὲρ τῶν χριστιανῶν.

unclear; if they were provoked by particular charges against the Christians or by civil unrest, Melito may have chosen the epithet 'God-fearers' for its apologetic note. The few surviving fragments of his *Apology* offer limited hints of his argument; they do suggest that he tried to claim civic loyalty by pointing to the correlation between the rise of Christianity and the security of the Empire since Augustus. To this end Melito distances 'our philosophy' from the 'barbarians' among whom it first flourished, preferring to claim a place among 'your nations' and a security alongside other forms of worship (θρησκεία) (Eusebius, *H.E.* IV.26.5–11); perhaps he found the claim to be a separate γένος one to be handled with care or avoided entirely.

In these texts we see two concerns in close combination; Christians are a 'race' (γένος), a term which both claims a cohesive identity and differentiates them from others, not least the Jews.[23] At the same time they are those who fear God, the God-fearers, a claim which in the contexts reviewed carries both a defensive and an offensive note, defensive against possible detraction, offensive against other such claims, again not least from the Jews. The background to these two ideas helps explain the force of the argument.

A race

Two trajectories seem to lead to the designation of Christians being 'a race'. First, Tertullian knows but also rejects the label 'the third race' (*tertium genus*) as a slur on the lips of the Christians' opponents (*ad Nat.* I.8; *Scorp.* 10.10); what he seems to find particularly unacceptable is the 'third' with its implications of last and least significant. Perhaps behind the accusation lies something like Suetonius's designation of Christians as a 'race' (*genus*) of men holding a new and mischievous (*malefica*) superstition', with its implication of alienation from and a threat to the state (*Vita Neronis* 16.2); in a world divided (according to one side) into barbarians and non-barbarians there was – as Melito may have realized – no room for a 'third' race.[24] Yet in this sense the

---

[23] Justin does not use the concept of 'the third race': O. Skarsaune, *The Proof from Prophecy* (NT.S 56, Brill: Leiden, 1987) 332.

[24] So D. van Damme, 'Gottesvolk und Gottesreich in der christlichen Antike', *Theologische Berichte III* (Benziger: Zurich, 1974) 157–68. A. Schneider, *Le Premier Livre Ad Nationes de Tertullien* (Inst. Suisse de Rome: Neuchâtel, 1968) 187–91 argues that the term originated with the Christians and was reinterpreted by the pagans, while H. Karpp, 'Christennamen', *RAC* II, 1114–38, 1124–5 argues for independent development.

term could also be used by the Christians to good effect, to claim both universality and independence of any other national or Empire cult;[25] another source for this, but notably without the use of the term 'race', was the New Testament sense of being a new creation.

However, behind the Christian affirmation also lies the Jewish. The sense of being a race or people is one proudly held in Jewish literature from the Maccabaean period, often in a context of suffering and persecution. The threat from the Assyrians is directed against 'the race of Israel' (Judith 6.2, 5, 19; 8.20, 32; 11.10), while Judith herself prays 'may your whole nation (ἔθνος) and every tribe know that you are God . . . and there is none other who shields the race (γένος) of Israel' (9.14). In her triumph Judith is acclaimed as 'the glory of Jerusalem, the great pride of Israel, the great boast of our race' (15:9), while she herself proclaims 'Woe to the nations who attack my race' (16:17). The same is true in the Maccabean literature: γένος joins the more widespread and older λαός in proclaiming a sense of identity in the midst of hostility and attempted annihilation, and in implying a contrast with all the other nations who give way to the oppressor's demands (2 Macc. 8.9; 14.8). The author admonishes his readers 'not to be disheartened by these events but to consider them as penalties not for destruction but for the discipline of our race' (2 Macc. 6.12), while the last of the brother martyrs prays that 'the wrath of the almighty which has justly fallen on all our race be halted with me and my brothers'.[26] A similar sense of internal loyalty is expressed when Tobit practises his acts of charity towards those who are of his γένος or ἔθνος (1.3, 16–17; 2.3), while in apologetic literature the term defines more clearly a particular pattern of life and a contrast with other peoples. The *Sybilline Oracles* speak of the Jewish people as 'the race of the most righteous' or 'of the pious', distinguishing them by their virtues and divine favour from all other peoples: 'There is a city . . . on earth, Ur of the Chaldees, from which stems a race of the most righteous men' (III. 219; see III. 573 discussed below and V. 249: 'the divine and heavenly race of blessed Jews')

---

[25] So van Damme, 'Gottesvolk', 160, but he is probably wrong to argue that this justification excludes any implied replacement of the Jewish people.
[26] ἔθνος is also used alongside γένος in this way (2 Macc. 10.8; 11.25, 27; 4 Macc. 4:19); on this theme see J. W. van Henten, B. Dehandschutter and H. J. W. van fer Klaauw, eds., *Die Enstehung der jüdischen Martyrologie* (SPB 38, Brill: Leiden, 1989) 127–8. See also Dan. 1.6 (LXX: the four are ἐκ τοῦ γένους τῶν υἱῶν Ἰσραηλ. Theod. follows the MT in only reading 'of the sons of Israel'); 3 Macc. 1.3; 7.10.

Although contemporary Jewish testimonies are lacking, it is possible that the Jews already spoke of themselves as the '*third* race', only to have the epithet taken over by the Christians.[27] For the latter, then, the definition of 'third' as a contrast to 'Greeks and Jews' would have been a Christian appropriation and redefinition of a term which originally had other connotations.[28]

Other elements of self-conscious separate identity parallel to those in the *Martyrdom of Polycarp* are also found in this literature. It was this setting that prompted the creation of the term 'Judaism' (ἰουδαισμός) as an all-embracing term to encompass the life and beliefs for which the battle was fought: 'those who for the sake of Judaism vied in acting the man' (2 Macc. 2.21; cf. 8.1; 14.38; 4 Macc. 4.26).[29] Perhaps inevitably, bound up with the threat of martyrdom there developed an understanding of Judaism and of the Jewish people set over against a hostile world which was bent on its destruction. Judaism demanded a loyalty of belief and life that could lead to death itself and set the Jewish people apart from all other peoples. It provided a citizenship or city life of its own, even when circumstances gave this no political reality. Language drawn from the city is common: the Jewish way of life is a 'citizenship' (πολιτεία, πολιτεύεσθαι) which is defined by its opposition to alien (or Greek) practices (2 Macc. 4.11; 8.17; 4 Macc. 5.16; 8.7; 17.9);[30] in 2 Macc. 14.37 Razis is, on account of his loyalty, named 'father of the Jews', perhaps an echo of the Roman title 'father of the Roman people', but one which is echoed by the charge brought by the mob against Polycarp with which we started.[31] In even closer parallel, in 4 Maccabees it is the martyrs who are called father or mother of the Jewish people: 'But the daughter of the God-fearing (θεοσεβής)

---

[27] So L. Baeck, 'Das dritte Geschlecht' in S. Baron and A. Marx, eds., *Jewish Studies in Memory of G. A. Kohut* (A. Kohut Memorial Foundation: New York, 1935) 40–6 who argues for a tannaitic origin to the rabbinic use of the phrase of those who have part in the Messianic period, possibly drawing on Hos. 6.2. Karpp, 'Christennamen' suggests a Jewish origin in Egypt in the contrast between Jews, Egyptians and Greeks.

[28] There are, of course, New Testament roots to this 'refinement'; see 1 Cor. 1.22 and P. Richardson, *Israel in the Apostolic Church* (SNTS.MS 10, Cambridge University Press: Cambridge, 1969).

[29] See Y. Amir, 'The Term Ἰουδαισμός (*IOUDAISMOS*); A Study in Jewish-Hellenistic Self-Definition', *Immanuel* 14 (1982) 34–41.

[30] 2 Macc. 6.1; 11.25; 13.14; 3 Macc. 3.4, 21, 23; 4 Macc. 2.8, 23; 3.20; 4.23; Esther 8.13. See M. Hengel, 'Die Synagogeninschrift von Stobi', *ZNW* 57 (1966) 145–83, 180–1.

[31] Livy, *Hist.* VI.14.5; see van Henten, *Die Enstehung*, 143–4 and above, p. 53 and n. 12.

Abraham remembered his bravery: O mother of the nation, avenger of the law and champion of piety (εὐσέβεια) and victor of the contest of the heart' (4 Macc. 15.29, cf. 7.1, 9).

Those who fear God

This brings us back to the second theme, the claim that Christians are those 'who fear God'. Here, while our particular interest is with the θεοσεβ- word group, we cannot ignore the near equivalent εὐσεβής/ εὐσέβεια, here rendered 'pious/piety'. This concept is a common one in Greek sources, both literary and epigraphical, and could encompass respect due to the gods, respect due to family and state, and the appropriate behaviour and attitudes. However, while both Jews and Christians did adopt it, there is some evidence that they particularly favoured θεοσέβεια as a more appropriate equivalent. Whereas pagan inscriptions are apt to celebrate their honorand as 'pious' (εὐσεβής), the claim that he or she was θεοσεβής seems to have been monopolized by the Jews.[32] At Sardis, for example, one of the donors of the mosaics decorating the synagogue – almost certainly a Jew – proclaims to posterity 'Aurelius Eulogios, God-fearing (θεοσεβής), I fulfilled a vow'.[33] Despite this preference, the development of the use of the terms may initially be viewed together.

Bertram's claim that both terms reflect the piety of Hellenistic Judaism (as opposed to that of the 'Old Testament') arises from their relative infrequency in the Septuagint, except in 4 Maccabees and, in the case of εὐσέβεια, in the Wisdom tradition.[34] The common Old Testament concept of 'fear (of God/the Lord)', ירא, is usually rendered by φόβος/ φοβοῦμαι, probably providing the model for at least the φοβούμενος formula used by Acts.[35] It is possible, but undemonstrable, that the rare use of θεοσεβής of the 'non-Jew' Job (1.1, 8; 2.3), and of θεοσέβεια in a 'non-Jewish' context by Abraham (Gen. 20.11) and Job (28.28) may

---

[32] So L. Robert, *Nouvelles Inscriptions*, 44; on the use of εὐσεβής in epitaphs see idem, *Hellenica* II (1946) 81.

[33] Robert, *Nouvelles Inscriptions*, 39. There are other examples at Sardis. See also above, p. 37–8.

[34] G. Bertram, 'Der Begriff "Religion" in der Septuaginta', *ZDMG* 12 (1934) 1–5; see n. 8 above.

[35] Gen. 22.12; Psalm 134.20 and frequently; see Overman, 'The God-Fearers', 20–1; for the formulae used in Acts see above, p. 49.

have been more influential in later Jewish and Christian usage than is now apparent;[36] both men continue to be remembered as pre-eminently God-fearing (Abraham: 4 Macc. 15.28; *T.Naph.* 1.10; Anon. in Eusebius, *Praep.Ev.* IX.17.3; Job: Ps. Aristeas in Eusebius, *Praep.Ev.* IX.25.4).[37] However, the development of the concept in 4 Maccabees takes us further.

The governing theme of 4 Maccabees, where the εὐσεβ- word group appears over sixty times, is a demonstration of how 'devout reason', εὐσεβὴς λογισμός, should be master of the emotions (1.1; 6.31; 17.1, 3; 13.1; 18.1–3, etc.), as evidenced by the readiness of each of the martyrs to die διὰ τὴν εὐσεβείαν (7.16; 9.6, 7, 23, 29, 30, etc.). This represents a combination of the Hellenistic commitment to 'reason' with the Jewish commitment to the Law, particularly as expressed in maintenance of food regulations (5.18, 24), and leads to the result that the Jews can be shown to have a pre-eminent claim to εὐσέβεια. θεοσεβ- is used in a broadly similar way, in contrast to the 'Old Testament' pattern just noted.[38] It is for this that the martyrs suffer, and this which in them conquers and wins a crown of victory (4 Macc. 7.6, 22; 15.28; 16.11; 17.15); as just noted, the mother of the seven martyrs is likened to Abraham as θεοσεβής (15.28; 16.11; cf. Judith 11.17).

A similar convergence with Hellenistic ideals is made by the *Letter of Aristeas*; here εὐσέβεια is both the answer to the questions of the true identity of beauty and of sound judgement, and is itself defined as the recognition of God's continuing activity and omniscience (§§ 229; 255; 210). Similarly, when *T.Reub.* 6.4 says that in sexual promiscuity there is place for neither understanding nor piety (εὐσέβεια), Jewish values are being expressed in Hellenistic terms. At times, then, 'piety' or 'to be pious' comes close to the Hebrew use of *hesed/hasid* as a self-designation of covenant faithfulness; for 4 Macc. 17.22 the martyrs are the pious (εὐσεβεῖς) whose blood is a source of salvation, while *T.Levi* 16.2 anticipates a generation that will 'persecute just men and hate the *pious*'. This becomes explicit in the *Third Sybilline* where the Jews are 'a holy

---

[36] θεοσεβής is also used at Exod. 18.21, while Job 6.14 unusually translates ἐπισκοπή.

[37] In Genesis Abraham (as a Jew?) is not 'God-fearing' but one who 'fears God' (ὅτι φοβῇ τὸν θεόν: 22.12), although he speaks of the lack of θεοσέβεια in Egypt. For the parallel between Job and Abraham see also *bSotah* 31a cited by Wilcox, 'The "Godfearers" in Acts', 106, who argues that Luke is putting Cornelius, like Simeon and Lydia, within this tradition.

[38] The two terms are used in parallel at 4 Macc. 7.6 and 17.15 and as *v.l.* at 7.22.

race of pious men' (εὐσεβῶν ἀνδρῶν ἱερὸν γένος), a piety expressed in their honour of the Temple, their sacrifices, their rejection of idols, their sanctification of the flesh with water, their honour of parents, and their rejection of marital infidelity and homosexuality (l. 573; cf. ll. 213; 769). Both the *Fourth* and *Fifth Sybillines* also see the Jews as a race or tribe of 'pious men' (εὐσέβων φῦλον), even at the point of their defeat by the Romans (IV. l. 136; cf. V. l. 36). This is a piety which is defined in terms of 'the common ethic' of trust in and reverence towards the one God, and a rejection of idolatry, but it is a definition which is fulfilled by the Jews alone (IV. ll. 24–6, 35, 156; V. l. 284); they, surely, are the 'pious' who will survive the judgement and inherit the earth (IV. ll. 40–6, 152–6, 187–90; V. ll. 281–3). Thus the Jewish claim to piety rejects all alternative claims.

In much of this literature θεοσέβεια/-ής is less common. It is comparatively infrequent in Josephus, although much has been made of his description of Poppaea, the wife of Nero, as θεοσεβής (*Ant.* XX. 8.11 [189–96]); this, however, is probably an appreciation of her support or patronage rather than a claim for any overt allegiance to Judaism on her part, and only serves to demonstrate the wide usefulness and reference of the term.[39] Neither does the term figure frequently in Philo although he does rate θεοσέβεια the fairest possession (*de Fuga* 27 [150]) and the greatest of the virtues (*de Opificio* 54 [154]).[40] However, in *Joseph and Aseneth* the θεοσεβ- word group alone is used to the complete exclusion of εὐσεβ-. Here it is Joseph who is 'God-fearing' (4.9), particularly in his refusal to kiss an 'alien' (8.5–8 ἀλλότριος) whose lips would have blessed 'dumb idols' and touched food and drink offered to them; neither could one who was 'God-fearing' sleep with his future wife before the wedding (21.1), while his brothers as θεοσεβεῖς are forbidden any form of retaliatory action (21.1; 23.9–10, etc.) such as

---

[39] On the passage see E. M. Smallwood, 'The Alleged Jewish Tendencies of Poppaea Sabina', *JTS* 10 (1959) 329–35; M. H. Williams, 'Θεοσεβής γὰρ ἦν: The Jewish Tendencies of Poppaea Sabina', *JTS* 39 (1988) 97–111. Josephus does not describe Izates as θεοσεβής although the question is how he may properly 'fear' God (το θειὸν σέβειν *Ant.* XX.2.4 [41]).

[40] It is the last word in *de Virt.* 34 [186]; according to Eusebius, Philo wrote περὶ εὐσεβείας, possibly to be identified with the *Hypothetica*.

[41] See C. Burchard, *Untersuchungen zu Joseph und Asenath* (WUNT 8, Mohr: Tübingen, 1965) 640 who says the word is *fast technisch für die Juden* and that it carries more weight than 'pious' (*fromm*). See also M. Philonenko, *Joseph et Aséneth: Introduction, Texte Critique, Traduction et Notes* (SPB 13, Brill: Leiden, 1968) 142–3. At *T.Jos.* 6.7 Joseph can claim the epithet in his self-control towards Potiphar's wife.

other people might take.[41] It is then an exclusive term applicable only to the Jews who 'fear (the true) God' and who observe the appropriate ethical behaviour; in theory it might be equally applicable to others who adopt this pattern of belief and behaviour, including Aseneth, although it is never explicitly applied to her (but cf. 8.7, a woman who is θεοσεβής should also not kiss a strange man). In the light of the parallels from Acts we should notice that Joseph can also be described as 'humble and compassionate and one who feared the Lord' (φοβουμένος τὸν κυριόν, 8.9; cf. 22.8; 27.2).

The evidence is uneven, just as is the survival of Hellenistic Jewish texts. Yet clearly the claim to be 'pious' carried an important apologetic note both within the Jewish community and in the face of pagan detraction. 'God-fearing', θεοσεβής, offered further advantages over εὐσεβής, for it pointed more directly to Jewish worship of the one God and rejection of idolatry, a theme already present in their use of the latter term. Therefore we should not be surprised that in a community context Jews proudly declared themselves to be θεοσεβής, just as their pagan neighbours celebrated their own εὐσέβεια.[42] We have seen this for a 'home' audience in the synagogue at Sardis where the epithet is claimed by a number of donors; yet it might be equally important for them to make a point of calling themselves 'God-fearing' in an appropriate setting of public display of loyalty to the city. Perhaps this was in the mind of the Jews of Miletus who inscribed on their theatre seats 'place of the Jews who are also *theosebioi*' (τοπος ειουδεων των και θεοσεβιον [*sic*]: *CIJ* II 748); they were turning the adjective into a party label and not, as so often claimed, including an adherent group of 'God-fearers'.[43] The theatre was the place for party claims as later centuries were to demonstrate;[44] it was also the place, as Acts 19.33–4 testifies, where doubts about such loyalty might readily be expressed. That the term could equally be used of, or claimed by those non-Jews who put into action their attraction for or active patronage of Judaism

---

[42] See above, p. 60.
[43] So Robert, *Nouvelles Inscriptions*, 41, 47 following Bertram, 'θεοσεβής', 125. There is no need to see a mistake for 'καὶ τῶν', 'and the Godfearers'. The bibliography on this inscription is vast – not least considering the small number of people who could sit in the area explicitly designated. See H. Hommel, 'Juden und Christen im kaiserzeitlichen Milet', *Sebasmata* II (WUNT 32, Mohr: Tübingen, 1984) 200–30 (reprinted from *Ist.Mitt.* 25 (1975) 167–95).
[44] See C. Roueché, *Performers and Partisans at Aphrodisias* (Society for Promotion of Roman Studies: London, 1992).

is self-evident; the Aphrodisias inscription fits well here – the label is an appreciation of patronage and not an acknowledgement of obedience to certain practices. As well as this more positive assertion, it would also counter any suggestions that such supporters were, as Tacitus said of converts, taught 'to despise the gods, disown their country, hold cheap parents, children and brothers' (*Hist.* V.5) – a succinct definition of the rejection of 'piety'. Yet it is equally self-evident that the Jews would be unlikely to restrict such an effective term to 'fellow-travellers'.

How far the choice of θεοσεβ- rather than εὐσεβ- became a matter of conscious preference among Jews – as *Joseph and Aseneth* might suggest – must remain uncertain. We also find it used in a number of first- and second-century pagan texts: according to Cassius Dio Marcus Aurelius showed himself to be θεοσεβής by even sacrificing at home on days when no public business was done (*Hist. Rom.* LXXII.34.2), while that Emperor himself rates the 'fear of God' alongside holiness and justice as the ultimate goals of reason (*Medit.* XI.20.2).[45] Dionysius of Halicarnassus describes Numa and Xenophon as 'righteous and God-fearing' (δίκαιος καὶ θεοσεβής: *Antiq. Rom.* II.60.4; *Ep.ad Pomp.* 4.2.7), just as Josephus describes David and the Maccabaean loyalists (*Ant.* VII.7.1 [130]; XII.6.3 [284]).[46] What does seem certain is that the terminology belongs to the religious claims and counter-claims of the period, with some roots in Hellenistic or diaspora Judaism.

Polemic and propaganda

Against this background we may return to the Christian sources of the second century. We have already seen how, in contrast to the insignificance of the concept in the New Testament and earlier Apostolic Fathers, the *Epistle to Diognetus* takes up its polemical value, denying any Jewish claims to 'θεοσέβεια' and reserving it for the Christians alone (3.1, 3; 4.5, 6; 6.4). However it is Justin Martyr who provides us with the broadest range of nuances that the term could carry. Not surprisingly Justin shows a slight preference for εὐσέβεια, while θεοσέβεια is restricted to the *Dialogue* with its context of debate with Judaism – thus confirming the significance of the term in a Jewish matrix. In his *Apology* Justin combines εὐσέβεια with φιλοσοφία as a self-evident norm in a calculated appeal to the contemporary political ideal of the

---

[45] Marcus Aurelius appears not to have used εὐσέβεια, etc.
[46] See below, p. 65 on Justin's combination with δίκαιος in *Dial.* 52.4; 53.6; 119.6).

philosopher-ruler: 'reason dictates that those who are in truth *god-fearing and philosophers* should honour and love the truth alone' (2.1–2; 3.2; 12.5; II *Apol.* 15.2).[47] This notion is entirely absent from the *Dialogue;* here εὐσέβεια is defined, instead, by its association with righteousness (δικαιο-),[48] and the Jews are condemned for thinking that such piety is fulfilled by washings or sabbath observance (12.3; 14.2). Indeed, any Jewish claims to εὐσέβεια are denounced (46.7; 95.2), while for Christians their piety along with their 'confession' (ὁμολογία) is a cause of their suffering (11.4; 131.2). For Trypho, Justin's Jewish opponent, however, Christian claims to εὐσεβεῖν are proved false by their failure to distinguish themselves from the pagans by religious observance: 'This in particular perplexes us, that you, who claim to be pious (εὐσεβεῖν) and consider yourselves different from the rest, do not distance yourselves from them in any respect' (10.3). This contest over who can properly claim εὐσέβεια is much more sharply expressed in Justin's use of θεοσέβεια. Christians, particularly Gentile Christians, are described as those who have become θεοσεβεῖς (52.4; 53.6; 131.5) or who have turned to θεοσέβειαν (τοῦ θεοῦ) from idolatry (30.3; 91.3; 110.4). By contrast, the Jews, who are tainted with idolatry (1 Kings 19.18!), fail to maintain an attitude of 'fear of God', although this was their proper vocation (46.6).[49] In the face of potential Jewish counter-claims Justin can affirm on behalf of the Christians: 'this happened by the marvellous foreknowledge of God, so that we might be found to be richer in understanding and *more God-fearing* than you who are neither esteemed nor lovers of God nor understanding' (118.3); it is the Christians, and not the faithless Jews, who constitute the nation (ἔθνος) promised to Abraham, sharing his faith, God-fearing and righteous (θεοσεβὲς καὶ δίκαιον 119.6).

The implicit – and sometimes explicit – countercharge to the claim to be pious or God-fearing is, of course, ἀσέβεια, impiety. As Athenagoras more sanguinely observes, ἀσέβεια belongs to those who fail to share your own θεοσέβεια (*Legatio* 14.7). For Justin the heretics can be indicted for impiety (*Dial.* 35.5; 80.3), but so also can the Jews

---

47 See H. Holfelder, 'Εὐσέβεια καὶ φιλοσοφία: Literarische Einheit und politischer Kontext von Justins Apologie', *ZNW* 68 (1977) 48–66; 231–51.
48 Combined with δικαιοσύνη in 23.5; 93.2; with δικαιοπραξία in 46.7; 47.2, 5.
49 In this section θεοσεβεῖν is identified with the exclusive centring on God which was the purpose of phylacteries.
50 See above, p. 55.

(46.5; 92.4), as we have seen they were also by *Diognetus*.[50] No doubt the Jews levelled the same accusation against the Christians: Justin complains that they seize upon the slightest weakness in exegesis as criminal and impious (115.6). Yet impiety was, of course, equally a charge laid against the Christians by their pagan neighbours (*Apol.* 4.7; 27.1; II *Apol.* 10.4); in this case it might be combined with the charge of being 'atheists' (II *Apol.* 3.2), a double accusation which Christians were proud to share with Socrates (*Apol.* 5.3). This confrontation between the charge of 'atheism' and the affirmation of being 'god-fearing' is one which we have already met in the *Martyrdom of Polycarp*.

That Christians are in fact θεοσεβεῖς served as a defence against such accusations of impiety and atheism, and is used as such by other Apologists of the second century.[51] While for Athenagoras piety (εὐσέβεια) concerning the divine is a widespread concern (*Legat.* 7.8; 28.2; cf. 13.1; 30.7), that Christians alone are God-fearing (θεοσεβεῖς) is warmly defended against charges of their being atheists (*Legat.* 4.2, 5; 12.3; 14.2; 37.1), and is denied of other claimants (12.2, the Epicureans).[52] For Theophilus of Antioch, too, the atheists are rather those who bring slanderous charges against 'those who are called God-fearers and Christians' (τοὺς θεοσεβεῖς καὶ χριστιανοὺς καλουμένομς, *ad Autol.* III.4). Like the other Apologists mentioned earlier, Theophilus describes his work as giving an account 'of my fear of God' (περὶ τῆς θεοσεβείας μου, II.1). Yet there are some hints that he was adopting and adapting the claims of the synagogue; in his account of the ten commandments as observed by the Christians he acknowledges the place of the Jews as a righteous seed of '*God-fearing* and holy men, Abraham, Isaac and Jacob' (III.9) and speaks of the Scriptures as books 'which belong to us, the God-fearers' (τὰ καθ᾽ ἡμας τοὺς θεοσεβεῖς γράμματα. II.30). Such assertions could well have originated on the lips of his Jewish peers.

It is not a large step from this contrastive and defensive use of θεοσέβεια to its becoming a general designation for the true Christian religion. Already in Irenaeus (*adv. Haer.* I.16.3) θεοσέβεια can be paralleled with ἀλήθεια in opposition to heresy, while the Christian women of the Apocryphal Acts refuse intercourse with their husbands

---

[51]   See P. Stockmeier, 'Christlicher Glaube und antike Religiositat', *ANRW* 23. 2, 872–909, 887–90 and 894 on the use of θεοσέβεια in response to the charge of atheism.

[52]   Tatian does not use εὐσέβεια in his *Oration* and speaks of θεοσέβεια as the proper attitude to God whose opposite is being hostile to God (θεομάχος) (*Oratio* 13.3; 17.3).

for the sake of 'the fear of God' (*Act. Ioh.* 63.6 – 64.7; *Act. Petri* 34.11). Yet one further text, the *Cohortatio ad Graecos* falsely attributed to Justin, although composed at the end of the third century when other authors were using θεοσέβεια widely and in this increasingly technical sense, epitomizes the picture we have been able to draw.[53] Avoiding εὐσέβεια altogether, Ps.Justin consistently defends 'our' or 'the true' θεοσέβεια against 'yours' which is falsely called (1.1; 2.1; 3.3, etc.). In fact the whole treatise is a defence of the Christians as alone preserving the true θεοσέβεια, accompanied by an indictment of the total bankruptcy of the Greeks, including Aristotle and Plato, who learned from Moses but apostasized from the 'true fear of God' (25.24; 36.33). There is also an implicit rivalry with Judaism: Ps.Justin is confident that the Christian 'fear of God' is to be found in the Scriptures and can claim all the antiquity of having been taught first by Moses (9.9 – 10.18). He knows too that some may object that 'these writings even now are to be found preserved in *their* synagogues and that we claim to have learnt the "fear of God" from them falsely' (13.5); yet, he responds, this is but an act of divine providence preserving the books which support '*our* θεοσέβεια'. It is not difficult to catch an echo of the earlier Jewish claim to be God-fearing and to possess the true 'fear of God' in the Scriptures. Seeking pagan support for the epithet, Ps.Justin appeals to a Greek oracle which, when asked who were the '*God-fearing* men', declared that 'only the Chaldaeans achieved wisdom, and then the Hebrews who hold God in holy awe as self-begotten and lord' (11.2, repeated at 24.28–9). Whether or not he drew this from Hellenistic Jewish sources, as he did some of his other testimonies, the oracle would have served a Jewish apologetic better than it does Ps.Justin.[54]

To successfully claim to be 'God-fearing' was to secure a multiple advantage; it offered a defence against charges both of impiety and atheism and of superstition – the two extremes which might normally

---

[53] M. Marcovich, ed., *Pseudo-Iustinus: Cohortatio ad Graecos, De Monarchia, Oratio ad Graecos* (PTS 32, de Gruyter: Berlin, 1990) accepts a date of between 260 and 302 (p. 4); θεοσέβεια is used very frequently by Origen a little earlier, see Bertram, 'Θεοσεβής, θεοσέβεια', 127.

[54] On his dependence on Jewish apologetics of the antiquity of Moses see Marcovich, *Pseudo-Iustinus*, 8–9; on this oracle see N. Zeegers-Vander Vorst, *Les Citations des Poètes Grecs chez les Apologistes Chrétiens du IIe Siecle* (Rec. de Trav. d'Hist. et de Phil. 4.47, Bibliothèque de l'Université: Louvain, 1972) 216–23 who argues that it is of Greek and not Jewish origin in the light of its citation by Porphyry (ap. Eusebius, *Praep.Ev.* IX.10.4).

be contrasted with true piety or εὐσέβεια, and which were levelled against Christians in the second century.[55] Unlike εὐσέβεια, it allowed an assertion of Christian monotheism and rejection of idolatry, an assertion inherited from its Jewish antecedents. Consequently it also carried an implicit or explicit denial that anyone else, particularly the Jews, could also claim the epithet. Yet this was only because they did so claim it. Indeed, as we have seen, both groups were making the same claim in a context of accusations or persecution, and both associated that claim with persecution and with suffering.[56] Both, too, were refusing the title to their opponents and claiming it for themselves as part of a cluster of terms asserting a rhetoric of identity, of belonging and of loyalty. Quite how this rhetorical competition was played out on the historical stage may remain uncertain, but those who pursue the history need to recognize the rhetoric: 'Who are the God-fearers?' was then an even more urgent and divisive question than it is now.[57]

---

[55] See J. J.Walsh, 'On Christian Atheism', *VC* 45 (1991) 255–77.
[56] P. Stockmeier, *Glaube und Religion in der frühen Kirche* (Herder: Freiburg, 1972) 32–7 recognizes that Jews and Christians shared the same pattern of response but does not note the implicit competition so implied.
[57] Since this essay has focused on the term θεοσεβής it does not try to answer directly the question of the interpretation of the references in Acts, which use a different terminology; the common appeal to the epigraphic use of θεοσεβής ignores both that difference and the wider and deliberate use of this epithet as it has been traced here.

5

Ignoring the Competition

'In the Graeco-Roman world emergent Christianity jostled with old-established religions like Judaism and traditional Graeco-Roman cults, but also with the cult of the Emperor, mystery cults, etc. How different was Christianity?'[1] This familiar picture is one of a crowded market-place where cults, like traders, elbowed each other into or out of the prime position to attract attention, adherents and status. Such a picture is a relatively recent one – at least, it was presented as such in a collection of essays *The Jews among Pagans and Christians* from a seminar series just ten years ago.[2] It sought to replace the view which we find in earlier *Histories of the Church*, of Christianity marching, vibrant, full of youth and vigour, into a world where traditional religion had lost its persuasive appeal, and the people were waiting, without solace, for a pattern of belief which would meet the deep needs of their intellects and hearts. That older view saw the Graeco-Roman world at the turn of the eras as gripped in an 'Age of Anxiety', the title of a book by E. R. Dodds:[3] no jostling here, but the confident possession of a market-place, agora or forum, where the only competitors were aged, weary, and self-evidently 'sick unto death'. So, for example, Adolf Harnack in his account of the *Expansion of Christianity in the First Three Centuries*, which was written and translated into English a century ago and which was to be one of the most influential 'Histories', wrote:

> When Christianity came upon the scene, indeed, the polytheism of the State-religion was not yet eradicated, nor was it eradicated for some time to come;

---

[1] This is a lightly edited version of a lecture for the Society for the Study of Early Christianity Conference on 'Competing Cults' at Macquarie University, Sydney, May 1998; the quotation comes from the Conference 'blurb'.

[2] J. Lieu, J. North and T. Rajak, eds., *The Jews among Pagans and Christians in the Roman Empire* (Routledge: London, 1992, 1994).

[3] E. R. Dodds, *Pagan and Christian in an Age of Anxiety* (Cambridge University Press: Cambridge, 1965).

but there were plenty of forces at hand which were already compassing its ruin . . . The onset against deities feathered and scaly, deities adulterous and loaded with vices, and on the other hand against idols of wood and stone, formed the most impressive and effective factor in Christian preaching for wide circles, circles which in all ranks of society down to the lowest classes . . . had, owing to experience and circumstances, reached a point at which the burning denunciations of the abomination of idolatry could not but arrest them and bring them over to monotheism. The very position of polytheism as the State-religion was in favour of the Christian propaganda. Religion faced religion; but whilst one was new and living, the other was old, nor could anyone tell exactly what had become of it.[4]

Few, I hope, would now repeat Harnack's enthusiasm, or rather triumphalism. What Harnack calls 'State-religion', a single, hyphenated noun, was hardly already facing its demise, nor is there much evidence that even the lowest classes were already in a position where it was self-evident that 'idolatry' was an abomination, waiting only for this to be proclaimed. On the contrary, the continuing vitality, and perhaps resurgence, of traditional religion in our period has been carefully detailed in recent scholarship, and is now widely accepted.[5]

Our opening quotation's inclusion of other cults, imperial and mystery, had already been anticipated by Harnack; he bundled them together under the heading 'orientalism', and saw in their 'syncretism' – such words are heavily loaded – the real preparation for the Christian preaching: here '. . . it possessed unconsciously a secret ally. All it had to do with syncretism was to cleanse and simplify it'.[6] More recent studies have been less interested in the religio-philosophical mood which Harnack thus branded syncretism or orientalism. Instead they have focused on the structural forms taken by what we may loosely call cults. A notable example of this would be the recent collection of essays edited by John Kloppenborg and Stephen Wilson, *Voluntary Associations in the Graeco-Roman World.*[7] The title reflects the problem of categorizing, for 'voluntary association' may make a modern reader think of the Girl Guides, the Red Cross, or the Rotarians; yet it does draw attention to

---

[4] A. von Harnack, *The Expansion of Christianity in the First Three Centuries* (ET Williams & Norgate: London, 1904–5) I, 27–8.
[5] See especially R. Lane Fox, *Pagans and Christians* (Penguin: Harmondsworth, 1986).
[6] Harnack, *Expansion*, 39.
[7] John Kloppenborg and Stephen Wilson, *Voluntary Associations in the Graeco-Roman World* (Routledge: London, 1996).

the phenomenon of allegiance to mainly locally based groups where membership was not by birth, as in Judaism, nor by default, as in what is commonly called 'paganism', but by individual choice. Such groups, sometimes corporately referred to by only one of the many terms used in the Latin sources, *collegia*, are known to us chiefly from inscriptions, both Greek and Latin, stretching from the classical through to the late imperial periods, as well as from the legislation which repeatedly, and perhaps ineffectively, regularly restricted their meetings. Some of these groups were more overtly 'religious', perhaps founded for the veneration of a particular deity, some less so, perhaps apparently serving the social needs of members or providing for their eventual funeral expenses and so saving them from the ignominy of the mass public grave. For New Testament scholars an influential article is that by Stephen Barton and Greg Horsley, 'A Hellenistic Cult Group and the New Testament Churches'.[8] That article discusses the many similarities in language, structure and ethos between such groups and the first Christian communities, at least as they must have been perceived by interested observers, and perhaps also by participants. Offering local loyalty, a sense of identity and belonging in an impersonal world, some degree of corporate care, communal life, meals and celebrations, status through the numerous offices to be held, and assurance of decent burial, such groups could indeed be included among the real competitors of early Christianity. Kloppenborg and Wilson's book includes in its ambit philosophical schools, early synagogues, the community of the Dead Sea Scrolls, the Asclepieion at Pergamum, and the mysteries of Mithras, showing just how pervasive patterns of local loyalty were, and how difficult it is to adhere to strict demarcations between them defined by practice or by belief. Here there is indeed much jostling going on, and such a rainbow of clothing and complexion that it becomes difficult to describe Christianity except as part of that rainbow.

Yet all this is only by way of introduction: it provokes both a question and an observation. The question: Why, without substantial new discoveries in the interim, was Harnack's picture of a race in which the front runner was clear from the start possible, whereas today we take for granted instead something more like the massed hordes of the Sydney

---

[8] S. Barton and G. H. R. Horsley, 'A Hellenistic Cult Group and the New Testament Churches', *JbAC* 24 (1981) 7–41; the authors were based at Macquarie University, home of the Conference.

fun run?[9] The observation forms the theme of this essay and looks at the early Christian writers themselves for their responses.

When we turn to the writings of the early church what sort of world do we enter? Who else peoples that world alongside the new believers? What threats are there to them as individuals but also as communities? In the words of advertising jargon, who are the market leaders, who represent the main competitors, what alternative products may entice away the loyalty of the faithful? If we had only the Christian literature how would we reconstruct the religious world of the early centuries of the Common Era? The short answer must surely be, a world very different from the jostling crowd of our opening quotation, or of much contemporary reconstruction of the religious vitality of the Roman Empire in the first and second centuries.

This difference is visible as soon as this literature traces Christianity's movement beyond the boundaries of Israel – Palestine into the cities of the Mediterranean world, namely in the Acts of the Apostles. Despite Luke's supposed affinity with the Gentiles, the cities he portrays as the scenes of Paul's missionary activities in Acts boast rather more synagogues than temples.[10] In Acts 14 the Temple of Zeus before the city gate at Lystra is introduced only because its priest initiates sacrifice to Paul and Barnabas (14.13), and, most famously and vividly, in Acts 19 there is the only moment of real competition, from those defending the honour of Artemis and her temple (19.27). In Athens Paul is repulsed by the concentration of idols (17.16), but in his subsequent speech he sees the altar to the unknown God more as an opportunity than as a source of competition, and we are left supposing that it is the philosophers who provide the real point of engagement (17.18). But in Thessalonica and Philippi, in Corinth and Beroea, we would hardly know that we were in a Greek city, and competing deities are notable by their absence.[11] The pervasive presence of 'religion' in the city, and the growing abundance of cults and associations which we are told were a mark of the period are nowhere to be seen.

---

[9]   Or any city marathon!
[10] On this and what follows see H. Moxnes, '"He saw that the city was full of idols" (Acts 17:16) Visualizing the World of the First Christians', in D. Hellholm, H. Moxnes and T. Karlsen Seim, eds., *Mighty Minorities? Minorities in Early Christianity – Positions and Strategies: Essays in honour of Jacob Jervell on his 70th birthday* (Scandinavia University Press: Oslo, 1995) 107–31.
[11] In Acts 16.17 the slave girl recognizes 'the Most High God', a conveniently multi-purpose epithet.

We might expect more from Paul's letters, for these more than Acts presuppose the non-Jewish background of most of those in the communities he founded. Yet we are disappointed. 1 Thessalonians describes the converts as having 'turned to God from idols to serve a living and true God' (1.9), but such language is formulaic and betrays little specific content; equally formulaic is the contrast between believers and the Gentiles who do not know God in 1 Thess. 4.4 where the Gentiles are characterized, or caricatured, as being controlled by lustful passions. A similar stereotyping is found in 1 Peter 4.3–5 with its colourful picture of licentiousness, passions, drunkenness, revels, carousing and lawless idolatry. Such stereotyping tells us nothing of the immediacy of the real world, nor about those other groups who met together, developed their own rules of behaviour, and found meaning for life.

Those familiar with the work of W. Meeks or G. Theissen no doubt will want to point to Paul's Corinthian correspondence.[12] There indeed food sacrificed to idols is a burning issue, and the possibility of being seen eating in the temple of an idol is a bone of contention (1 Cor. 8; 10.14–22). Such meals could have been part of the social experience of members of 'associations' or of 'competing' cults, and it is often pointed out that membership of such would be of social and commercial importance, particularly for the more elite in the Corinthian congregation. Such 'social' reconstructions may indeed be right, and throw valuable light on our understanding of the Pauline letters, but the parallels and illustrations have to be drawn from outside of the New Testament: Paul's failure to elaborate or to address the issues of competition is for us the more significant element.

This silence about the 'competition' even in the more missionary writings of the New Testament is continued in the writings of the second century. The Apostolic Fathers – Ignatius, Polycarp, the Didache, Clement of Rome – offer no real contribution to our theme. This is not because they are purely pastoral, for if the competition were real one would expect it to form a pastoral concern, and even these writings are aware of some forms of competition, as we shall see. However, it is with the later writers from the middle of the second century, the Apologists, that we begin to find an explicit and even polemical acknowledgement

[12] W. Meeks, *The First Urban Christians* (Yale University Press: New Haven, 1983); G. Theissen, *The Social Setting of Pauline Christianity* (ET T&T Clark: Edinburgh, 1982).

of the antithesis between Christianity, as it now begins to be called, and the religious world of the Gentiles.

It is a matter of dispute whether the Apologists really were writing for the outside world, either in general terms or for the emperor and other authorities, which is what they claim in their texts, or whether this is only a guise when in practice their real audience was internal; but this need not trouble us here. In each case, to address the alternatives against which Christianity defined itself would, it might be assumed, demand some acknowledgement of their character. And indeed, each of the Apologists does attack or pillory both the worship offered by the Gentiles and the recipients of that worship. Yet if we were, once again, to reconstruct the religion of the cities of the Empire from these attacks we would come up with a strange and distorted account. For example, Athenagoras wrote his *Embassy* in around 177 CE, yet when he attacks 'pagan' worship it is with a description which explicitly appeals to Homer, Plato, Pindar and Euripides as his authorities; when he wants to give a 'recent' example, 'yesterday or the day before' (*Legatio* 28.6), it is the tragedian of the fourth century BCE, Euripides, whom he cites. His most recent 'authority' appears to be Apollodorus, a writer of the second century BCE, and it is possible that most of his information is drawn from that author.[13]

This does not mean that Athenagoras has no contemporary knowledge. He refers to the miracles associated with the statues of Proteus Peregrinus and Alexander of Abonuteichos (*Legatio* 26). Both of these cult-founders are familiar from the writings of the near contemporary pagan satirist, Lucian of Samosata.[14] Lucian is roundly contemptuous of them, and his accounts could even be read as presenting Peregrinus and Alexander and their 'new religious movements' as competitors of Christianity; he refers to the gullibility of the Christians in the *Peregrinus* (13), and the eponymous hero dies a spectacular death which has been seen as a parody of Christian martyr accounts (32–34). But the Christian writer, Athenagoras, does not present them as active rivals: for him they are merely further examples of an unchanging problem of (what he did not yet call) 'paganism'.

Much of Athenagoras's ire is fired with denouncing the worship of idols of silver and gold. This is a common theme in the Christian

---

[13] So W. Schoedel, ed., *Athenagoras, Legatio and De Resurrectione* (OECT, Clarendon Press: Oxford, 1972) 71 n.

[14] Lucian, *Peregrinus; Alexander the False Prophet.*

Apologists (cf. *Epistle to Diognetus* 2). It has venerable antecedents going back, with little material change, to the prophetic denunciations of Isaiah 44–46 in the sixth century BCE; the same 'self-evident' mockery of worshipping the same wood on which a man (*sic*) cooks his dinner is repeated by various texts in various places thereafter. The term 'idol' (εἴδωλον) used in this sense is something that the Christians took over from their Jewish past, and it was they and not their pagan contemporaries who thought – or assumed for their own purposes – that worship and sacrifice were made to the image alone; we may suspect that such arguments would carry little force with most of Athenagoras's Gentile readers, pagan and Christian convert alike. It is a purely literary polemic, preaching to the converted, and drawn not from real contemporary experience but from the dusty texts of the past.

Much is often made of the new so-called 'oriental' cults as potential competitors of Christianity in this period, particularly those dedicated to Isis and to Mithras. Athenagoras does indeed refer at some length to Isis, but his knowledge of her story is drawn from Herodotus (*Legatio* 28). The same is true of the Apologist Aristides, writing perhaps a little earlier. He classifies the 'races' of humankind, and defines them by their religious traditions and loyalties; yet for him it is the Egyptians who are characterized by the worship of Isis, not the Greeks into whose world her cult had long since moved (*Apology* 12.2). We can suspect from his account of the Egyptians that his knowledge is entirely 'bookish' – it repeats what ethnographers had long been saying, that the Egyptians worshipped gods in the form of animals; his bibliography is more than a little out-of-date. This is no urgent issue for him.

Mithras is mentioned in our period only by Justin Martyr in the middle of the second century, perhaps appropriately as a writer then living in Rome. Here he does imply some degree of competition, for he sees the Mithraic use of bread and a cup of water as a demonic imitation of the Christian eucharist (*Apol.* 66.4), and their use of a cave as the place of initiation in supposed recollection of Mithras's cave-birth as demonic plagiarism of Isaiah and Daniel (*Dial.* 70.1; 78.6). Demonic inspiration of pagan religion is a common theme (cf. Minucius Felix, *Octavius* 26–7), but the competition they offer is not one in the lives and emotions of individuals and groups, but in the intellectual construction of the divinity.

Even more detail is found in Minucius Felix at the end of the second century. He argued for the folly of worshipping deities who had begun their lives as human beings and who had been 'upgraded', who wept, wailed and died, who engaged or provoked engagement in wild and orgiastic behaviour. He knows that the rites of Isis, once Egyptian, 'are now even practised in Rome' (*Oct.* 22.1), that the Galli castrate themselves in honour of Cybele, that Jupiter's tomb is visited even 'today' (23.13); his description, or rather vilification, of Roman deities and religious practice is rich and detailed – but it probably could have been written by anyone who had read their classical and more recent writers. These are not competing cults; it is the full panoply of Roman religion as a literary, even if also as a popular, reality which is to be attacked, not because it competes with Christianity, but because its folly has to be demonstrated in order to defend Christian piety.

It also represents something more, and this becomes much stronger in subsequent writers. The introduction of a mid-nineteenth-century edition of Tertullian's *On Idolatry* paints a wonderful, elaborately detailed picture of religion in the city, or what it calls 'heathen life'. Simply to quote from its conclusion:

> Thus hedged in with idolatry, unable to enter the streets or market-place without seeing things which to him were an abomination, the Christian of Tertullian's day might well feel the world to be filled by Satan and his ministers, and tremble lest he make shipwreck of his faith among the rocks and shoals of idolatry.[15]

Not competition, then, but the ever present snares of the devil; the world not in which the Christian is engaged in healthy market competition but from which the Christian fled and sought protection. The picture just quoted is, incidentally, drawn not from independent sources but entirely from Tertullian's tirade against idolatry and its multifarious manifestations. And not a competing cult is to be seen.

Thus far we have focused on the Graeco-Roman cults, but we should not ignore Judaism, for most major cities of the Empire would have had at least one Jewish community or synagogue. To outsiders the Christian churches must have looked much like synagogues, not as buildings but as communities organized for weekly meeting, imageless

---

[15]   G. Currey, *Tertulliani Libri Tres, De Spectaculis, De Idololatria, et De Corona Militis* (Cambridge University Press: Cambridge, n.d.) xxvi–xxvii. See also C. Edwards, *The Politics of Immorality in Ancient Rome* (Cambridge University Press: Cambridge, 1993) 33 for the way that Christian polemics against Roman vice and pagan immorality have shaped later 'historical' accounts of society 'as it was'.

'worship', study of sacred texts and corporate care. To explore the early Christian writers' perception of or picture of these Jewish communities would take more than a short essay – and it has taken a book for me to explore just a few.[16] That the Jewish synagogues also offered some competition to the early Christian groups has also become part of the modern reconstruction, once again in contrast to older views which largely 'wrote the Jews off' after the end of the first century from histories of the church and of the Roman Empire. Why was this older view which excluded the Jews from our jostling crowd possible? Not because the Christian writers fail to mention the Jews: they are a real problem for a number of them and occupy writings of every genre. Yet curiously the Jews whom these writers attack are not members of the synagogue across the market-place, but the Jews of the past, of Scripture. It is often supposed that the Letter to the Hebrews was written to counteract the appeal of contemporary Judaism, yet its arguments about the superiority of Christ do not draw on contemporary reality, nor even on the Jerusalem Temple, but on the Tabernacle of the wilderness wanderings as described in the Scriptures (Heb. 8–9). Similarly, the *Epistle of Barnabas*, surely written after 70 CE and the destruction of the Temple, and probably not in the Land of Israel but in a Diaspora city, is concerned about Temple, sacrifice and food-laws.[17] The *Epistle to Diognetus* mocks:

> When they [the Jews] believe themselves to be fulfilling their sacrifices to him by means of blood, fat and burnt offerings, and fancy that they are doing him honour by such rites, I cannot see that there is anything to choose between them and those who lavish similar attention on things that are deaf. (*Diog.* 3.5)

Yet this letter was written in a Diaspora city where no Jews offered sacrifices, and at a time when even in the Land of Israel the Temple had long been destroyed.

The reason for this focus on the Jews of Scripture in Christian writings is evident and not disputed. The Christians claimed to revere as Scripture the same texts as did the Jews; they claimed to be the heirs of God's promises through the prophets of the biblical tradition; some even claimed to be the true Israel, the authentic people of God. Yet the

---

[16] J. M. Lieu, *Image and Reality: The Jews in the World of the Christians in the Second Century* (T&T Clark: Edinburgh, 1996).

[17] On *Barnabas* see J. Carleton Paget, *The Epistle of Barnabas: Outlook and Background* (WUNT 2.64, Mohr: Tübingen, 1994).

Christians did not observe the Law as prescribed in Scripture; they did not observe sabbath or circumcision, sacrifice or purity; and so they defended themselves by seeking to 'prove' that such practices were not God's intention, perhaps never had been; that observance of them was not a sign of piety but of impiety. The Jews of the 'Old Testament', as Christians came to call it, are the opponents for Christian Apologists because the Old Testament was a problem. Yet is this sufficient explanation for why Christian writers almost totally fail to address also the Jews who were their contemporaries, the Jews who, as modern scholarship suggests, may have been competing for the same adherents, perhaps even attracting members from the Christian community into the synagogue? Probably not. Neither can it explain why they ignore the competing cults whose local expressions are becoming increasingly well documented: the traditions of Graeco-Roman paganism did not present the Christians with the same conceptual and theological problems as did the Jewish Scriptures.

Yet here is a clue: it is 'the traditions' which count; the Apologists look not to the market-place but to the library. They conclude with a message of stern warning to more classically inclined readers:[18]

> For what did it profit Homer to have composed the Trojan War ... what good did their tragedies do to Euripedes and Sophocles, ... or their comedies to Menander and Aristophanes ... or their histories to Herodotus and Thucydides? (Theophilus of Antioch, *ad Autolycum* III.2)

It is hardly the intention of this essay to suggest that there were no 'competing cults' as Christianity emerged within the Roman Empire. It would be flying in the face of so much contrary evidence to return to the old picture of a paganism consisting only of the traditional deities and their myths and rituals, of a paganism that was self-evidently no longer credible or satisfying. That picture could be drawn only by taking the Christian writers at their word, a method that is naive. This alternative may be naive without further elaboration, but it offers a starting-point. The Christians lived in two worlds: the world which they shared with their neighbours, the world of competing cults, a world that is so often hidden from our direct gaze; and the world that they constructed through their texts, a world in which the Christian

---

[18] The Society for the Study of Early Christianity at Macquarie University is sponsored largely from within the Department of Ancient History.

worship of God brooked no competition. In order to understand how it was that Christianity emerged and eventually 'reconstructed' the world we have to ask what was it like to live at once in two such different worlds?

Part II

Women and Conversion in Judaism and Christianity

6

The 'Attraction of Women' in/to
Early Judaism and Christianity:
Gender and the Politics of Conversion*

It has been a truism of scholarship that women were particularly attracted to Christianity, and that women numbered significantly among its earliest members – although such claims are rarely accompanied by statistical elaboration.[1] This claim is frequently presented, whether implicitly or explicitly, as a correlative to the idea that Christianity – often as personified by Jesus or less frequently by Paul – was 'good' for women, paid them particular attention, or at least offered them opportunities not otherwise available; to caricature, the ideal of 'the feminist Jesus'. The politics of such a view are self-evident, for much study of the subject has developed within a context where women were struggling to establish a proper role for themselves within the contemporary church; to this end they have sought an egalitarian past to act as a model for present polity. While other enthusiastic assertions about the distinctiveness of early Christianity and/or of the teaching of Jesus have been somewhat tempered in recent years, this one, for those same reasons, has continued to be repeated. It is the purpose of this discussion neither to prove nor to disprove that claim, something which with our evidence may not be possible, but rather to explore the rhetoric which surrounds it and to expose the hazards of the naive use of sources which often accompanies it.

* First published in *JSNT* 72 (1998) 5–22. Reprinted by permission of Sheffield Academic Press.

---

[1] See, for example, such diverse voices as J. Bremmer, 'Why did Early Christianity Attract Upper-Class Women?', in A. A. R. Bastiaensen, A. Hilhorst and C. H. Kneepkens, eds., *Fructus Centesimus: Mélanges offerts à Gerard J. M. Bartelink à l'occasion de son soixante-cinquième anniversaire* (Instr.Pat. XIX, Kluwer Academic: Dordrecht/Steenbrugis: Abbey of S. Peter, 1989) 35–47, 37–8 [Harnack] 'convincingly demonstrates the great importance of women; women were apparently in the majority in the early Church'; H. Chadwick, *The Early Church* (Penguin: Harmondsworth, 1967) 58–9; R. Stark, *The Rise of Christianity* (Princeton University Press: Princeton, 1996) 95; S. Heine, *Women and Early Christianity* (SCM Press: London, 1987) 86. For Harnack see below, n. 44.

To do so is not totally new: a range of recent studies has shown that such wishful thinking about Jesus' or Paul's 'liberalism' is deeply flawed, resting on a naive use of the early Christian sources, particularly regarding Jesus, and on a, perhaps less naive, misuse of the Jewish sources, taking as descriptive of the first century, the prescriptive construction of a world by the second-century male scholarly elite we know as the rabbis.[2] This latter step resulted from the desire to show not just that Jesus' or Paul's attitude was affirmative – which in twentieth-century terms is not easy to argue – but that it was far superior to or at least more liberated than their contemporaries, particularly within Judaism.[3] This particular story has often been told: to establish the 'uniqueness' of Jesus – in his attitude to women as in other matters – scholars have drawn a negative picture of Jewish values of the time. That, too, we may recognize as 'political' – affirmation by denigration – and it is deeply to be regretted that feminist analysis recognized too late its entrapment in such a schema.[4]

Yet, ironically, it has also been possible to claim that women were particularly attracted to Judaism and were a majority among full converts.[5] This does not only suggest that claims for the novelty of early Christian attitudes are over-simplistic, it also allows for a useful comparison of evidence and argument.

Drawing this conclusion for Judaism on the basis of the predominance of women among stated proselytes in Frey's *Corpus of Jewish Inscriptions*, B. Blumenkranz, in a study of missionary activity in Christianity and Judaism, felt it necessary to emphasize that this was because conversion to Judaism was easier for women than for men, and 'not because of any greater susceptibility for the Jewish religion by the female nature'.[6]

---

[2] See A.-J. Levine, 'Second Temple Judaism, Jesus, and Women: *Yeast of Eden*', *Biblical Interpretation* 2 (1994) 8–33, reprinted in A. Brenner, ed., *A Feminist Companion to the Hebrew Bible in the New Testament* (The Feminist Companion to the Bible 10, Sheffield Academic Press: Sheffield, 1996) 302–31.

[3] E.g. B. Witherington, *Women in the Ministry of Jesus* (SNTS.MS. 51, Cambridge University Press: Cambridge, 1984) 10.

[4] See K. von Kellenbach, *Anti-Judaism in Feminist Religious Writings* (Scholars Press: Atlanta, 1994).

[5] See next note. This is still assumed by B. Brooten, *Women Leaders in the Ancient Synagogue* (Scholars Press: Chico, 1982) 144–7.

[6] B. Blumenkranz, 'Die christlich-jüdische Missionskonkurrenz (3. bis 6. Jahrhundert)', in *Juifs et Chrétiens, Patristique et Moyen Age* (Variorum: London, 1977) ch. 10 (reprinted from *Klio* 39 (1961) 227–33) 228, 'und nicht etwa in einer größeren Empfindlichkeit der weiblichen Natur für die jüdische Religion'.

Blumenkranz is not alone in claiming that conversion to Judaism was more difficult for men, by implication because it involved circumcision, derided in the Graeco-Roman world and possibly hazardous in adult life. Yet such a view is self-evidently male and does not think to ask what conversion would involve for a woman from her perspective; neither does it draw on any comparative study of the relationship between the perceived difficulty or offensiveness of the conversion ritual and the numbers converting.

Yet the question of 'female susceptibility' needs more discussion. There is a long tradition of associating women with religiosity, particularly of a marginal kind, a tradition that, as we shall see, goes back to the Graeco-Roman sources; Blumenkranz may be recognizing such an assumption for the rhetoric it is, and would be right to do so. Yet it is also a modern popular perception that more women are attracted to 'new religious movements' (NRMs) – and not just a popular perception, for detailed studies have been devoted to the issue.[7] Given this parallel, what can be contributed by contemporary sociological analysis of 'women and religion'? Rodney Stark in his recent account of *The Rise of Christianity* posits a 2:1 imbalance of women to men in early Christianity as not unreasonable on this basis.[8] Yet quite apart from the problems of retrojection, over-hasty generalizations should be avoided: there is as yet no consensus in sociological analysis and explanation of the numbers of women in NRMs, and recent study suggests that there is considerable variation between different movements and over time within them.[9] Similarly, sociological analysis of gender differences in conversion is also in its relatively early stages. In general terms, analysis of 'conversion' has moved away from the passive 'Damascus Road' model to models which stress the active involvement of the individual and of their social context in what is a process;[10] this too is good reason for rejecting a model which understands women's attraction to early Christianity, or indeed to Judaism, purely in terms of 'what it did for them'.

---

[7] See Y. Y. Haddad and E. B. Findly, *Women, Religion and Social Change* (SUNY: Albany, 1985) xii; L. Davidman and J. Jacobs, 'Feminist Perspectives on New Religious Movements', in *Religion and the Social Order: The Handbook on Cults and Sects in America* 3B (JAIPress Inc.: Greenwich, 1993) 173–90.

[8] R. Stark, *The Rise of Christianity*, 101.

[9] L. L. Dawson, 'Who Joins New Religious Movements and Why: Twenty Years of Research and What We Have Learned', *SR* 25 (1996) 141–61, 155.

[10] See B. Kilbourne and J. T. Richardson, 'Paradigm Conflict, Types of Conversion and Conversion Theories', *Sociological Analysis* 50 (1988) 1–21.

A consequence of this, however, is that suggesting that there are gender differences in the experience and/or the articulation of conversion need not entail adopting a highly contentious biologistic perspective – namely that such differences are among the biologically and not just socially constructed determinants of gender, Blumenkranz's 'weiblichen Natur'. In the modern context the differences that there do seem to be between men's and women's participation in and experience of religion have been shown to be related to the nature of the language of religious experience and to the structure of the religion concerned; equally important, and not unrelated, is the perceived social location of religion, at least in the modern world, as belonging to the private sphere.[11] This is certainly suggestive for the analysis of early Christianity, if not of Judaism, but should not be too simplistically retrojected into that context. The question of where early Christianity was seen and saw itself as located in the rhetorical division between public and private is a complex one although it undoubtedly is strongly gendered,[12] but the division does not fall along the same lines as in the modern world. Once again to speak of the division as a rhetorical one demonstrates the need to think of 'politics' at every level of such analysis.

In practice our evidence makes it difficult to describe the overt motivations for conversion in the ancient world.[13] Within Christianity, from Paul to Justin and then to Augustine we have a number of accounts by male converts of their spiritual journey; it is a journey that involves sudden conviction, but it is also one which either has or soon acquires a strong intellectual content. We have no such autobiographical accounts, and, arguably, no biographical conversion accounts by

---

[11] Cf. E. H. Thompson, 'Beneath the Status Characteristic: Gender Variations in Religiousness', *JSSR* 30 (1991) 381–94; Thompson also suggests the socialization of women in terms of the values associated with religion: 'the feminisation of religion'. I am less sure whether this is applicable to antiquity, although the polemic of pagan authors against marginal cults adopts this as a rhetorical device: see below, pp. 90–2 and also p. 98 n. 66 for S. Juster's analysis of eighteenth-century New England which follows this model.

[12] See K. J. Torjesen, *When Women Were Priests: Women's Leadership in the Early Church and the Scandal of their Subordination in the Rise of Christianity* (Harper: San Francisco, 1993) 53–88, 126–8; M. MacDonald, *Early Christian Women and Pagan Opinion* (Cambridge University Press: Cambridge, 1996) 30–41; U. Wagener, *Die Ordnung des 'Hauses Gottes': Der Ort von Frauen in der Ekklesiologie und Ethik der Pastoralbriefe* (WUNT 2.65, Mohr: Tübingen, 1994) 94–6, 235–45.

[13] See the debate between R. MacMullen, 'Conversion: A Historian's View', *The Second Century* 5 (1985/6) 67–81 and W. S. Babcock, 'MacMullen On Conversion: A Response', *The Second Century* 5 (1985/6) 82–9.

women.[14] For Judaism we have no comparable material of any kind.[15] While modern scholars seem to have little difficulty in recognizing the intellectual dimension in the conversion, for example, of Justin, even if his account is undoubtedly stereotyped, few explore whether women would have found Christianity intellectually attractive: they are more interested in what it did for women.[16] But, despite both ancient and modern rhetoric about women's (limited) intellectual tendencies, women too, in all traditions, responded to intellectual challenge – from Hypatia to Beruriah to the ascetic women commented on by Galen, and to the women who adopted teaching roles in both Montanism and Gnosticism.[17] The tendency to ignore such possibilities is merely part of the objectifying of women which is both the major weakness of contemporary debate and the most significant characteristic of the earlier sources.

Leaving these methodological issues we may turn to the evidence usually cited and to its interpretation. That for Judaism is probably more diverse. Reference has already been made to the predominance of women 'proselytes' in Frey's *Corpus Inscriptionum Iudaicarum*. Yet the problem here is not simply the small numbers involved: Frey found eleven proselyte epitaphs, six of which were women's – the numbers would now need modification but do show the same balance.[18] It is also

---

[14] This is contentious since some would argue for women behind the *Acts of Thecla* if only at an oral stage; see below, pp. 95–6.

[15] On *Joseph and Aseneth* see below, p. 94, but this is a novel and scarcely representative of many women's experience.

[16] G. Bardy, *La Conversion au Christianisme durant les premiers siècles* (Théologie 15, Aubier: Paris, 1949) treats women separately (220) from his general exploration of the intellectual and spiritual motivations for conversion (121–61).

[17] On 'learned women' within rabbinic Judaism see D. Boyarin, 'Reading Androcentrism against the Grain: Women, Sex and Torah Study', *Poetics Today* 12 (1991) 29–53; on women teachers in the philosophical tradition see Wagener, 'Hauses Gottes', 89–92; for Galen see R. Walzer, *Galen on Jews and Christians* (Oxford University Press: London, 1947) 15; on women's contribution to Montanism see C. Trevett, *Montanism: Gender, Authority and the New Prophecy* (Cambridge University Press: Cambridge, 1996) 151–97; on women's intellectual part in Gnosticism, denied by but evidenced by Epiphanius, see J. Goehring, 'Libertine or Liberated: Women in the So-Called Libertine Gnostic Communities', in Karen L. King, ed., *Images of the Feminine in Gnosticism* (Sudies in Antiquity and Christianity, Fortress Press: Philadelphia, 1988) 329–44.

[18] See above, p. 84 and n. 6; Blumenkranz noted that six out of eleven proselyte inscriptions in Frey were of women, and that this was out of a total of *c*.300 inscriptions. P. W. van der Horst, *Ancient Jewish Epitaphs* (Pharos: Kampen, 1991) gives the number of proselyte epitaphs as fourteen or fifteen – seven or eight from Rome, one from Venosa, five from

one of geographical spread. There are no proselyte epitaphs from Egypt, and apparently no explicit references to proselytes in the papyri.[19] Yet we know of converts to Judaism there, and the literary sources, particularly Philo and *Joseph and Aseneth* to which we shall return, take their existence for granted. We do not know why and when people did or did not identify themselves as proselytes. Those who hold that Judaism did have missionary success must conclude that proselytes are included, anonymously, among other Jewish or 'pagan' epitaphs: Ross Kraemer has argued that when someone is specifically identified on an epitaph as 'Jew' they may in fact be a proselyte, as is explicitly the case in a few inscriptions.[20] Yet the self-designation 'Jew' is also rare in the Egyptian epitaphs.[21]

Yet where we do have the designation 'proselyte' we need to note the 'story' of the epitaph. In a much-discussed inscription the proselyte is a 3½-year-old foster child, Irene;[22] in another, from Cyrenaica, Sara, presumably a 'conversion name', aged 18, is in a family (?) group and probably either adopted or a slave.[23] Another is set up by the proselyte's *patronus*,[24] another by her brother,[25] and yet another by her sons.[26]

Jerusalem and one from Caesarea Maritima; to these would now have to be added three names from the Aphrodisias inscription, and one in G. Lüderitz, *Corpus jüdischer Zeugnisse aus der Cyrenaika* mit einem Anhang von Joyce M. Reynolds (B.TAVO, Reichert: Weisbaden, 1983). These represent only about 1 per cent of the total number of Jewish inscriptions. About nine of these are of women.

19 See P. van Minnen, 'Drei Bemerkungen zur Geschichte des Judentums in der griechisch-römischen Welt', *ZPE* 100 (1994) 253–8, 253–4.

20 R. Kraemer, 'On the Meaning of the Term "Jew" in Graeco-Roman Inscriptions', *HTR* 82 (1989) 35–52. See below nn. 22, 27, 30.

21 *CIJ* 1537 and 1538 both in dedications from the Temple of Pan at El Kanais; see W. Horbury and D. Noy, *Jewish Inscriptions of Graeco-Roman Egypt* (Cambridge University Press: Cambridge, 1992) 208 for a discussion of these.

22 *CIJ* 21 = D. Noy, *Jewish Inscriptions of Western Europe, II, Rome* (Cambridge University Press: Cambridge, 1995) no. 392. Either she or her mother is also designated 'Jewess'; with this we might compare the description of children as 'pious' and even as 'ruler [of the synagogue]'.

23 Lüderitz, *Corpus*, 12 (pp. 26–7); Sara is the last of four people, the other three, presumably Jewish (although only one, Joses, bears a Jewish name), being 4, 15, and 58 years old.

24 *CIJ* 462 = Noy, *Inscriptions*, II, no. 62 (third/fourth century): Felicitas, renamed Peregrina. Matching this is that of Nicetas set up by his *patrona*, Dionysia: *CIJ* 218 = Noy, *Inscriptions*, II, no. 218. Both are third/fourth century and use the terms *proselita/us*.

25 *CIJ* 222 = Noy, *Inscriptions*, II, no. 224 for Chrysis, by her brother Mannacius.

26 *CIJ* 642 = D. Noy, *Jewish Inscriptions of Western Europe, I, Italy, Spain, Gaul* (Cambridge University Press: Cambridge, 1993) no. 9, for Aurelia Soteria, described as *metuens*, set up by her sons.

Conversely, not often counted as evidence for women, is that of a male proselyte set up by his mother.[27] Clearly the epitaphs are equally saying something about the allegiance of the dedicator, and gender is of secondary significance. Conversion is to do with family relationships; the perceived threat it offered in the ancient world was of destroying such relationships, and so the advertisement of conversion by members of the family, is not simply a statement about the dedicatee. Epitaphs, like other inscriptions, had a political function.[28]

Proselyte epitaphs are absent from Asia Minor, although there are three male proselytes on the well-known inscription from Aphrodisias, and a long list of those called 'God-fearers' which notably includes no female names. Discussion, however, has raged over other Jewish inscriptions mentioning women, particularly where women hold office within, or act as benefactors to the synagogue – thus undermining the claim that in Judaism women were not allowed to participate in the public life of the synagogue.[29] Some of these women are not born Jews: Julia Severa at Acmonia who provides the building for synagogue use almost certainly is not a convert since she appears later as High Priestess of the imperial cult; Tation at Phocaea who is given a crown and a seat of honour perhaps is, as also may be Rufina who is identified as Jewess as well as 'ruler of the synagogue'.[30] Neither they nor those who set up the inscriptions honouring them see fit to mention their status – hence the scholarly debate. It need hardly be emphasized that both benefaction and the public advertising of it, as well as the reciprocal giving of honours, is a political process, and the role of women in this process probably belongs to the well-attested distinctive politics and exploitation of the public/private spheres in Asia Minor.[31]

[27] *CIJ* 68 = Noy, *Inscriptions*, II, no. 491, 'Cresces Sinicerius Jew proselyte . . . The mother did for her sweet son what he himself should have done for me.'

[28] Conversely, R. S. Kraemer, *Her Share of the Blessings: Women's Religions among Pagans, Jews, and Christians in the Greco-Roman World* (Oxford University Press: New York, 1992) 122–3 suggests that the failure of Rufina (*CIJ* 741, discussed below) to mention husband or father indicates that she had broken those family links on her conversion.

[29] Decisively argued by B. Brooten, *Women Leaders*.

[30] Tation was honoured by 'the synagogue of the Jews' for her gift of a 'house' to the Jews (*CIJ* 738). Rufina (*CIJ* 741) sets up her own inscription. Kraemer, *Blessings*, 119, 121–2 raises the possibility that both may be proselytes because of the otherwise unnecessary mention of Jews / Jewess.

[31] See R. van Bremen, *The Limits of Participation: Women and Civic Life in the Greek East in the Hellenistic and Roman Periods* (Gieben: Amsterdam, 1996).

There can be no comparable epigraphic evidence for Christian women in the formative period. Yet it is worth noting that although Montanism is often seen as offering women a scope and an equality no longer available in catholic Christianity, epigraphic remains do not point to their predominance in the movement.[32]

Yet given the accidents of survival of epigraphic evidence we need also to draw on the literary evidence. Here again the field needs tidying and setting out more clearly. None of the literary evidence is concerned to provide an objective statistical account of adherents to the religions concerned. That may seem obvious, but it is sometimes so treated. Pagan writers do speak of the attraction of women to Christianity (e.g. Origen, *c.Cels.* III.18; 44, Minucius Felix, *Oct.* 8.4);[33] they also speak of the attraction of the uneducated masses and of children. Celsus speaks of 'thieves, burglars and poisoners' although few have argued that they too were represented in unusual numbers in the early church.[34] They equally speak of the attraction of women to other esoteric religious groups, although they do not single out Judaism in this regard.[35] Such evidence is clearly tendentious – which need not mean that it is never true – and it is equally clearly political. There is a whole rhetoric involved of 'superstition', irrationality, subversion, the undermining of the proper structure of the family and therefore also of the state, infiltration into the private, and so on, all of which has been well analysed elsewhere. Once again this only establishes that discourse concerning the conversion of women serves a political and propagandic end of characterizing the religion concerned and its relationship with the norms of society; it also provides justification for (re-)asserting control.

Livy's account of the Bacchanalia crisis in 186 BCE is paradigmatic here (XXXIX.8–18). Understood as an irrational and dangerous cult, the more dangerous because it does not belong to the public sphere of normal political decision and action, it is indelibly linked with women: key figures are Aebutius's mother, his aunt and his mistress, who describes

---

[32] See C. Trevett, *Montanism*, 196. W. Tabbernee, *Montanist Inscriptions and Testimonies: Epigraphic Sources Illustrating the History of Montanism* (PMS 16, Mercer: Macon, 1997) considers the ten out of twenty-eight 'definitely montanist' inscriptions of women 'a high percentage' (560, 568).

[33] Caecilius in *Oct.* 8.4 is characteristic in blaming women's inherent credulity; see further MacDonald, *Early Christian Women*, 49–126.

[34] Although Tertullian might sometimes make us suppose otherwise: *de Pud.* 22.

[35] E.g. Lucian, *Alexander* 42; Tacitus, *Annal.* XIII.32 where the woman attracted by 'an alien superstition' is put under her husband's control.

the cult as first of all a ritual for women (13.8). As the story develops, the men who are after all involved are not 'true men', but are made 'effeminate'(16.1).³⁶ Once it becomes viewed as an instrument of political instability, both the instigators and its character are described in very different terms: now we read that the heads of the conspiracy (*coniuratio*) are four men, who, contrary to the earlier account, are 'the supreme priests and founders of the cult' (17.6–7).

Josephus's account of the expulsion of the Jews under Tiberius in 19 CE follows the same rhetoric (*Ant.* XVIII.3.4–5 [65–84]). Both Tacitus (*Annal.* II.25–28) and Suetonius (*Tib.* 36) couple together 'Egyptian and Jewish rites' as the targets of Tiberius's proscription, and possibly hint at their proselytizing activities as responsible.³⁷ Josephus first gives a graphic account of the sexual seduction and exploitation of a devotee of the Isis cult, Paulina, with the connivance of the priests of the cult, leading to Tiberius's destruction of the Temple of Isis. He follows this with the *financial* (only) exploitation of the Roman 'proselyte', Fulvia, by a 'scoundrel Jew' which occasions the expulsion of the Jews. Thus Josephus adopts the theme of the susceptible woman convert to explain both incidents, but distances them from each other by ascribing sexual deceit only to the followers of Isis.

A similar discourse is repeated within Christianity itself: Christian authors from the second century on polemize against fringe or what they deem heretical groups by describing the role of women, often seductive or morally questionable, within them or by claiming women's susceptibility to the founder's wiles.³⁸ Robin Lane Fox accepts such descriptions – 'The afternoons were long in a Gnostic's company';³⁹ characteristically of much (male) scholarship, he acknowledges that it is a stereotype in the literature 'that strange teachings appealed to leisured women who had just enough culture to admire it and not enough education to exclude it',⁴⁰ yet he proceeds to treat this as a historically valid explanation. Yet what we are dealing with is a rhetoric which

---

³⁶ 13.10: The men involved engage in lustful practices with each other, and entry was restricted to boys under 20; they certainly would be untrustworthy soldiers and unlikely to 'fight with the sword for the chastity of your wives and children' (13.13–14). For the young men cf. Lucian, *Alexander* 41.

³⁷ For a discussion see M. Goodman, *Mission and Conversion: Proselytizing in the Religious History of the Roman Empire* (Clarendon Press: Oxford, 1994) 68, 83.

³⁸ The *topos* is already implied in 1 Tim. 5.13–15; see Wagener, 'Hauses Gottes', 219–21.

³⁹ R. L. Fox, *Pagans and Christians* (Penguin: Harmondsworth, 1986) 311.

⁴⁰ Fox, *Pagans and Christians*, 310.

identifies women with non-normative or marginalized religion. In the same way, in the fourth century John Chrysostom berates those Christians within the church at Antioch whose wives are frequenting the synagogue: 'You let them entangle themselves in accusations of ungodliness, you let them be dragged off into licentious ways. For as a rule, it is harlots, the effeminates, and the whole chorus from the theatre who rush to that festival.'[41] It is over-credulous to rely on this 'political' rhetoric as further evidence of the attraction of women to Judaism.[42]

Lane Fox is not alone among historians in going along with some of this rhetoric; it has become common to argue that women were prominent in heretical movements, notably Montanism or Gnosticism, driven there as they were marginalized by the progressive patriarchalization of the church. The question whether heresy attracted women or the attraction of women determined the identification 'heretical' is indeed a moot one;[43] but we should be wary lest we are being seduced by this rhetoric which associates women with 'uncontrolled' religiosity, often with sexual overtones.

Thus we are dealing with a 'political' rhetoric. Indeed much of the supposed evidence of the significance of women in early Christianity – and this goes back to Adolf von Harnack whom many later scholars merely repeat[44] – is rather of women as a topic of concern in the early church. This does not point to the numerical dominance of women so much as to women as a problem, and particularly as a symbol of the tension between separate identity and social respectability, which is characteristic of early Christian literature; we should, therefore, view it with a 'hermeneutic of suspicion'. Thus, already in the first century Paul appears to associate problems of the unbridled use of 'tongues' with the problem of women (1 Cor. 11–14);[45] believing him, Antoinette C. Wire reconstructs their context in the Corinthian church as one

---

[41] Chrysostom, *Hom.ad Iud.* II.4, translation from P. Harkins, *Saint John Chrysostom, Discourses Against Judaizing Christians* (Fathers of the Church, Catholic University of America: Washington, 1979) 44.
[42] As do Kraemer, *Blessings*, 108 and L. Feldman, *Jew and Gentile in the Ancient World* (Princeton University Press: Princeton, 1993) 376.
[43] Heine, *Women and Early Christianity*, 130–4 accepts women's attraction to Gnosticism; see further Trevett, *Montanism*, 196.
[44] In *The Expansion of Christianity in the First Three Centuries* (ET Williams & Northgate: London, 1904–5) I, 217–39.
[45] The gendering of the problem is achieved as much by the structure of this section and by the inclusio between ch. 11 and 14.33f. as by explicit association.

where ascetic charisma offered women a freedom, and thus grounds for their attraction to the church.[46] Such a reconstruction is not impossible: studies of ecstatic religion have suggested that ecstasy occurs as a phenomenon when women are marginalized and acts as a means of negotiating non-structural power.[47] Yet caution is due; it may also be the case that certain types of religious behaviour are being gendered rhetorically in order to control them.

No Christian source explicitly celebrates the number of women joining their ranks. For Judaism, Josephus does something like this when he says of Damascus, 'all their wives but for a few had gone over to the Jewish worship' (B.J. II.20.2 [559–61]), although his precise meaning remains obscure.[48] Likewise he describes how the queen of the independent kingdom of Adiabene and her household were converted to Judaism by a passing merchant, Eleazar (Ant. XX.2.1–4 [34–48]). Yet what is important in these two cases is not just that they are women, but that they are powerful women whose influence is an indispensable element in the eventual outcome of the broader events described. We may put under the same heading Josephus's reference to Poppaea, the wife of Nero, who helped certain Jewish emissaries to Rome 'for she was a God-fearer' (Ant. XX. 8.11[195]): this cannot mean that she was a convert nor even one of those elusive and, I would argue, illusory God-fearers beloved by modern scholarship.[49] Josephus is doing his best to claim her without going beyond the boundaries of what his readers would find credible: women are appropriate 'patrons' in a literary context.

The idea that women, and particularly women of note, were attracted to Christianity has drawn its evidence first from the Acts of the Apostles, where specific mention is made of the conversion of Lydia, the seller of purple, at Philippi, and of noble women at Thessalonica, Beroea and Athens (17.4, 12, 33f.). The similarity between Josephus and Acts here is striking, but that it is evidence of historical realism is less certain. As

---

[46] A. Clark Wire, *The Corinthian Women Prophets: A Reconstruction through Paul's Rhetoric* (Fortress Press: Minneapolis, 1990).

[47] See I. Lewis, *Ecstatic Religion: A Study of Shamanism and Spirit Possession* (Routledge: London, 1989 [1971]).

[48] S. Cohen, 'Respect for Judaism by Gentiles in the Writings of Josephus', *HTR* 80 (1987) 409–30, 417 treats them as adherents and not converts.

[49] See J. Lieu, 'Do God-fearers make Good Christians?', in S. Porter, P. Joyce and D. E. Orton, eds., *Crossing the Boundaries: Essays in Biblical Interpretation in Honour of Michael D. Goulder* (BIS 8, Brill: Leiden, 1994) 329–45 = pp. 31–47 above.

has often been noted, the two writers share a number of historio-graphical techniques; close to this issue, both present Gentile patronage of synagogues in similar terms, more characteristic of the end than of the beginning of the first century. Both are types of apologetic if not to the outside world, at least in awareness of it; both are claiming that the story they tell is not subversive, that it has won respect without surrender-ing its distinctiveness or its occasional incompatibility with aspects of Roman society. The sympathy of powerful women seems to be a non-threatening way of articulating such a combination of respectability with independence. This does not mean it is entirely imaginative. As is regularly noted, Hellenistic women appear to have enjoyed far more freedom of action and possibility of influencing events than their classical foremothers; participation in 'alternative' religious groupings was a means of giving expression to the independence and status wealth afforded.[50] However, it has been noted also that in the Greek novels of the second century this increased social influence is even more exaggerated, and that in Jewish novels women take over the whole stage: Esther, Judith, Susannah and Aseneth.[51] It seems probable that the narratives of Josephus and of Acts also share this novelistic tendency, however it is to be understood.[52]

Of these the prime exemplar is Aseneth: the daughter of the Egyptian priest, she ends up married to Joseph, a basic plot the author drew from Gen. 41.50. To do so – exposing a problem that did not occur to the author of Genesis – she first has to convert to Judaism, the theme that constitutes the bulk, the first twenty chapters, of this intriguing novel. Thus a woman is the topic of our most detailed Jewish conversion narrative.[53] Yet this is hardly evidence that women did provide the majority of such converts, although if it tackles the problem of 'mixed marriages' a non-Jewish wife would presumably be more acceptable than a non-Jewish husband. Rather, Aseneth joins the 'cast list' of women heroines in the hellenistic novels. The social context of their prominence

---

[50] See van Bremen, *Limits of Participation*; also T. Ilan, 'The Attraction of Aristocratic Women to Pharisaism during the Second Temple Period', *HTR* 88 (1995) 1–33.

[51] See L. Wills, *The Jewish Novel in the Ancient World* (Cornell University Press: Ithaca, 1995) 12–13.

[52] Wills, *Jewish Novel*, explicitly treats the conversion of the House of Adiabene as a novel; the Fulvia narrative also bears strong novelistic marks.

[53] Despite some recent debate I am assuming the Jewish provenance of the novel; I am most persuaded by arguments which date it in the first two centuries of the Common Era.

has been much debated, but their role seems best understood not as evidence of a predominantly female readership nor of women's prominence in society but as a projection of male concerns.[54]

Such literature is perhaps but one symptom of what has been seen as a growing concern with the 'subjective self' and with the body as an expression of this within the early Empire, as also with the relationship between individual and civic structures, with consciousness of alienation, and with the longing for private or domestic happiness.[55] Christianity did not generate but located itself readily and participated within this development. As 'natural' symbols of vulnerability it is not surprising that women should play a rhetorical role in this process nor that they should provide a means for exploring the nature of conversion understood in individual and private terms.

In this context we should consider Thecla, the heroine of a Christian 'novel', an episode, perhaps originally independent, within the second-century apocryphal *Acts of Paul* which gives an alternative account of Paul's activities with a strong ascetic or encratic ethos. Thecla is converted by Paul's preaching, the essence of which is the rejection of marriage. Deserting home and fiancé she follows Paul, endures and triumphs through various adventures, sets up an independent mission, with hair cut short and dressed in male clothing, and duly dies revered and holy. A 'women's' setting has sometimes been posited for this and related literature, and it has been seen as evidence of alternative patterns of early Christianity, which were eventually to be either marginalized or institutionalized.[56] Understood as the reflection or articulation of a reality for some at least, Thecla has been seen as evidence for the ascetic appeal of early Christianity for women: Christianity authorized them to reject marriage and so to remove themselves from male control.[57] Certainly in

---

[54] B. Egger's 'literary gynocentrism but factual androcentrism' referred to by Wills, *Jewish Novel*, 225, n. 86. However, in 'Looking at Chariton's Callirhoe', in J. R. Morgan and R. Stoneman, eds., *Greek Fiction: The Greek Novel in Context* (Routledge: London, 1994) 31–48, Egger is more positive about the possibilities for exploring feminine readings of the novels.

[55] See Wills, *Jewish Novel*, 19. J. R. Morgan, 'Introduction', in Morgan and Stoneman, eds., *Greek Fiction*, 8 comments that 'novel and cult were operating in the same general market'.

[56] Stevan L. Davies, *The Revolt of the Widows: The Social World of the Apocryphal Acts* (Southern Illinois University Press: Carbondale, 1980).

[57] Gail Corrington, 'The "Divine Woman"? Propaganda and the Power of Chastity in the New Testament Apocrypha', *Helios* 13 (1987) 151–62.

the fourth century and beyond, asceticism offered Christian women a route to self-determination and a form of power, and this development has been easily related to the rhetoric of the body and to sexuality.[58] But we are less secure in reading back such concerns to earliest Christianity at least as part of social reality, even if the literary exploration is beginning to be in place.

The story of Thecla is notable for its ambivalence. Her adoption of Paul's gospel of asceticism is inevitably seen as subversive by society, not least by her erstwhile fiancé and later by another would-be lover – although it is her mother who calls for her to be burnt. To some extent she suffers what Paul ought to. His message is also directed to the young men, and at least inspires Onesiphorus to give up his home and possessions to follow Paul, reducing his family to hunger: yet no one protests at this. Again, it is through a woman that, within the conventions of the age, the issues of vulnerability, of risk, of sexual chastity, and of alienation from civic structures, can be explored: those issues, again, which have been seen as central to the Greek novels and other literary genres of the period. Moreover, for all the heartening realism that has been descried in Thecla's painfully developing independence from her 'fixation' on Paul, her 'conversion' is to the ascetic renunciation of her own sexuality, and Paul is the necessary if unresponsive mediator of that sublimation.[59] Whatever the origins of the Thecla tradition, it can only be read as text which both entertains and explores the relationship between society and Christianity; it tells us little about 'real' women's conversion to Christianity in the second century.

Bound too by the confines of their textuality are the rabbinic references to the conversion of women to Judaism. Although a number of texts treat the procedures for female conversion or initiation, and the potential consequent legal questions, it is characteristically nigh impossible to determine what sort of reality is reflected by these debates – although the second-century (?) development of proselyte baptism has been reasonably linked to the real need for such a rite for women in

---

[58] Virginia Burrus, 'Word and Flesh: The Bodies and Sexuality of Ascetic Women in Christian Antiquity', *JFSR* 10 (1994) 27–51.

[59] See *Acts of Paul* 9–10, 19–20 where Thecla sits like a spider at the window, and later rolls on the ground where Paul has sat in prison; by 34–37 she baptizes herself, her faith is in God, and not in Paul, and her teaching mission is an affirmation of self-determination. For the desire of the man as the agent for conversion compare Aseneth's passion for Joseph.

the light of developing ideas of Jewish identity.[60] Not surprisingly, the issues raised reflect the male concerns of the rabbinic writers and there is nothing to imply that there were more female than male converts.[61] More interesting are the quasi-narrative accounts or anecdotes involving women proselytes, although these too are outnumbered by the men. In a number of such we meet influential women, most typically the Roman matrona, although usually as an enquirer rather than as a convert; in rabbinic sources Helena of Adiabene is virtuous and a benefactor but, unlike her sons who circumcise themselves, never explicitly a proselyte.[62] There are, however, also a disproportionate number of prostitutes, starting of course with Rahab.[63] The superficial parallel with the Synoptic Gospels is deceptive, although perhaps enough to confirm their literary function in both contexts; but these prostitutes demonstrate, and are suitably impressed by, the virtue of the rabbis who resist their wiles. Interestingly, prostitutes drop out of Christian accounts of conversion after the Synoptic Gospels, offering further confirmation that they say more about our authors' views on women than about social reality. Once more we find sexuality in our rhetorical nexus – women, power, sexuality and religion, a heady and familiar combination.

Thus, for all its variety, the evidence often cited for the attraction of women to Judaism or Christianity is not this; they are sources for different political agenda. They tell us more about the rhetoric of language about religion, about sexuality, and about vulnerability and change, and the interconnection of these. The gendering of conversion is a matter of rhetorical and not of statistical analysis. The move from rhetoric to social experience must remain hazardous.

For all this, some comments might be possible. This essay has already rejected any model which starts with 'the good' that Christianity or Judaism could offer women, for such models tend to personify Christianity, usually in the person of Jesus or Paul, when recent study suggests that both Jesus and Paul were ambiguous regarding this issue,

---

[60] See S. Cohen, 'The Rabbinic Conversion Ceremony', *JJS* 41 (1990) 177–203; J. Lieu, 'Circumcision, Women and Salvation', *NTS* 40 (1994) 358–70, 364–7 = pp. 101–14 below.

[61] See T. Ilan, *Jewish Women in Greco-Roman Palestine: An Inquiry into Image and Status* (TSAJ 44, Mohr: Tübingen:, 1995) 211–14; B. J. Bamberger, *Proselytism in the Talmudic Period* (KTAV: New York, 1968 [1939]) 54ff.

[62] Ibid.

[63] See Leila L. Bronner, *From Eve to Esther: Rabbinic Reconstructions of Biblical Women* (Gender and the Biblical Tradition, Westminster/John Knox: Louisville, 1994) 146–7, 149–50; *Sifre Num.* 115; *bMen.* 44a; for Rahab see *bZeb.* 116a–b.

and that any place women had in their movements was ancillary to their definition of those movements. Similarly, it is not easy to establish a correlation between women's conversion to Judaism and the surviving teaching *about* women. Instead, early Christianity – as also Judaism – must be viewed as a dynamic and constructive process within which its members were not acted upon but were creative participants. Such a positive view would note the evidence already discussed that in some parts of the Empire influential women were able to use religion, including non-civic religion, to negotiate a role for themselves in society.[64] This would not be a case of Christianity or Judaism offering a message of liberation to enslaved women, but of women seeking a social framework for the independence that was de facto theirs, and finding it in the growing ambiguities that were breaking down the public/private divide, ambiguities that were inevitably characteristic of these new religious movements.[65] Thus, such ambiguity offered a framework for women to exercise roles that already were developing within society but that existing conceptual frameworks did not legitimate.

Despite the cautions voiced earlier against over-hasty parallels with more recent experience, this would cohere with sociological exploration of interrelationships within the nexus of social change or instability, marginalization, religious innovation, and the independent role of women.[66] This does not mean that we need to posit widespread social instability, for there is evidence enough of social changes in the first centuries CE, and of the tensions between these new conditions and of continuing conservative values, as witnessed once more by the novels. Neither does it mean that, as the pagan polemicists and Christian writers alike feared, the activity of women was bound to lead to social collapse. It is a matter of debate whether the role of women in NRMs is only innovative or not also conservative and integrative. It has become customary to see the developing church as characterized by an increasing patriarchalization – once again women are perceived only as victims, those acted on. It does no service either to historical reconstruction or

---

[64] See nn. 29–31 above, but also the cautions of R. van Bremen, *Limits of Participation*, who stresses that such women remain within and represent family power networks.

[65] See above, p. 86 for the ambiguities here.

[66] See Haddad and Findly, *Women, Religion and Social Change*, xii; see also S. Juster's analysis of the concurrence of a 'feminizing' of religion and religious language, of an independent role for women, and of social instability or marginalization in eighteenth-century New England, *Disorderly Women: Sexual Politics and Evangelicalism in Revolutionary New England* (Cornell University Press: Ithaca, 1994).

to the political agenda to deny that women too were able to use and therefore to shape Judaism and Christianity as vehicles of their own identity. Yet any such suggestion should not be mistaken for the positivistic claims that in the past have bedevilled the journey.

However, such a reconstruction would belong to a different essay, and would no less come under the strictures of the subtitle of this one. For what we have discovered is that gender and religion are inseparably interrelated in the construction of each.

BIBLIOGRAPHICAL NOTE

See the note following the next essay, p. 114.

7

Circumcision, Women and Salvation*

The title of this essay sets its own agenda when considered in the form of a syllogism. What is the relationship between circumcision and women, what between circumcision and salvation, what then between women and salvation? Merely to raise the question in this form is to indicate the ambiguity which might surround any answer, at least within the sort of debate with which New Testament scholarship is familiar. The immediately obvious solution would be to object that the question, together with the presuppositions and concerns which apparently inspire it, is born of a modern consciousness inappropriate to the critical study of the past: that it is an imposition on the text.[1] However, we may for the moment postpone the hermeneutical questions such an objection should provoke: the title is inspired not by the modern agenda of 'women's rights' or feminism but by that of the second century.

In his debate with Trypho the Jew, Justin Martyr amasses arguments against the Jewish Law, most of which were to become standard in later Christian rhetoric. He wants to demonstrate that the provisions of the Law which for Trypho are eternal[2] – Trypho specifies sabbath, circumcision, new moons, purity – were in truth late and temporary, and so he makes the familiar appeal to the righteous worthies who lived before Moses and who failed to observe them – Abraham, Isaac, Jacob, Noah and Job. He then continues, 'I might also cite Sarah, the wife of

* First published in *NTS* 40 (1994) 358–70. Reprinted by permission of Cambridge University Press.

---

[1] For discussion of this see E. Schüssler Fiorenza, 'Remembering the Past in Creating the Future: Historical-Critical Scholarship and Feminist Biblical Interpretation', in A. Y. Collins, ed., *Feminist Perspectives on Biblical Scholarship* (SBL, Scholars Press: Chico, 1985) 43–63, 44–8; eadem, 'The Ethics of Biblical Interpretation: Decentering Biblical Scholarship', *JBL* 107 (1988) 3–17.

[2] Justin's use of the phrase 'eternal just enactments' in 46.2 must be an ironical echo of his opponent's assessment.

Abraham, Rebecca, the wife of Isaac, Rachel, the wife of Jacob, and Leah, and all the other such women up to the mother of Moses, the faithful servant, who observed none of these – do you think they will be saved?' (46.3).[3] Trypho's answer effectively renders the women invisible – a familiar tactic: 'But wasn't Abraham along with his household circumcised?', he retorts. At this point Justin, with some exasperation, has to remind Trypho – and the reader – that he had already dealt with circumcision earlier in the debate. As we turn back to that earlier point in the debate, in chapter 23, we find ourselves again on what was to become well-worn ground in future polemic. Not only were the righteous men of old not required to observe the law, but nature itself knows nothing of it. Then, after quoting Gen. 17.14, 'Every person (ψυχή) shall be cut off from that race who is not circumcised on the eighth day',[4] Justin continues:

> Furthermore, that the female sex is unable to receive fleshly circumcision demonstrates that this circumcision was given as a sign and not as a work of righteousness. For God made women equally able to observe all that is right and virtuous. We see that in physical form male and female have been made differently, but we are confident that neither is righteous or unrighteous on this basis but only on the basis of piety and righteousness (23.5).

The logical link between these two passages, although separated in the *Dialogue*, is significant. Justin was not the first to argue that the Law, given by or through Moses relatively late in God's dispensation, was not integral to God's purposes (Gal. 3.15–26). Circumcision offered a separate problem since it was already enjoined upon Abraham, as Trypho himself pointed out. This is where the women offered a solution – unlike Noah or Job they are part of what biblical scholarship calls 'the salvation history'. However, they not only antedate the giving of the Law but are also excluded by nature from the requirement of circumcision given to Abraham and his male line. Hence Justin provides us with our syllogism – circumcision, women, salvation.

Yet it is the apparent novelty of Justin's argument which attracts attention. Not only has he observed something which Paul and countless

---

[3] Note, however, that the women are defined in terms of their menfolk who are the significant characters.

[4] Justin's text here, in contrast to the LXX, aids his argument. In the LXX the text reads 'every uncircumcised *male* who does not circumcise his uncircumcised flesh on the eighth day, that person shall be cut off from that race'. Justin uses the same text as here in *Dial.* 10.3.

of his commentators have failed to note – to which we must return; later church tradition maintained and developed most of Justin's other arguments against the Law, particularly the appeal to the uncircumcised righteous men of old, and yet pointedly ignored this one: why?[5] Was the argument from the independent spiritual potential of women, who could not, however, be circumcised, one which could be understood, which would be a self-evident concern; or, like Trypho, would most who listened fail to make any sense of it: in a patriarchal society would it have seemed a meaningless question?

This is a question which can be asked because so often we find that Justin is not an innovator in his arguments with his Jewish opponent. Frequently he betrays not only dependence on earlier Christian tradition, but equally knowledge of contemporary Jewish exegesis of Scripture, even when this has survived otherwise only in later written sources.[6] In the present case he himself prefaces his arguments by appealing to words of his 'guru', the old man who converted him (23.3).[7]

Circumcision and women in contemporary interpretation

Whatever the origins of the rite it is clear that in the post-exilic period, and particularly from the second century BCE, circumcision becomes a key concept in defining the Jewish religious community – in time it becomes almost coterminous with 'covenant'. The same is true for outsiders: pagan observers see Judaism as characterized by circumcision even though other nations observed the same practice; Persius need

---

[5] Tertullian, *adv.Iud.* II.10–14 notes that Adam was not created circumcised (cf. Justin, *Dial.* 19.3) and appeals to Abel, Noah, Enoch, Melchizedek and Lot who were pleasing to God before Abraham. Only Cyprian adds to these two arguments, 'that sign does not benefit women' (*tunc quod illud signaculum feminis non proficit adv.Iud.* I.8). Zeno of Verona does develop a contrast between Eve and Mary, who is both the source of salvation and a woman for whom physical circumcision was impossible; for him circumcision denotes not salvation but the 'place and chief source of sin' (*locum caputque criminis monstrat: Tract.* I.3. 8–9, 19). For Aquinas this was why circumcision was limited to males (F. Dexinger, 'Beschneidung: III, Nachtalmudisches Judentum', *TRE* V. 722–4, 724). Most commentators on Justin's use of the Old Testament also ignore these arguments, an exception being W. Shotwell, *The Biblical Exegesis of Justin Martyr* (SPCK: London, 1963) 124–5.

[6] There is a considerable bibliography on this: see O. Skarsaune, *The Proof from Prophecy: a Study in Justin Martyr's Proof-text Tradition* (NT.S 56, Brill: Leiden, 1987); K. Hruby, 'Exégèse Rabbinique et Exégèse Patristique', *RSR* 47 (1973) 341–69.

[7] This applies explicitly to the argument from nature.

speak only of 'the circumcised sabbath' (*Sat.* 5. 184).[8] At one level
Christians could be said simply to adopt the same perspective: Paul, of
course, refers to the Jews as 'the circumcision', just as he refers to non-
Jews as 'the uncircumcision', perhaps reflecting current name-calling.[9]
That male circumcision alone is involved is never questioned – barring
an erroneous remark by Strabo – and, indeed, is implicit in the Greek
term used;[10] any awareness of the consequences for women of this
identification of Judaism with (male) circumcision, however, is hard to
come by.

Two questions must for the moment be set to one side; first, that
women's obligations under the Law were more limited than those of
men, women being exempt in principle from such positive precepts as
were fixed by time. This has been widely analysed and discussed, and is
often seen as rendering women less than full participants within the
covenant community.[11] Secondly, society and the world-view of the time
were self-evidently patriarchal: is this to be accepted as a given or to be
treated with a hermeneutic of suspicion? We should not forget that,
contrary to later rabbinic opinion, women were involved in circumcision
– in the Maccabean literature it is the women who face death for
circumcising their sons (1 Macc. 1.60; 2 Macc. 6.10). Our question,
however, is the explicit connection of circumcision – or its impossibility
– with women's status as members of the covenant community, a
covenant the sign of which was circumcision.

Given the assumption of a patriarchal society, few will be surpised to
find there is little on which to build an answer. We need consider only
three discussions. First, whatever is said, or fails to be predicated, of
women, they are not described as 'uncircumcised' עֲרֵלָה.[12] Indeed in
bAbZ. 27a, there is a debate about who may perform circumcision,
repointing the infinitive absolute construction הִמּוֹל יִמּוֹל of Gen. 17.13

---

[8] 'Recutita sabbata'; in M. Stern, *Greek and Latin Authors on Jews and Judaism* (Israel
Acad. of Sci. & Hums.: Jerusalem, 1974–84) I, 436–7. Pagan authors are, of course,
aware that the Jews were not alone in being circumcised, and some claim that the Jews
adopted the practice from the Egyptians (so Herodotus, *Hist.* II.104. 1–3; Diodorus
Siculus, *Bibl.Hist.* I.28. 3; (Origen) *c.Cels.* I.22; = Stern, *Authors* I, 2, 169; II, 233).
[9] See J. Marcus, 'The Circumcision and the Uncircumcision', *NTS* 35 (1989) 67–81, 73–9.
[10] Strabo, *Geog.* XVI. 2.37; 4.9; XVII. 2.5 (Stern, *Authors* I, 300, 312, 315). ἐκτέμνειν is used
of women.
[11] See J. R. Wegner, *Chattel or Person: The Status of Women in the Mishnah* (Oxford
University Press: New York, 1988) 146–59; see further below, pp. 111–12.
[12] In the post-Talmudic period the epithet referred to a non-Jewish woman, sometimes to
a Christian as opposed to a Muslim.

as 'let the circumcised circumcise' (הִמּוֹל יִמּוֹל). That the qualification 'circumcised' is *not* to be applied to a non-Jew who was circumcised is a fairly common assertion to be found already in the Mishnah;[13] here it is supplemented by the parallel that the qualification *is* to be applied to a Jewish woman who was not, 'for a woman should be classed among the circumcised'.[14] Yet this discussion is Amoraic, and the lack of other parallels means it cannot be over-pressed.

An apparent and, in date, more pertinent exception is provided by Philo. Discussing Gen. 17.10 'every male among you shall be circumcised', he asks, why does God command that only the males be circumcised, particularly when the Egyptians circumcise both males and females at puberty (*Quaest. in Gen.* III [47]).[15] For Philo, it should be remembered, the Egyptian use of circumcision, seen by some observers as the origin of the Jewish practice, served as a defence against pagan mockery (*de Spec.Leg.* I.1 [1–3]). Philo's answer is in line both with contemporary biology and with his own well-known assessment of the female: first, the male takes more pleasure in sexual intercourse and so needs to be taught to suppress undue impulses; secondly, the male, who in procreation provides the skill and cause, needs a check to his pride, while the female, who supplies only the bodily parts through her menstrual fluids, has no temptation to arrogance. Circumcision of the relevant organ signifies the suppression or removal of such untoward emotions.[16] Independent of any other assessment of this line of argument, it is notable for its total failure to explore the covenant dimension of circumcision, and does little to help us understand Justin.

A final exception, however, proves more promising. This comes in *Genesis Rabbah* 46, also commenting on Genesis 17. Among the questions discussed are some which were also being debated outside rabbinic

[13] See *mNed.* 3.11, 'uncircumcised is used as a name for the gentiles' and so is inapplicable to an uncircumcised Israelite but is applicable to a circumcised gentile. Here there is no reference to women.
[14] דאשה כמאן דמהילא דמיא; others, relying on the words 'you shall keep my covenant' (Gen. 17.9), disagree because a woman is not 'subject to the observance' (so the Soncino translation; lit.: 'not daughter of circumcision') (דאשה לאו בת מילה היא); the similar argument in *bHull.* 4b as to who may perform shechita offers no parallel to the place of women.
[15] Only extant in the Armenian. The LXX of Gen. 17.10 renders the subject πᾶν ἀρσενικόν.
[16] Philo is not alone in linking circumcision with procreation; *Gen.Rabb.* 46.4 makes a direct link because God's covenant with Abraham included the promise of progeny. When Josephus says the purpose of circumcision was to prevent mixing, he too may be making this sort of connection but with a view to the prohibition of intermarriage.

circles. Why was Abraham circumcised so late in life? so as not to discourage proselytes (46.2). Why, Abraham himself asks, if circumcision is so precious, was it not assigned to Adam; will it not impede others coming and joining? Other texts pose the same question, often through the mouth of 'an outsider'; interestingly, both the proselyte Aquila and a Roman *matrona* are said to have asked why it was not included among the ten commandments.[17] Justin is also aware of the objection: earlier in the *Dialogue* he commented that if circumcision were necessary God would not have created Adam uncircumcised (*Dial.* 19.3). *Genesis Rabbah* goes on to argue why it must be the circumcision of the body, despite Biblical references to the uncircumcision of the ear (Jer. 6.10), of the lips (Exod. 6.30), and of the heart (Jer. 9.25), texts again familiar from Christian debate (Justin, *Dial.* 28.3).[18] Coming to Gen. 17.14, 'And the uncircumcised male (עָרֵל זָכָר) who has not circumcised . . . shall be cut off from his people', the question is asked 'Is there such a thing as an "uncircumcised female" (עָרֵל נְקֵבָה)?' Merely to ask the question is to demonstrate it to be meaningless, for עָרֵל remains in the masculine despite the feminine form of נְקֵבָה; rather, the specific and apparently unnecessary mention of 'male' is a further indication of the 'point at which circumcision takes place'.[19] The next chapter continues with a discussion of the changes made to Abraham and Sarah's names, a debate familiar to Justin who attributes it to Jewish teachers and dismisses it with contempt (*Dial.* 113.2).[20]

In this section *Genesis Rabbah* clearly reflects debate, a debate with one eye at least on relations with outsiders, on issues surrounding circumcision and Abraham, issues which were also part of Justin's agenda. It would be wrong merely to explain these parallels as implicit rebuttal of Christian polemic.[21] These issues were already

---

[17] In *Gen.Rabb.* 11.6 the same question is asked by a philosopher, in *Pes.Rab.* 23.4 on Exod. 20.10 by a pagan, and the questions by Aquila and the Roman matron are added.

[18] See O. Skarsaune, *Proof from Prophecy*, 294, 70–2 who argues that Justin is developing earlier polemic.

[19] *Gen.Rabb.* 46.5; the argument is repeated at 46.13 in the name of R. Isaac, a fourth-generation Tanna, and so contemporary with R. Judah. It is there followed by a reference to those who disguise their circumcision, with specific mention of those who did so in the time of 'ben Kozebah'.

[20] Justin, dependent on the Greek, believes it to be a matter of an additional α for Abraham, and ϙ for Sarah.

[21] So M. Friedländer, *Patristische und Talmudische Studien* (Breitenstein: Wien, 1878) 96–9; K. Hruby, 'Exégèse Rabbinique', 348–50, neither of whom refer to the 'female' argument.

part of an existing debate and polemic, one into which Christianity entered, and one which was further exacerbated following the Bar Kochba revolt.[22]

We find evidence of this in Philo who speaks of those allegorists who preferred the spiritual to the literal observance of circumcision (*de Migr. Abr.* 16 [89–93]). Despite his rejection of their praxis, he himself reflects a 'wisdom' type of approach which finds sources for the knowledge of God within creation, an approach which could easily come into tension with the exclusiveness of the special revelation with which circumcision was bound up. Even the pagan Strabo complains that the insights of the Jewish understanding had been corrupted by the superstitions such as circumcision (and female excision) introduced after the time of Moses.[23] Taking the offensive on the other side, *Jubilees* retaliates by tracing the commandments back to the patriarchs before Moses, rooting the festivals in nature herself, and confidently asserting that the angels themselves are circumcised – all as part of an uncompromising attack on those who fail to circumcise their sons (*Jub.* 15.25–34). Such evidence suggests that there were others than Christians for whom the dependency of certain affirmations of Jewish identity on particular historical moments or revelation became an argument for their contingency – particularly in the need to relate to the outside world.

Women proselytes

Yet if these other elements in the argument were already potential areas of debate within Judaism, would this also be true of the 'uncircumcised woman'? It does seem that the context where this could become a concern would be conversion. It has frequently been noted that before the end of the first century CE it is obscure what conversion meant for a woman, and how a woman convert differed from a female firm sympathizer (or 'God-fearer').[24] In most cases, perhaps, inclusion in the community was simply through marriage to a Jewish husband,

[22] See Skarsaune, *Proof from Prophecy,* 293–5; 324–6. The revolt is explicitly mentioned in *Gen.Rabb.* 46.13 (see n. 19) and forms a significant undercurrent to Justin's *Dialogue.*
[23] *Geog.* XVI.2.37 = Stern, *Authors* I, 295.
[24] So S. Cohen, 'Respect for Judaism by Gentiles according to Josephus', *HTR* 80 (1987) 409–30, 430; 'The Origins of the Matrilineal Principle in Rabbinic Law', *AJSR* 10 (1985) 19–53, 53.

or – more ambiguously – adoption as a slave;[25] but for other women, particularly those who remained married to their pagan husbands, with all the consequences that might entail for possible observation of the commandments, there was, as far as we can tell, no clear ceremony and perhaps no clear or agreed idea of conversion. This accords oddly with the fact that both literary and inscriptional evidence indicates that there were women who were reckoned by some or by themselves to be proselytes, and that we are often told in the secondary literature that Judaism was attractive to women.[26] It is true, of course, that for Josephus the women of the court of Adiabene, including the Queen, Helena, did convert (μετακομιζέσθαι εἰς τοὺς νόμους, *Ant.* XX.2.3 [35]). Yet, how in practice did they differ from other women who 'adopted Jewish ways', if the latter also abandoned idolatry? Izates presumably followed a similar pattern of observance to them – both the women of the court and Izates are said to have been taught τὸν θεὸν σέβειν (*Ant.* XX.2.3, 4 [34, 41]) – but until he was circumcised he was not a Jew.[27] For Aseneth in *Joseph and Aseneth* it is abandoning idolatry which marks the crucial step: she is not said either to be taught the other laws or to observe them. The lack of clarity in Josephus's other references to women attracted to Judaism also points to the inherent ambiguity in their situation.[28]

[25] So Cohen, 'Crossing the Boundary and becoming a Jew', *HTR* 82 (1989) 13–33; in *de Virt.* 39 [219] – 40 [220] Abraham is the standard of proselytes, Tamar, who joined by marriage, the prime example of women who moved from darkness to light. On inscriptional evidence from Cyrenaica of possible slave women who have become Jewish through adoption see G. Lüderitz, *Corpus jüdischer Zeugnisse aus der Cyrenaika* mit einem Anhang von Joyce Reynolds (B.TAVO, Reichert: Wiesbaden, 1983) nos. 12, 31d, 43c.

[26] See B. Brooten, *Women Leaders in the Ancient Synagogue* (BJS 36, Scholars Press: Chico, 1982) 144–7. See now above, pp. 83–99.

[27] It is interesting that the text already discussed, *Genesis Rabbah* (46.10), tells the story of Monobases and Izates who circumcise themselves on reading Gen. 17.11. Rabbinic sources know of Helena's piety but not of her conversion. On the impossibility of harmonizing Josephus and the Rabbinic traditions see L. Schiffman, 'The Conversion of the Royal House of Adiabene in Josephus and Rabbinic Sources', in L. Feldman and G. Hata, eds., *Josephus, Judaism and Christianity* (Brill: Leiden, 1987) 293–312. Schiffman suggests that Josephus's account may stem from propaganda designed to affirm the validity of the House of Adiabene's conversion against doubts by Jews of Nisibis (307).

[28] Josephus appears to treat the Roman Fulvia as a proselyte (νομίμοις προσεληλυθυῖαν τοῖς Ἰουδαϊκοῖς) but the construction of the sentence obscures the relation between her becoming such and her meeting the three charlatans who duped her (*Ant.* XVIII.3.5 [81–4]). Presumably she was not included in the subsequent exclusion of Jews from Rome. The women of Damascus who according to *B.J.* II.20.2 [559–61] 'had gone over to Jewish worship' (ὑπηγμένας τῇ Ἰουδαϊκῇ θρησκείᾳ) are unlikely all to have been proselytes. See Cohen, 'Respect for Judaism', 417, 420.

Things become clearer in the second century, particularly in Palestine. As has been convincingly argued recently, particularly by Martin Goodman and Shaye Cohen, the end of the first century and beginning of the second witnessed a sharpening of the question of the status of proselytes and a formalizing of conversion procedures.[29] The destruction of the Temple, the imposition of the *fiscus iudaicus*, which unlike the Temple tax was also demanded of women, its regularization under Nerva, and the developing pattern of rabbinic authority would all lead to this. This is matched by internal evidence of the development of immersion within the conversion procedure and of a pattern of requirements and procedure for conversion in the second century. If the ambiguity of the position of women converts did not raise questions before, now, in a setting of clearer definition and procedures, it might. Were women who converted, perhaps sometimes influential women, any less part of the Jewish community for not being circumcised?

Here we may turn to the oft-quoted debate in *bYebamot* about whether circumcision or immersion have priority in conversion, a debate often cited, wrongly, in defence of a supposed conversion without circumcision, and set, possibly rightly, in the time of Akiba.[30] Here the conversion procedure for the female proselyte – bathing but not circumcision – is treated as in no way secondary to that for males. Championing the significance of immersion for the male proselyte, R. Joshua can even appeal to the 'mothers' who bathed but were not circumcised, presumably the women who left Egypt but shared in the ablutions at Sinai.[31] The answer is clear; although not circumcised, proselyte women were fully members – in Justin's terms, 'saved'.

That some of Justin's arguments are drawn from traditions and debates regarding proselytes, seems beyond doubt. Earlier in the same chapter (23) he addresses his hearers as 'Trypho and you who wish to become proselytes', and makes the appeal 'remain as you were made' as if, contrary to the general presentation in the *Dialogue*, they were not Jews. This may be inspired by the argument from nature and reflect his

---

[29] M. Goodman, 'Proselytising in Rabbinic Judaism' *JJS* 40 (1989) 175–85; idem, 'Jewish Proselytizing in the First Century', in J. Lieu, J. North, T. Rajak, eds., *The Jews amomg Pagans and Christians in the Roman Empire* (Routledge: London, 1992) 53–78; S. Cohen, 'The Rabbinic Conversion Ceremony', *JJS* 41 (1990) 177–203, who argues that the needs of women may have been one of the factors in prompting a structured ceremony.

[30] *bYeb.* 47a. For the date see Cohen, 'Rabbinic Conversion Ceremony', 186–7.

[31] However, the propriety of arguing 'from the impossible', i.e. from the non-circumcision of the women, is contested.

dependency on earlier material.[32] Although the evidence is more ambiguous, Justin's appeal to the matriarchs may also reflect their role – or at least Sarah's – in traditions regarding proselytes. Sarah was credited with converting female proselytes alongside Abraham, and a number of proselytes known to us through their epitaphs took her name.[33] It would be entirely in keeping with Justin's techniques elsewhere in the *Dialogue* to take an issue from contemporary debate and use it against his Jewish opponents in a new context.

If the various threads are drawn together what does become clear is that when Justin argued against circumcision by appealing to women's experience he was not asking a question which, within the world-view of the time, could not be asked. The ambiguity for women inherent in male circumcision as the covenant marker, although invisible to general perception of the time, could demand attention. Indeed, Scripture itself – Genesis 17 – invited it, particularly when encountered by new experiences or read in a new framework, in this case as provided by those women who were not born into the covenant and who sought to join it.

Hermeneutical consequences

While seeking to answer a particular historical question this essay also provides the prolegomena for a number of further issues; in an area of considerable confusion, attention to the historical questions and texts offers a heuristic framework for exploring such issues. Some of these may be briefly sketched.

[32] He acknowledges his dependency on the 'old man' to whom he owed his conversion. In ch. 46, which introduces the righteous women, discussion centres on those aspects of the Law which can be observed in the post-destruction situation, and also considers those who believe in Jesus and adhere to the Law. These too might be seen as loosely 'missionary' situations.

[33] Generally, the literature of the period shows no consistent way of dealing with Sarah and the others, even when rewriting or commenting on the Genesis narratives. However, in some traditions Abraham and Sarah convert proselytes – Abraham the men and Sarah the women – on the basis of an exegesis of Gen. 12.5 where Abraham brings to Canaan 'those whom they had made' (*Gen.Rabb.* 39.14 in the name of R. Hunia). Among the proselytes who take the name 'Sarah' should be noted Beturia Paucla who died at the age of 86 after sixteen years as a proselyte and whom the communities of Campus and Bolumnus honoured as 'mother of the synagogue' (*CIJ* 523). Sarah is the third most popular female name in surviving Jewish sources, and the most popular one to be found in both Palestine and the Diaspora: see G. Mayer, *Die jüdische Frau in der hellenistisch-römischen Antike* (Kohlhammer: Stuttgart, 1987) 41–2.

1. First, to return to the potential objections against any anachronistic collusion with modern concerns in critical study of the past: the texts studied here illustrate well how all reading of Scripture is an encounter between the experience of the reader and the text itself. New experiences or frameworks reveal potentialities in the text which may never have been part of the authorial intention. Gen. 17.10–14, with its repeated identification of male circumcision with the covenant, itself raises the legitimate question of women's participation; the congruity between ancient and modern readers in recognizing this in different contexts and with different hermeneutics can hardly be ignored.

2. Granted the validity of Justin's question, 'Can women be saved?', how is it to be answered? Are or were women members of the covenant community? That the very logic of the understanding of circumcision points to the exclusion of women as full members of the covenant community has become a sharply contested issue, certainly since the early Reform Movement in Frankfurt in 1845 and more recently under the stimulus of Jewish feminist analysis.[34] As such it has generated largely unsuccessful attempts both to deny the original exclusivity of circumcision and to interpret it as representing the supplanting of an earlier matriarchal culture.[35] More pertinently, it has also been rightly emphasized that Jewish women were considered Jews, were obligated to observe many of the commandments, and frequently fulfilled roles within community life that the literary sources have led (and continue to lead) modern interpreters to deny them.[36] Social reality and experience

[34] The implicit exclusion of women was one of the arguments forwarded against the maintenance of circumcision: see S. Holdheim, *Geschichte der Enstehung und Entwicklung der jüdischen Reformgemeinde in Berlin* (Berlin, 1857). J. Plaskow, 'Bringing a Daughter into the Covenant', in C. Christ and J. Plaskow, eds., *Womanspirit Rising* (Harper & Row: New York, 1979) 179–84 charts the attempt to develop parallel rites for girls to affirm their place in the covenant. See also L. Archer, *Her Price is Beyond Rubies* (JSOT.SS 60, JSOT Press: Sheffield, 1990) 29–34.

[35] I. Peritz, 'Women in the Ancient Hebrew Cult', *JBL* 17 (1898) 111–48, 136 argued that originally both men and women were circumcised; see also U. Winter, *Frau und Göttin* (Vandenhoeck & Ruprecht: Freiburg, 1983) 41–3. For circumcision as symbolizing supplanting see S. Teubal, *Sarah the Priestess: The First Matriarch of Genesis* (Swallow: Athens, Ohio, 1984); G. Lemer, *The Creation of Patriarchy* (Oxford University Press: New York, 1986) 190–3; C. Delaney, 'The Legacy of Abraham', in M. Bal, ed., *Anti-Covenant: Counter-Reading Women's Lives in the Hebrew Bible* (Almond Press: Sheffield, 1989) 27–41 who notes parallels with the Kronos myth in the (almost-) sacrifice of the son, the 'castration', and the establishment of a new religion.

[36] See B. Brooten, 'Judinnen zur Zeit Jesu', *ThQ* 161 (1981) 281–5 who shows that Christian misreading of the sources is often also involved in claims that women were severely restricted in their participation in religious life; eadem, *Women Leaders in the Ancient*

should not be too easily identified with theological perception and presentation, although a dynamic relationship between the two is to be expected.

3. The issue has played an equally important role in Christian scholarship. The assertion has frequently been made that 'a woman could not enter the covenant relationship through circumcision' or even that 'women were not, *theologically speaking*, members of Israel at all' (my italics).[37] The argument usually is that the abolition of circumcision signalled a fundamental change for women. So for E. Schüssler Fiorenza 'if it was no longer circumcision but baptism which was the primary rite of initiation, then women became full members of the people of God with the same rights and duties'.[38] However, not only do the assertions about women's place in Judaism demand a more nuanced treatment as just suggested, but closer analysis must lead us to question whether the abolition of the demand for male circumcision did have such a fundamental effect on the position of women within Christianity. The arguably pre-Pauline formula in Gal. 3.28, 'In Christ there is neither Jew nor Greek, neither slave nor free, and not male and female', has been celebrated with enthusiasm as the cornerstone of early Christian egalitarianism, particularly within feminist exegesis. Yet the rhetoric of Galatians remains unaffected by the last clause of that confession.

Synagogue (BJS 36, Scholars Press: Chico, 1982). It is also important to distinguish between the expectations of male-authored legal sources, the situations implied by narrative or prophecy, and the realities of women's experience, see P. Bird, 'Images of Women in the Old Testament', in N. Gottwald, ed., *The Bible and Liberation* (Orbis: Maryknoll, 1983) 252–88. However, see also above, p. 104 and n. 11.

[37] Both quotations come from the debate over the ordination of women to the priesthood in the Church of England: the 1972 ACCM Report on 'The Ordination of Women to the Priesthood' quoted in J. Field Bibb, *Women Towards Priesthood* (Cambridge University Press: Cambridge, 1991) 108; M. Thrall, *The Ordination of Women to the Priesthood: A Study of the Biblical Evidence* (SCM Press: London, 1958) 44. See also J. and G. Muddiman, *Women, the Bible and the Priesthood* (MOW: London, 1984) 3, who speak of only adult males being properly members; also the more nuanced discussion of M. Hayter, *The New Eve in Christ: The Use and Abuse of the Bible in the Debate about Women in the Church* (SPCK: London, 1987) 67–70 who sees a development by which women lost *theological status* 'in later Judaism', and argues that it was women's susceptibility to regular uncleanness which excluded them from eligibility for the priesthood.

[38] E. Schüssler Fiorenza, *In Memory of Her: A Feminist Theological Reconstruction of Christian Origins* (SCM Press: London, 1983) 210; B. Witherington, *Women in the Ministry of Jesus* (SNTS.MS 51, Cambridge University Press: Cambridge, 1984) 127 offers a similar argument. It is easy to see how this can then be used to justify a female ministry in the Christian church which has transcended the Law.

Circumcision does represent the defining question in the identity of the covenant people of God, but it is a people who are perceived only as male: the implied readers of Galatians are undoubtedly male. Gal. 5.2, 'Therefore, brethren, we are not children of the slavewoman but of the free . . . So I Paul tell you that if you have yourselves circumcised Christ is of no benefit to you', is in a very real sense, in the assumption that those addressed might do just that, no less patriarchal than Exod. 12.48, 'no uncircumcised shall eat of the Passover', a verse which has been seen as typifying the theological invisibility if not the disqualification of women. The question remains unanswered what the focus on circumcision as the defining issue in the self-identity of authentic Christianity over against Judaism meant for women?[39] We may equally properly ask, but find few answers, what the differentiation of Christianity from Judaism meant for those women who, we are so often told, were particularly attracted to Christianity (as also to Judaism).

4. If the abolition of circumcision within the Christian church did not significantly change the status of women, why not? Here we might consider the way that rituals are not just theological symbols but are performative and must be seen in a total social context. Circumcision has been seen by authors ancient and modern as symbolizing and maintaining male dominance: it symbolizes integration within the community and the public role accorded to the male, while the voluntary shedding of blood assumes a quasi-sacrificial and quasi-redemptive character.[40] What new symbols maintained that dominance in the early

---

[39] This has been rarely asked, but see L. Portefaix, *Sisters Rejoice: Paul's Letter to the Philippians and Luke–Acts as Received by First-Century Philippian Women* (CB.NTSer 20, Almquist & Wiksell: Stockholm, 1988) 136, who argues that circumcision would present women with both anxiety and added tension within a mixed marriage. That in some settings women were treated on equal terms with men, probably in Corinth and even in Paul's assumption of mutual responsibility in 1 Cor. 7, is not being denied here. However, the impulses behind this are less clear and are not related to the debates over circumcision.

[40] See the articles by Teubal, Lemer and Delaney cited above in n. 35. On the necessity of the shedding of blood in circumcision see G. Vermes, 'Circumcision and Exodus IV. 24–26', in *Scripture and Tradition in Judaism* (SPB 4, Brill: Leiden, 1973) 178–92, who argues that the Pauline association of baptism with sacrifice through participation in the sacrificial death of Christ is a development from the Jewish doctrine of circumcision. L. Archer has recently attempted to present as the 'flip-side' of male circumcision the woman's involuntary, 'natural' shedding of blood, blood which is deemed impurity and which excludes her from participation in the sacred and in some senses from the community, thus reinforcing the private as her proper sphere: 'Bound by Blood: Circumcision and Menstrual Taboo in Post-Exilic Judaism', in J. M. Soskice, ed., *After Eve: Women, Theology and the Christian Tradition* (Marshall Pickering: London, 1990)

church, a dominance which swiftly if not immediately becomes the norm? What new theological constructs prevented others from following the lead implied by Justin's insight?[41]

In default of an immediate answer it must here suffice to close by answering Justin's question with a new syllogism provided by the deutero-Pauline I Tim. 2.15, 'But she [a woman] will be saved by child-bearing if she continues in faith, and love, and holiness with self-control'.[42]

BIBLIOGRAPHICAL NOTE

This and the preceding essay belong to the wider debate about the place of women in the development of early Christianity. Generally, an earlier confidence about recovering the 'historical' role of women has been succeeded by more attention to the rhetorical strategies of the texts, both in their own right and as standing in the way of any easy exercise in reconstruction. The general bibliography grows rapidly: for an introduction see R. Kraemer and M. R. d'Angelou, *Women and Christian Origins* (Oxford University Press: Oxford, 1999). S. Cohen, 'Why Aren't Jewish Women Circumcised?', *Gender and History* 9 (1997) 560–78 has also taken up some of the specific issues and texts discussed here and has developed them further.

38–61; eadem, '"In thy blood live": Gender and Ritual in the Judaeo-Christian Tradition', in A. Joseph, ed., *Through the Devil's Gateway: Women, Religion and Taboo* (SPCK: London, 1990) 22–49. Although there are problems with her analysis, an examination of the fate of menstrual taboos within Christianity would be revealing; see S. Cohen, 'Menstruants and the Sacred in Judaism and Christianity', in S. Pomeroy, ed., *Women's History and Ancient History* (University of North Carolina Press: Chapel Hill, 1991) 273–99; D. Wendebourg, 'Die alttestamentlichen Reinheitsgesetze in der frühen Kirche', *ZKG* 95 (1984) 149–70, 159, 164–7.

[41] There is nothing to suggest that Justin himself recognized the implications of his own argument.

[42] For a careful analysis and argument that the text does mean what it appears to mean see S. Porter, 'What Does it Mean to be "Saved by Childbirth"? (I Timothy 2.15)', *JSNT* 49 (1993) 87–102.

Part III

Theology and Scripture in
Early Christian Views of Judaism

8

History and Theology in
Christian Views of Judaism*

In his still influential study of 'the relations between Christians and
Jews in the Roman Empire (AD 135–425)' M. Simon pin-pointed the
heart of the issue in the following terms: 'The problem of Jewish
expansion and of the spread of its influence is bound up with that of
anti-Semitism'.[1] These words, written in the postscript fifteen years
after the first publication of the book, were reaffirming, against the
rejection by some of the term 'anti-Semitism', his earlier assertion – 'the
most compelling reason for anti-Semitism was the religious vitality of
Israel'.[2] In his own context Simon was forcefully countering the prevalent
view which saw the Judaism of the period as turned in on itself and, as
far as any external impact went, moribund, – 'strangers in a pagan
world'.[3] His arguments for the religious vitality of Judaism were
sufficiently persuasive to have become increasingly familiar in modern
discussions of the world of early Christianity. Perhaps equally significant
is Simon's interpretation of the Christian polemic in terms of anti-
Semitism or anti-Judaism; this is rarely found in earlier discussions of
Christian–Jewish polemic in the patristic period, whereas now it is
regularly proposed – as in this judgement by Hruby: 'the attitude of the
church fathers to Jews and Judaism is synonymous with anti-jewish
polemic and with Christian anti-Judaism'.[4] Simon himself saw no

---

* First published in Judith Lieu, John North and Tessa Rajak, eds., *The Jews among Pagans
and Christians in the Roman Empire* (Routledge: London, 1992) 79–96. Reprinted by
permission of Routledge.

1 M. Simon, *Verus Israel* (ET Littman Library. Oxford University Press: Oxford, 1986
[1964/48]) 395.
2 *Verus Israel*, 232.
3 For example, E. Schürer, *Geschichte des jüdischen Volkes im Zeitalter Jesu Christi* (Hinrichs:
Leipzig, 1901) 703, So sind die Juden immer mehr das geworden, was sie ihrem Wesen
nach waren: Fremdlinge in der heidnischen Welt.
4 K. Hruby, *Juden und Judentum bei den Kirchenvätern* (Theologischer Verlag: Zurich,
1971) 6.

difficulty in defending the term 'anti-Semitism', even while acknowledging that, in contrast to its modern form, it had relied neither on a theory of race nor on an economic basis, and while also firmly distancing himself as a historian from any attempt 'to connect the Nazis' anti-Jewish persecutions too closely with Christian teaching'.[5] This last quotation comes from the 1964 postscript; the issue of modern anti-Semitism rarely surfaces in the first publication of the book, and then only in contrast with that of the first centuries or when labelling the attempt to present an 'Aryan' Christianity rid of its Jewish heritage as a renewal of the 'Marcionite' heresy.[6]

It is in this area that scholarship has become more nuanced, and perhaps more self-critical; it might be better to speak of 'Christian' scholarship, for many of those who work in this area come from a Christian theological background and have contemporary theological concerns which infuse their historical interests – a good example is Wilken's introduction to his study of Cyril of Alexandria where he speaks of his theological interest in anti-Judaism and of his growing current contacts with contemporary Judaism.[7] A consequence is that the choice of the term 'anti-Semitism' (as opposed to 'anti-Judaism'), particularly in a book title about the early church or, even more, about the New Testament, has become something of a polemical issue determined by more than merely the recognition that the term is a nineteenth-century coinage with a specific, outmoded, conceptual background. Indeed, since the mid-1970s there has been an explosion of literature in the subject, and few authors are able to avoid at least a sidelong glance at the continuing heritage of the earliest Christian attitudes to the Jews.

A further landmark for English-speaking scholarship was Rosemary Ruether's study of the 'theological roots of anti-Semitism' with the arresting title *Faith and Fratricide*;[8] while the main part of the book focuses on the New Testament and Patristic periods, her concluding chapter demands a fundamental rethinking of Christian identity and theology. Her key contention behind this demand is that anti-Judaism is neither superficial nor peripheral to Christian thought, but that from

---

[5] *Verus Israel*, 203, 397.
[6] *Verus Israel*, 238.
[7] R. Wilken, *Judaism and the Early Christian Mind* (Yale University Press: New Haven, 1971) ix.
[8] R. R. Ruether, *Faith and Fratricide* (Seabury Press: New York, 1974).

the New Testament period onwards it was inseparable from developing Christian self-identity, and that its continued vitality within Christian tradition provided the fertile ground for the Nazis' adoption of a racial and secular anti-Semitism. Her presentation of a straight-forward continuity within the Christian tradition (but not so much from earlier *pagan* 'anti-Semitism') has provoked valid criticisms of over-generalization and of a lack of attention to detail, and has been followed by more careful analyses; equally contentious has been her isolation of Christology, the Christian proclamation of Jesus as the promised Messiah, as the reverse side of anti-Judaism and so as the heart of the problem – 'Is it possible to say "Jesus is the Messiah" without, implicitly or explicitly, saying at the same time "and the Jews be damned"?'.[9] Other scholars have sought to show that disputes between Jews and Christians about the status of Torah or about the interpreta-tion of the (Hebrew) Scriptures were more fundamental than those about the messianic status of Jesus. Yet it is significant that despite all the acknowledged weaknesses of the book, it continues to provoke respect, discussion, and, most notably, responses which bring together the historical and the contemporary theological dimensions of the problem.[10] Another inescapable part of the contemporary picture is the growth of attempts by Christian as well as by Jewish theologians to struggle with the understanding of God and of the justice of God in the light of 'Auschwitz'.

It is in this context that historical setting and theological evaluation – both of the modern interpreter and of the original source – combine in an unresolved tension. In her survey Ruether paid only limited attention to the particular social setting of the different Christian writers. However, as in the broader study of the New Testament and early church, this concern has come to be a significant feature of recent study. As of course already argued by Simon, it was the presence of contemporary Judaism that sharpened the polemic of early Christian writers; but this can be given a more local and specific focus, as already by Wilken for Cyril of Alexandria, and subsequently for John Chrysostom.[11] Inevitably

---

[9] *Faith and Fratricide*, 246.
[10] A. T. Davies, ed., *AntiSemitism and the Foundations of Christianity* (Paulist Press: New York, 1979).
[11] R. Wilken, *Judaism and the Early Christian Mind*; idem, *John Chrysostom and the Jews: Rhetoric and Reality in the Late Fourth Century* (University of California Press: Berkeley, 1983).

this leads to a further question: how does the pressure of the immediate situation relate to the continuing heritage of a writer's (or preacher's) words? Melito of Sardis has been labelled the 'first poet of deicide'; the virulence of his attack against Judaism may well owe more than a little to the vitality of Judaism in his home city as now attested by archaeology.[12] How far should this awareness colour our assessment of him in view of the later legacy of the charge of deicide (although not on the authority of Melito)?

For many the issue is more pressing when we go back to the New Testament; in the Fourth Gospel Jesus declares the Jews to be children of a father who is the devil and who was a murderer from the beginning (John 8.44; there is probably a covert reference to Cain). With its 'Evangelical' authority that charge too has had a long legacy – it is taken up by many later church writers – and, together with the overall presentation of the Jews in that Gospel, has earned John the label 'the father of the anti-Semitism of the Christians'. Recent study has proposed conflicting interpretations of the Gospel's attitude to the Jews; for some the hostility reflects the sharpness of polemic and pain occasioned by the recent radical break between Jews and Christians within John's own community, itself reflected in the references to exclusion from the synagogue (John 9.22; 12.42; 16.2). For others the 'Jews' of John 8 are a cover for 'Judaizers' (see below) in the Johannine community – they are Jews who had believed in Jesus (as in 8.31) but whose faith is found wanting; it is an internal hostility and has nothing to do with the 'real' Jews. For others again, the 'Jews' are but representatives of the 'world' which, within the characteristic dualism of the Gospel, represents for the author the ultimate hostility to God and to believers. Not only are scholars undecided as to the appropriate interpretation of John's words in their original context, they are equally undecided whether such an interpretation, particularly the second or third, would properly absolve the Gospel of the charge laid against it. Yet it is clear that a concern prompted by the contemporary situation overshadows if it does not inspire the historical-critical task – 'through careful study, Christians can isolate what genuine forms of anti-Judaism really colour the major

---

[12] A. T. Kraabel, 'Melito the Bishop and the Synagogue at Sardis: Text and Context', in D. G. Mitten, J. G. Pedley and J. A. Scott, eds., *Studies Presented to George M. A. Hanfmann* (P. von Zabern: Mainz, 1971) 77–85, (but see now above, pp. 13–14).

writings and, by examining their historic genesis, neutralise their potential for harm'.[13]

The fate of Judaism in early Christian thought

This discussion may well seem to have taken us away from our proper concern with the situation under the Roman Empire. Yet the last two paragraphs indicate both that there is a considerable 'unfinished agenda' in the analysis and interpretation of the Christian witnesses to the role of Judaism in the religious interaction of the Roman Empire, and that the setting of a significant part of that analysis and interpretation combines both historical and theological worlds, in the modern period no less than in the early church.

That this is true of the early church needs little demonstration. The picture of Judaism after the end of the first century CE as passive if not moribund and as playing no active religious role in relation to Christianity has found its way into 'histories' of Judaism and of the period generally. Whether or not modern scholars espousing this view were gullibly seduced by the patristic sources, this is certainly what those sources would have their readers believe. Yet that image drew its conviction from theological necessity and is effectively refuted not simply by modern archaeological discoveries but by the very same sources themselves.[14] The sheer variety and impact of the polemic against Judaism and against those who succumb to its attractions betray the authors' actual experience even though it may be at variance with the image they want to project.[15] For these early Christians it is now the church that has replaced the Jews as the heirs to God's promises, the church

---

[13] Davies, *AntiSemitism*, xv, here of the New Testament but the sentiment could be repeated of the later texts. For John see E.Grässer, 'Die Juden als Teufelssöhne in Johannes 8,37–47' in W. Eckert, N. Levinson and M. Stöhr, eds., *Antijudaismus im Neuen Testament?* (Kaiser: Munich, 1967) 157–70, and the discussion on pp. 210–12; see now also R. Bieringer, D. Pollefeyt and F. Vandecasteele-Vanneuville, eds., *Anti-Judaism and the Gospel of John* (Van Gorcum: Assen, 2000); the same question could be asked of Matthew or of Luke–Acts. For a patristic source compare P. Harkins, *Saint John Chrysostom. Discourses against Judaizing Christians* (The Fathers of the Church 68. Catholic University of America: Washington, 1977) x, 'Even if he (Chrysostom) was motivated by an overzealous pastoral spirit, many of his remarks are patently anti-Semitic. For these objectively unChristian acts he cannot be excused even if he is a product of his times.'

[14] On the former see T. Rajak, 'The Jewish Community and its Boundaries', in J. Lieu, J. North and T. Rajak, *Jews among Pagans and Christians*, 9–28.

[15] This is one of the main themes of Simon, *Verus Israel.*

that is properly 'Israel' (or the 'new Israel'), the church that is the covenant partner with God. The reverse side of this must be that the Jews are no longer God's people, that they have lost God's election, often by their own wilful rejection of it. Here we need not pause over the many variations and different nuances on this theme, for example how much value is given to Israel's past history 'before Christ', its overall tenor is plain and could be richly documented.[16] Nor can we pause to speculate how an alternative tradition of interpretation might have developed, namely the early Christian conviction that they too were entering into God's covenant promises (1 Peter 2.4–10; Rom. 9–11).

What did happen was that 'history' itself appeared to validate this Christian perception of the rejection of the Jews through the destruction of Jerusalem in 70 CE, through the loss of Temple and sacrificial cult, and through the apparent 'confirmation' of this loss after the failure of the Bar Kochba revolt. Of course, Jewish tradition was also able to intepret the defeat as punishment, but without according it ultimate finality, and even the Christian writer Hegesippus apparently saw it only as the punishment for the murder of James the brother of Jesus (in Eusebius, *H.E.* II.23.18). However, Origen represents the Christian consensus when he says that the Jewish nation had to be overthrown and God's invitation to blessedness transferred to others, and attributes this 'to what they had dared to do against our Jesus' (*c.Celsum* II.8; IV.22). For many writers the time gap between the crucifixion and the destruction of Judaism becomes eclipsed, but Origen acknowledges it as forty-two years graciously given by God for repentance. Both the dispersion of the Jews, 'their scattering to all nations of the whole world', and their unceasing suffering since are the consequence of their sin against Jesus (Eusebius, *Dem.Evang.* I.1.6); like many other writers Eusebius here ignores the antiquity of the dispersion and ties the scattering to the loss of Jerusalem as divine punishment. In the same way we can accord Tertullian no historical integrity when he says the Jews began to have synagogues in the dispersion when they did not believe in Jesus (*adv.Iud.* 13). For these authors, that the Jews have ever since continued to suffer, 'wandering, banished from their soil and sun, having neither man nor God as king' (Tertullian, *Apol.* 21.5), is part of the same theological necessity and obviously would not reflect the self-perception of Tertullian's Jewish neighbours with their long-established

---

[16] Hruby, *Juden und Judentum*, 27–54.

history in North Africa or elsewhere. Small wonder then that Christian authors provide a model which effectively excludes the Jews from active participation in the history of the Empire – something in which they are aided by rabbinic sources' lack of historical interest.[17]

The consequences of this theological conviction can be seen in the violent literary reaction to the Emperor Julian's plans to rebuild the Temple in Jerusalem – for this would undermine a central pillar of the church's own self-understanding (e.g. Ephraem, *Hymni adv.Jul.* IV.20–21), something that may have been part of Julian's conscious intention.[18] On the other hand, the fact that the Jews continued to exist, even after the Christianization of the Empire had seemed to prove the victory of the church, demanded an explanation and provoked Augustine's influential declaration that they must continue as a testimony to Christian truth (*Civ.Dei* XVIII.46; *adv.Faust.* XVI.21).[19]

The continuing existence of 'the Jew' proved a very real problem for these early Christian writers. Given their prolific literary activity, it is not surprising that they can be an invaluable source of information about contemporary Judaism – and they have long been used as such. Yet this information invariably comes from contexts in which the authors had quite different concerns of their own. So, for example, Origen attests the continued payment of the *fiscus iudaicus* until at least the middle of the third century, as well as the authority accorded by the Romans to the ethnarch 'as if he were a king'; he also mentions the blind eye turned towards sentences of death passed by Jewish courts according to their law. He does so, in his discussion of the History of Susannah (*ad Afric.* 14), to demonstrate the freedom that the Jews as a captive people might be allowed, and we may trust him when he says that he speaks from firsthand knowledge. Jerome offers a dramatic description of the anguish of the Jews, permitted on one day of the year to come and weep over the destruction of their city and Temple (*Comm.in Zeph.* I.15–16). Schürer closed the first volume of his 'History of the Jewish people in the time of Jesus Christ' with a long quotation of this description together with its grim ascription of the suffering to

---

[17] It is not a very big step from the sentiments of Eusebius or Tertullian to the historical statement that after the disasters of the revolt against Rome the Jews became increasingly 'strangers in the Gentile world', quoted above, p. 117.

[18] So Wilken, *John Chrysostom and the Jews*, 138–48.

[19] B. Blumenkranz, 'Augustin et les Juifs – Augustin et le judaïsme', *Rech.Aug.* 1 (1958) 225–41.

their killing of the servants of God and of the Son of God.[20] Yet when Jerome speaks of the broken down women and old men who come as demonstrating 'the wrath of God' in their bodies and clothing, when he asks whether any who see it can doubt that it is a 'day of distress and anguish, a day of calamity and misery', and again when he speaks of them as weeping over 'the high pinnacles' of the Temple, from which they killed James – an echo of the interpretation found in Hegesippus – he draws his vocabulary from the text on which he is commenting, Zeph. 1.15f. When he goes on to say (17–18) that after the destruction of Jerusalem 'their blood was poured out like soil over the whole area and their bodies remained unburied like dung over the face of the earth', he is again quoting his scriptural text, just as he is when he says that they suffered this 'because they had sinned against the Lord'. Contemporary reality (assuming that the Jews were still with limited exception excluded from Jerusalem) is serving, and at the same time is coloured by, the needs of the exegesis of the 'Old Testament'.

Such exegesis, particularly of the prophets, although directed at an internal or 'home' audience, plays a significant role in Christian anti-Jewish polemic; the prophecies of doom are regularly interpreted as directed against the Jews; those of hope and promise are seen as finding their fulfilment in the Christian church. Undoubtedly this makes what is said about the Jews tendentious, but not necessarily pure fantasy: it is in Jerome's commentary on Ezekiel that we hear of the Jewish traditions, for which he, probably following their practice, uses the Greek term *deuteroseis*,[21] although he dismisses them as 'myths'; he also reports that 'the Hebrews say' that the Babylonian teachers wear parchments around their forehead on which is written the decalogue – it may have been the case that phylacteries were rarely worn in Palestine in his time, although such evidence as there is contradicts the inclusion of the decalogue (*in Ezek.* XI.36; VII.24). Augustine's report, in commenting on Deut. 11.20, that *mezuzoth* were not in frequent use may well be right, although this is undoubtedly coloured by his assertion, as he considers contemporary

---

[20] *Geschichte*, 705f. This has been retained in the revised edition (G. Vermes and F. Millar, eds., *History of the Jewish People in the Age of Jesus Christ* (T&T Clark: Edinburgh, 1973) 557) although with a counterbalancing note of hope, and has been quoted by other 'histories' since.

[21] See F. Millar, 'The Jews of the Graeco-Roman Diaspora between Paganism and Christianity, AD 312–438', in Lieu, North and Rajak, eds., *Jews among Pagans and Christians*, 97–123, 114–15. Jerome also uses the term elsewhere as do other writers of the period.

elaborate houses, that the injunction that they be fixed to the door post *could* not be followed literally (*Quaest. in Hept.* V.17); that the injunctions of the Law could not be followed literally is, of course, even more a theological statement about the Christian understanding of the Law's true significance. On the other hand, when Eusebius says that the Jews no longer have King, leaders, chief priests, prophets, Pharisees or Sadducees or others of old revered by them (*in Isa.* I.81), he is guided by his 'text', Isa. 22.2–3, 'all your rulers have fled together'. By contrast, Origen, this time commenting on the New Testament, on Matt. 23.2– 3, declares that one can see 'even now among the Jews', scribes and Pharisees sitting on the chair of Moses (*Comm. in Matt.* IX). We cannot assume from this that Origen is deliberately referring to contemporary rabbis as Pharisees or even witnessing to the historic link between them; again it is his text that guides him, and as his exegesis develops it soon becomes clear that he is as much concerned with those within the church who teach only a literal interpretation of the Scriptures as he is with the Jewish teachers whose characteristic method, in his view, this is.

Yet when read sensitively, each of these authors does on occasion offer valuable information about the situation, life or beliefs of the Jews of their day. This is particularly true of Origen and Jerome, both of whom had contacts with contemporary Jewish teachers, to whom they are often indebted for exegesis of the Scriptures;[22] nonetheless, their indebtedness apparently did little to soften either their frequent use of a scriptural lens or the harshness of their polemic against the Jews or against those influenced by them. On the other hand, other authors also must have been aware of well-established Jewish communities in their midst and yet betray much less direct knowledge. Tertullian's anti-Jewish polemic is particularly virulent but he offers only a few hints of contemporary Jewish communities in Carthage, and these mainly as illustrations of some other point;[23] when he is writing against the Jews they become for him the people of the Old Testament who rejected and persecuted the prophets that spoke of the coming of Jesus, and who eventually rejected both him and the church. It has been well argued

---

[22] See N. de Lange, *Origen and the Jews: Studies in Jewish Christian Relations in Third Century Palestine* (Cambridge University Press: Cambridge, 1976); S. Krauss, 'The Jews in the Works of the Church Fathers', *JQR* 5 (1892) 122–57; 6 (1893–4) 82–99, 225–61.

[23] For example in *de Ieun.* 16 where he speaks of Jews having left their 'Temples', praying in the open air when they fast; *ad Nat.* I.13 about those who follow Jewish festivals, sabbath, *cena pura*, etc. It has also been argued that Tertullian shows contacts with Jewish Haggadah.

that his polemic is sharpest not in his work against the Jews but in his attack against Marcion, the second-century 'heretic' who rejected the Old Testament and drove a wedge between the creator God there encountered and the Father revealed by Jesus Christ. Marcion's views were undoubtedly attractive to many and provoked a barrage of refutations; forced to justify the church's retention of the Jewish Scriptures while rejecting the literal observance of many of the precepts within them, and in order to preserve the consistency and unity of God's character, the early Christian writers presented the initial recipients of those Scriptures, the Jews, as consistently blind to God's word, unable to see in their own Scriptures the promised coming of Christ, needing the injunctions of the Law to control their many vices, or perceiving only its literal meaning, which even then they disobey.[24] Thus it is that the Jews of Christian polemic are so often a uniform, stylized type, trapped within the Old Testament, first within the charges brought against the people by the prophets, and secondly within the regulations which they can only interpret literally and yet cannot observe literally, in the past because of their own character, in the present because of the loss of the Temple. So, for example, in the fourth century, contemporary Jewish claims to celebrate the Passover validly are 'proved' fraudulent, for the Temple is laid waste, they no longer have any priests, the stipulated victim is not to be found, God rejects animal sacrifice (e.g. Isa. 1.11), and the people are in any case deserted by God (Zeno of Verona, *Tract.* I.19; 28; 51). It is this theologically moulded 'scriptural' mask that gives rise to the false impression that the authors are blind to the real face of contemporary Judaism.

Conflict and contact

In none of this intertwining of historical experience and theological rationale, of the interpretation of the past and the realities of the present, can we ignore the encounter between Judaism and Christianity as a meeting not of two strangers, but of two who were irrevocably bound up with each other. Of course the problems of identity, definition and distancing were not fully reciprocal; Judaism was more of a problem for Christianity than Christianity for Judaism, although the latter probably engaged in more debate and polemic than the surviving Jewish sources

---

[24] See D. Efroymson, 'The Patristic Connection', in Davies, ed., *AntiSemitism*, 98–117.

betray. Yet the question of boundary, relationship and opposition is nowhere clearer than in the existence of what, in the absence of a better term, we must call Judaizing. As Simon already argued, it was often the vitality and so the attraction of contemporary Judaism that provoked the strength of the reaction and of what he termed anti-Semitism. It is equally often pointed out that many of the attacks against 'the Jews' are in reality directed against 'Judaizing Christians' – Christians adopting Jewish beliefs or practices. As we have already seen, this is hinted at in Origen's exegesis of Matt. 23 and even more clearly in his interpretation of Matt. 16.5–12 where those who eat 'the bread of the Pharisees' are those Christians who do not recognize that the Law is spiritual or discover the things of which the Law is a shadow (*in Matt.* XII.5). Reflecting this awareness of the true provocation of the polemic, Chrysostom's Sermons *Adversus Iudaeos* ('Against the Jews') have recently been translated under the more eirenic title *Against Judaizing Christians.*[25] Here particularly the relation between reality and theological perception, or between different perceptions needs careful disentangling.

The (theological) perception of the early Christian writers (at least outside the New Testament) is of two separate entities, Judaism and Christianity, which have been separated virtually from birth. It is a model implicitly adopted by Simon when in Part 2 of his book he discusses the polemics under the heading of 'The Conflict of Orthodoxies'; for him the conflict is the aspect of Jewish – Christian relations 'involving the *orthodox* members of each group' (p. xiii, my italics). The other, equally significant, aspect comes under the heading 'Contact and Assimilation' (Part 3) or 'contacts resulting in *syncretism*' (p. xviii, my italics). This image of 'orthodoxy – conflict *versus* contact – syncretism' is the same as that projected, for example, by Jerome in his argument against the continuing observance of the Law by converts to Christianity from Judaism. In a passage whose lack of clarity suggests he is not speaking from personal knowledge, he introduces the Ebionites 'who pretend that they are Christians'; in an attempt to identify them he goes on to speak of a contemporary heresy 'throughout all the synagogues of the East among the Jews', called 'of the Minaei' or, popularly, 'the Nazaraeans'. They believe in Christ as Son of God, in the virgin birth, his suffering under Pilate and his resurrection. For all this, 'while they wish to be both Jews and Christians, they are neither

---

[25] See n. 13.

Jews nor Christians' (*Epist.* 112.13). We need not here pursue the question how this report relates to others about the Ebionites, Nazaraeans, or other 'Jewish Christian' groups, nor how the statement that 'even today they are cursed by the Pharisees' relates to the application and history of the so-called 'benediction against heretics' or *birkath ha-minim*. The most revealing point is that for Jerome neither they nor anyone else can be both Jew and Christian, but that, if we can trust Jerome, this is precisely how they did see themselves and indeed, if they were to be found in the synagogues despite being cursed by contemporary 'Pharisees', how they actually lived.

In a different setting, the Christians of Antioch who observed the Sabbath, joined in Jewish fasts and festivities, and respected the awe and sanctity of the synagogue 'were not marginal renegades who came to church only infrequently – they appear to be regular members of his [John Chrysostom's] congregation who thought they could remain members of the Church while observing Jewish rites and customs'.[26] For Chrysostom, however, the Jews are bent on bringing destruction to the Christian flock, and those who succumb are 'mixing what cannot be mixed' (*adv.Iud.* IV.3.6).[27] Such testimonies could be multiplied,[28] although it is hard to determine when we are being persuaded by the rhetoric of the speaker to see a more substantial threat than numbers justified. Origen warns Christians listening to him on a Sunday against bringing up what they had learnt the previous day in the synagogue (*Hom.in Lev.* V.8); yet when he interprets Exod. 12.46, 'in one house shall it (the Passover) be eaten', as a prohibition against 'eating' in church and in the synagogue of the Jews or, equally, in church and in the synagogue of heretics (*Sel.in Exod.* 12.46), we may suspect he is guided as much by text and rhetoric as by contemporary, contrary, practice.

Behind these perceptions lies a complex reality. What Chrysostom, Origen and others testify to is ordinary Christians participating in Jewish life. By contrast, Jerome's appeal to the Ebionites belongs to a series of descriptions of groups with apparently fixed identities, and with beliefs (for example a 'low' Christology) or practices (observance of all or part of the Jewish Law) which in the patristic writers' eyes betray too close a

---

[26] Wilken, *John Chrysostom and the Jews*, 175–6.

[27] Harkins, *Saint John Chrysostom*, xxxix, follows Chrysostom (I 4,7) when he speaks of the 'demi-Christians'.

[28] Simon, *Verus Israel*, 306–38; Wilken *John Chrysostom and the Jews*, 66–83.

convergence with Jewish belief and practice. Sometimes such groups are presented as close to the Jews, sometimes as bitterly hostile. From the time of Irenaeus they are categorized as 'heretical', and, like other heretical sects as seen through Christian eyes, soon acquire names implying a specific allegiance or origin – Symmachians, Nazaraeans, Ebionites – genealogies (usually going back to apostolic or immediately post-apostolic times), and other marks of a fixed identity, namely specific beliefs and adherence to particular (sectarian) writings.[29] They figure not only in catalogues of heresies but also in other settings as sources or illustrations of particular views (their millenarian beliefs: Jerome, *Comm.in Zech.* III.9; *Comm.in Joel* III.7–8) or practices (being both circumcised and baptized: Augustine, *adv.Cresc.* I.31.36), and as a threat to other Christians (Augustine, *de Bapt.* VII.1.1). In modern scholarship these groups are commonly labelled 'Jewish Christian', a confusing term since it can also be applied to the earliest stages of Christianity in general, to patterns of Christian theology with Jewish roots or parallels, or to Christians of Jewish birth. Patristic sources are more likely to label them by 'sect' or to call them 'Judaizers' (so Jerome in the references just given where they are associated with 'the Jews': 'the Jews and our *iudaisantes*').

A different group – or a different perception – appears in the shadowy figures who feature in rabbinic literature as the 'sinners of Israel' (*posh'e yisrael*); it has been forcefully argued that since these people are sometimes treated more openly than informers, than those who deny Torah or resurrection, or than those who separate themselves from the community, they represent 'Jewish Christians' who continued to observe Sabbath, festivals, circumcision and certain dietary and purity laws.[30] Similarly, while a simplistic identification of the 'heretics' or *minim* of rabbinic sources with Jewish Christians is now widely rejected, it still seems likely that they included some Jewish Christians. This does not mean, however, that we can readily identify them with the same 'Jewish Christian' groups as those of the Christian heresiological writings.

The perceptions or presentations of the Christian writers offer little clarity and lead naturally into the terminological confusion of modern

---

[29] See A. F. J. Klijn and G. J. Reinink, *Patristic Evidence for Jewish Christian Sects* (NT.S 36, Brill: Leiden, 1973) for a full analysis of the texts.

[30] A. Mamorstein, 'Judaism and Christianity in the Middle of the Third Century', *HUCA* 10 (1935) 226–63.

scholarship. Even the evidence we have cited suggests, first, that some people within the churches were attracted by Judaism for a variety of reasons, many probably not 'theological' in terms of the arguments explored earlier in this discussion, and shared in certain public aspects of Jewish life. How they perceived their activities or were viewed by other Jews within the synagogues is left to our imagination, but our imagination should be coloured by the fact that Judaism had long had a fascination for outsiders within the Graeco-Roman world and that visitors to the synagogue were rarely repulsed even when active proselytism was not favoured.[31] It is usually assumed that these 'Judaizers' – although the term is probably too specific for this group – were of Gentile origin (as, of course, were the majority of Christians). In fact, the genealogical model, so loved by the anti-heretical writers of the early church, is frequently transferred to this group so as to speak of a continuous tendency to 'judaize' from the opponents of Ignatius (to whom we shall return) to those of Chrysostom discussed above, although such an interpretation introduces a uniformity that not even the sources attempt.

Despite the superficial 'concreteness' of the descriptions of the second group, namely 'Jewish Christians' with fixed, theologically grounded, identities and presumably independent structures, the traces they have left are hardly less elusive than those of the first group. It has been left to modern scholarship to try to recreate the reality behind the conflicting descriptions given by the church fathers and to determine which writers betray any genuine knowledge; it is a matter of unresolved debate whether members of such groups were of Jewish or Gentile birth, and whether some can be traced back in historical continuity to the more positive attitudes towards the abiding validity of the Jewish Law ascribed in the New Testament to Peter or to James, while others are products of later 'syncretizing' tendencies. The church fathers may have done most to mislead by combining a genealogical model with an institutional model of 'counter-churches'; although they apply that model even more determinedly to gnostic groups, the gnostic literature from Nag Hammadi does little to support such clear 'gnostic' self-consciousness and suggests that often the 'gnostics' were still within the church, while maintaining a critical distance from some of its institutions. In our case

---

[31] See M. Goodman, 'Jewish Proselytizing in the First Century', in Lieu, North and Rajak, eds., *Jews among Pagans and Christians*, 53–78.

an agreed definition, identification and analysis of comparable 'sectarian' Jewish Christian literature has yet to be achieved.[32]

Image and reality

Fortunately it is not our task here to attempt to clarify the picture any further. It is enough that the picture that has emerged so far is one of considerable complexity. In each case we must ask not so much how clear are the boundaries between Christianity and Judaism, but more particularly who is drawing them and for whom. We may illustrate the question by turning to one of the earliest post-New Testament sources, Ignatius of Antioch. Travelling from that city, where he was bishop, to Rome, where he was to be martyred (soon after 110 CE), Ignatius wrote letters to six churches on his route; some of these he had visited, while from the others he had received delegations and news. The burning concern with unity which infuses these letters has as its reverse side a polemic against false belief. The dominant point of conflict is the reality of Jesus Christ's humanity and death, dominant perhaps in reality but also because of its consequences for any understanding of Ignatius's own, eagerly anticipated, martyrdom. However, in two letters, those to the Magnesians and the Philadelphians, the problem is of 'Judaism'.

We may leave aside here two important questions, first whether Ignatius is reflecting the situation in Antioch, which he knew somewhat better, or the situation in the churches of Asia Minor to whom he writes; secondly whether there is but one heresy in these churches, which combines Judaizing elements with a docetic Christology, or whether the problem in Magnesia and Philadelphia is 'simply' that of Judaizing.

Writing to the church at Magnesia, which he had not personally visited, he says, 'If up to now we live according to Judaism, we confess that we have not received grace'; 'It is impossible to speak of Jesus Christ and to judaize. For Christianity did not put its faith in Judaism but Judaism in Christianity' (*Magn.* 8.1; 10.3). He warns the Philadelphians, of whose situation he did have personal experience, 'if anyone interprets Judaism to you, do not listen to him; for it is better to hear

---

[32] Work, and so the literature, in this area is now growing fast, and so this paragraph has inevitably included gross simplifications. For some of the debate see *Aspects du Judéo-Christianisme* (Colloque de Strasbourg 23–5 avril 1964) (Presses Universitaires de France: Paris, 1965), and for a more recent bibliography, F. Manns, *Bibliographie du Judéo-Christianisme* (Fransiscan Print. Press: Jerusalem, 1979).

Christianity from a circumcised man than Judaism from an uncircumcised' (*Philad.* 6.1). For Ignatius there are two separate and contrary entities, *Ioudaismos* and *Christianismos*; the former term we meet already in the Maccabaean literature (2 Macc. 2.21; 8.1; 14.8; 4 Macc. 4.26), perhaps representing a significant step in combining life and beliefs within a single term. *Christianismos* comes first in Ignatius (also *Rom.* 3.3) and appears to be modelled on *Ioudaismos* by antithesis. If we ask what 'Judaism' actually means for Ignatius we get a remarkably circumscribed answer, particularly when we recall that Antioch was the home of a large and flourishing Jewish community of whom he must have had some knowledge. *Philad.* 6.1 (just quoted) depends for its irony on an assumption that Judaism is irreversibly characterized by circumcision.[33] Not surprisingly, the other characteristic is Sabbath: those who 'converted' from Judaism to Christianity, either the prophets or the first disciples, no longer sabbathized (*sabbatizontes*) but lived 'according to the lord's (day)' (*kata kuriaken zontes*) (*Magn.* 9.1).[34] Again Ignatius does not elaborate what he means by this and it is left to modern scholarship to draw links with his emphasis elsewhere on the communal meetings of the church, which he accuses his opponents of avoiding, and to speculate how the assertion relates to their teaching or practise. For Ignatius Judaism and Christianity are two separate systems with typical 'phenomenological' characteristics – for Judaism, the same characteristics as were most noted by the pagan world, circumcision and sabbath. The only relationship between the two is a one-way passage which virtually renders Judaism obsolete. Such is the separation that the prophets belong to Christianity and not to Judaism (*Magn.* 8.2) – there can be no common ground between the two.

So Ignatius; yet it is equally clear that this does not represent the real situation which he was addressing. As is also the case with his docetic opponents, the problem he is addressing is one within the church; at Philadelphia he found himself in an exegetical debate with other

---

[33] Unless we are to speculate about 'Judaizers' who advocated a Judaism without the requirement of male circumcision. This is not impossible, but the antithesis seems to be more the expression of Ignatius's perception of the two entities and the one-way relation between them than a report of the 'heretics'' views. (On this and what follows see now J. M. Lieu, *Image and Reality: The Jews in the World of the Christians* (T&T Clark: Edinburgh, 1996) 23–56).

[34] Or perhaps 'the lord's life'; there is no noun with the fem. adjective 'lord's'. 'Day' provides a better contrast with the reference to sabbath, although the main emphasis is a way of life.

members of the church about the Old Testament where he failed to prove his point (8.2). Inevitably, then, modern scholars speak of the problem within these churches (or perhaps in reality at Antioch) as one of 'Judaizing', although interpretations of the character of this Judaizing vary greatly; it was members of the church who were appealing to the Scriptures, 'interpreting' or accepting interpretations of Judaism, and perhaps 'sabbathizing'. It was a situation of weak or poorly defined boundaries, whether those were the boundaries between the Jewish and Christian communities or, more probably, the internal boundaries within the Christian community which encompassed a broad range of possible belief and practice. This, however, is not Ignatius's perception; for him 'Judaizing' is 'Judaism' and is incompatible with Christianity. To put it anachronistically, Ignatius is working with the model of orthodoxies – orthodoxies which, despite his well articulated theology of the church, are determined by visible social and structural characteristics; the members of the churches, however, were living within a different pattern but not one that merits the term 'syncretism' or assimilation.

Only in very broad terms can we see a continuity of problem and response between Ignatius and Chrysostom; certainly the situation of the latter cannot be read into that of the former – we do not know what the Christians of Magnesia were doing on the Sabbath, if anything. Not only were Judaism and Christianity not the homogeneous entities the polemical writers present, but the situation of both the Jews and the Christians changed radically through the centuries, and so, too, must have the varying patterns of relations between them. Clearly this is not to imply that at any point during this period the boundary between Judaism and Christianity was imaginary. Even though we must avoid reading back into the first and second centuries later conceptions of orthodoxy, nonetheless, Ignatius's perception represents the dominant and formative perception of the developing self-consciousness of the church, as it was expressed in literature, liturgy, creed and structures. External factors, too, reflected and confirmed the same reality: the Christians knew that it was as Christians that they were persecuted, while they were denied the privileges of protection they saw enjoyed by the Jews. Even here not everyone may have shared the same perception; Christian writers warn their audience against accepting the protection of the synagogue during persecution (*Mart.Pion.* 13). If some accepted such protection rather than apostasizing into paganism it was presumably because for them Judaism was an acceptable spiritual home (see Jerome, *de Vir. Illust.* 41); they would not have agreed with Origen's exegesis of the three servants whose questions prompt Peter to deny Jesus, as first the Jewish synagogue, secondly the Gentiles and thirdly the heretics (*Comm. in Matt.* CXIV on Matt. 26.69–75). Here, however, the numbers appear to be very small compared with the anxieties about and supposed evidence of Judaizing.

Rather, we see here as throughout, that the relationship between Jewish and Christian groups in the Roman Empire, and between 'Judaism' and 'Christianity', was a complex, contradictory and rarely stable one. An attractive rhetorical conclusion would be that the theological relationship projected by the church fathers is simple, consistent and unchanging! It may be truer to say that the dialectic between practice (?history) and theology shares in the same complexity.

BIBLIOGRAPHICAL NOTE

This was the earliest of the essays in this collection, and a number of the themes have been taken up in subsequent essays included here, and in Lieu, *Image and Reality*. For the general theme the bibliographical note on p. 29 is also relevant here. M. Taylor, *Anti-Judaism and Early Christian Identity: A Critique of the Scholarly Consensus* (SPB 46, Brill: Leiden, 1995) offers a sustained critique of (Christian) scholarship's explanation of 'anti-Judaism' in early Christian writings as a response to the threat of Judaizing or of the success of contemporary Judaism, and puts more emphasis on the theological functions of 'Judaism' for Christian self-understanding.

9

Accusations of Jewish Persecution in Early Christian Sources with particular reference to Justin Martyr and the *Martyrdom of Polycarp**

For in truth your hand was lifted high to do evil, for even when you had killed the Christ you did not repent, but you also hate and murder us . . .

(Justin Martyr, *Dialogue* 133.6)

The charge that the Jews actively sought the death of Christians lies at the heart of the oft-rehearsed scholarly debate over Jewish involvement in the persecution of Christians, a debate which need only be cursorily signalled here. Harnack's vivid account, summarized in his words 'as a rule [*sic*], whenever bloody persecutions are afoot in later days, the Jews are either in the background or in the foreground',[1] offers a useful starting-point. True, it is an account which easily can be shown to rely more on rhetoric than on wealth of evidence, which even when taken as historical record is remarkable for its paucity:[2] in fact, it was not historical evidence so much as Harnack's own understanding of Christianity's discovery of its true identity that shaped his narrative. Yet it is an account which has left a long legacy; W. H. C. Frend's rhetoric is equally well known: 'In the persecutions which were to wrack Asia in the reign of Marcus Aurelius the Jew was often in the background [*note*

---

* First published in G. N. Stanton and G. G. Stroumsa, eds., *Tolerance and Intolerance in Early Judaism and Christianity* (Cambridge University Press: Cambridge, 1998) 279–95 (and originally given at the British–Israeli Colloquium on 'The Limits of Tolerance in Judaism and Christianity in Antiquity', Jerusalem 1994). Reprinted by permission of Cambridge University Press.

---

1 A. von Harnack, *The Expansion of Christianity in the First Three Centuries* (ET Williams & Norgate: London, 1904–5) I, 64–7, 66.
2 See D. Hare, *The Theme of Jewish Persecution of Christians in the Gospel according to St. Matthew* (SNTS.MS 6, Cambridge University Press: Cambridge, 1967) 66–79.

the echo of Harnack]. For nearly another century he [*sic*] continued to stir up trouble wherever he could'.[3] This is only a high point of a continuing theme in the early part of Frend's account, and has evoked an angry response from the critics, one which betrays that more than historical fidelity to the sources is at stake.[4]

The historical question can not be ignored, and it is undoubtedly one that has been obscured by an inappropriate tendency to see Jewish–Christian interaction, even in the Diaspora, in isolation from the wider context of the Graeco-Roman city, despite the emphasis in recent study of Jewish communities on their social integration within the city. However, a better starting-point might be not 'Jewish persecution of Christians' but 'Christian accusations of Jewish persecution'. Most of our sources for the former, 'historical', question are those accusations, yet rarely, if ever, do they come in 'historical' contexts. Hence the primary task must be to analyse the literary and theological nature and function of such accusations. Thus the initial question must be not about the Jews – 'Did they persecute Christians?' – but about the Christians – 'Why did they perceive Jews as persecutors?' This may be part of a much wider debate: the precise nature of the persecution of Christians, its legal – or otherwise – base, and its extent before 250 CE are heavily contested.[5] However, what is beyond dispute is that Christians perceived and presented themselves as persecuted.[6] Again, it is important to ask why was this so and how this self-presentation functioned.

In exploring this issue we shall leave aside the New Testament material because of the ambiguity as to when and whether it is appropriate there to speak of 'internal' or of 'external' action or perception, a problem

---

[3] W. H. C. Frend, *Martyrdom and Persecution in the Early Church* (Blackwell: Oxford, 1965) 259.

[4] See the review by F. Millar in *JRS* 56 (1966) 231–6; T. Barnes, 'Tertullian's "*Scorpiae*"', *JTS* 20 (1969) 105–32, 132 ; and the spirited self-defence by Frend, 'A Note on Tertullian and the Jews', in F. L. Cross, ed., *Studia Patristica* X (*TU* 107, Akademie Verlag: Berlin, 1970) 291–6. A summary and assessment of this aspect of the debate is made by D. M. Scholer, 'Tertullian on Jewish Persecution of Christians', in E. Livingstone, ed., *Studia Patristica* XVII.2 (Blackwell: Oxford, 1982) 821–8.

[5] See the classic debate between G. M. de Ste Croix, 'Why were Early Christians Persecuted?', reprinted in M. I. Finley, ed., *Studies in Ancient Society* (Routledge & Kegan Paul: London, 1974) 210–49, and A. N. Sherwin-White, 'Why were Early Christians Persecuted? An Amendment', in Finley, *Studies*, 250–5, continued by G. M. de Ste Croix, 'Why were Early Christians Persecuted? A Rejoinder', in Finley, *Studies*, 256–62.

[6] See J. Perkins, "The Apocryphal Acts of the Apostles and the Early Christian Martyrdom', *Arethusa* 18 (1985) 211–30, 222.

exemplified by Gallio's response to Jewish complaints in Acts 18.12–17. Only from a later perspective could such tensions be seen unequivocally as defining 'the synagogues of the Jews [as] the fount-heads of persecution'.[7] We may also leave aside the hostile role of the Jews in the later *Acts* of martyrdom of the saints, a role which frequently led to generalizing statements about Jewish responsibility by those who edited them: sixty years ago James Parkes exposed the flimsy grounds on which such statements were made and demonstrated how few *early Acts* lay the blame at the feet of the Jews, and that even in these few instances the tendency is to the general rather than to the specific.[8] So too, it is only accusations of persecution that are relevant, and not the ubiquitous complaints of Jewish rejection of Christian preaching; similarly, charges that the Jews spread their own 'slanders' concerning Jesus or his followers, some of which may be traced in the sources, or the more questionable assertion that they were responsible for pagan slanders against Christians, are not enough to establish *persecution*.[9]

The persecution of the righteous

Despite Christian attempts to deny any parallel between their own experience and that of the Jews, both the fact of persecution as a response to their perceived exclusivity, and their interpretation of it through the martyrological tradition, can only be understood within a Jewish frame-work.[10] This is something that Christian authors – and we shall start with Justin Martyr – were able to affirm, but only when refracted through their own interpretative lens:

> For you murdered the righteous one and the prophets before him [cf. Isa. 57.1; Jas. 5.6]. And now you reject those who put their hope in him and in God, the almighty and creator of all, who sent him. (*Dial.* 16.4)

---

[7] Tertullian, *Scorp.* 10: this passage has inspired much of the debate referred to in n. 4, although the next words, 'among whom the apostles suffered beatings' does seem to restrict the reference to apostolic times.

[8] J. Parkes, *The Conflict of the Church and the Synagogue* (Soncino Press: London, 1934) 121–50.

[9] On the former see already Justin, *Dial.* 17.1; 108.2; 117.3; J. Maier, *Jesus von Nazareth in der talmudischen Überlieferung* (Wissenschaftliche Buchgesellschaft: Darmstadt, 1978); for the latter, particularly that Christians participated in cannibalistic and sexual orgies, see Tertullian, *ad. Nat.* I.14; Origen, *c. Cels.* VI.14; A. Henrichs, 'Pagan Ritual and the Alleged Crimes of the Early Christians', in P. Granfield and J. Jungmann, eds., *Kyriakon: Festschrift J. Quasten* (Aschendorff: Münster, 1970) I, 18–35.

[10] See Frend, *Martyrdom and Persecution*, 31–78.

Here Justin stands within a tradition concerning the fate of the prophets that early Christianity inherited from Judaism, a tradition in which it is characteristic of a prophet to be rejected, persecuted and even murdered by his (*sic*) contemporaries. In its original context, this portrayal is an integral element within, and is inseparable from, the broader tradition of the obstinacy of those to whom the prophet is sent, of the warnings and judgement given by God, and of the climactic appeal for repentance; in Christian hands it easily became a demonstration of Jewish inveterate rejection of God's message, a rejection which might even have reached the point of no return. Justin, of course, was not the first to use the theme: whether or not part of Jesus' own self-understanding, it is taken up by New Testament (cf. Luke 6.23; Matt. 23.29–31; Luke 11.49f.) and by later writers.[11] In Justin, however, it offers a key to the understanding of Jewish rejection both of Jesus and of those who followed him, which is developed in a number of directions.

First, to extend the passage just quoted:

> Accordingly, these things have happened to you in fairness and justice, for you have murdered *the righteous one* and the prophets before him. And now you reject those who put their hope in him and in God, the almighty and creator of all, who sent him, and, as far as you can (ὅσον ἐφ᾿ ὑμῖν), you insult, cursing in your synagogues those who believe in the Christ. For you do not have authority to act murderously against us, on account of those who now hold power, but as often as you were able, that you did. Wherefore God through Isaiah calls to you, 'Behold how *the righteous one* is destroyed . . . [Isa. 57.1–4]'. (*Dial.* 16.4)[12]

In the next chapter Justin goes on to accuse them not only of murdering 'the only blameless and righteous man', but that when 'you knew that he had risen from the dead . . . you not only did not repent of the wicked deeds you had committed' – the prophetic theme is again unmistakable – but sent out messengers with charges against Christianity 'so that you might make not only yourselves guilty of injustice but also all other people' (17.1). This charge is further substantiated by Isa. 52.5, 'Through you my name is blasphemed among

[11] See O. Steck, *Israel und das gewaltsame Geschick der Propheten: Untersuchungen zur Überlieferung des deuteronomischen Geschichtesbildes im Alten Testamentes, Spätjudentum und Urchristentum* (Neukirchener Verlag: Neukirchen-Vluyn, 1967); on the early Christian use of the tradition (99–109), Steck adds 1 Thess. 2.15; Jas. 5.10; *Barn.* 5.11; Ignatius, *Magn.* 8.2; *3 Cor.* 9f., and the passages from Justin to be discussed below.

[12] For the recognition they do not have the power they would like, see *Dial.* 95.4.

the nations', by Isa. 3.9–11, 'Let us bind (δεῖν) the *righteous one* for he is distasteful to us', and by Isa. 5.18–20.

Similarly, in *Dial.* 93.4 the litany starts with '*your*' rejection of God, continues that '*you* proved to be always idolators and murderers of the righteous [pl.]', and proceeds via '*your*' killing of Christ to '*your*' cursing of those who prove him to be the Christ and even '*your*' attempt to show him to be cursed.[13] The second person plural, 'you/your', does not only belong to the *Dialogue* form; it establishes a continuity of character and responsibility which has its roots and authority in the Scriptures and which reaches, without a break, to the present. In 136.3–137.4, Justin again starts from Isa. 3.9–11, this time appealing to what he claims to be the correct LXX text, 'Let us *do away* (αἴρειν) with the righteous';[14] once more he traces a history of disobedience which continues through their rejection of Jesus to their infamous 'reviling of the son of God . . . and despising of the King of Israel, as your rulers of the synagogue teach, after the prayer' (137.2).

In this material a number of themes are being developed, each of which could be traced further through other early Christian writings: first, the 'murder of the prophets' is extended to include both Jesus and his messengers, a process which encourages or colludes with the suppression of any role by the Roman authorities in the death of Jesus; secondly, a significant step in the argument is provided by the appeal to Isa. 57.1, the murder of the *righteous one*, a text that Justin had already used as a proof-text in *Apol.* 48.5, but which is now combined with Isa. 3.9–11; thirdly, this tradition can be used either as a basis for an appeal to repent or, and more frequently, as an assertion that they rejected the opportunity to repent; and fourthly, Isa. 52.5 is here used by Justin – as it is later by Tertullian (*adv.Iud.* 13.26; *adv.Marc.* III.23.3) – of Jewish defamation of Christians. Much later, Jerome still uses the same passage, but has to acknowledge that the words 'among the nations' are not part of the Hebrew text; therefore he refers the verse instead to Jewish cursing of Christians in the synagogue (*in Esaiam* XIV.52.4), an issue with which it had been already rhetorically associated, but not as a proof-text!

---

[13] In *Dial.* 96.2 'your cursing' is activated by the Gentiles in the killing of Christians; see below, pp. 147–8.

[14] Contra. 17.1 (p. 138 above) where he cites Isa. 3.10 as δήσωμεν, in agreement with the surviving LXX tradition. In 137.3 he defends his reading of the LXX against theirs.

That Justin was seriously convinced of Jewish hostility to Christians is not to be doubted; however, the *frequent repitition* of the theme owes as much to its function within one, or more than one, theological schema, as it does to its historical primacy.

Fulfilment of prophecy

If the charge of 'always' murdering the righteous belongs to direct polemic, the appeal to the fulfilment of prophecy had a wider potency, and its significance in Justin's *Apologies* shows how much was at stake. There he appeals again to Isa. 5.20:

> For evidence that these slanders which are uttered against those who confess the Christ were foreknown and that those who slander him and say it is good to keep the old customs would be afflicted, hear what is succinctly said through Isaiah, 'Woe to those who call what is sweet bitter, and what is bitter sweet' [Isa. 5.20]. (*Apol.* 49.7)

Despite this assertion, Justin explicitly blames the Jews for persecution at only two points in the *Apology*, 31.6; 36.3. In both cases the contexts are important: in chapter 31 he is establishing the credibility of Christianity by appealing to prophecy, and the credibility of that appeal by reference to the *Jewish* Scriptures which are authenticated by a double line of tradition. Here he recounts the story of their translation into Greek by the Egyptians, 'among whom the books have remained even to this day', and also claims their universal distribution among the Jews.[15] He pre-empts this from becoming a counter-argument in favour of the Jews by continuing, 'However, the Jews when they read do not understand what has been said, but consider us enemies and hostile, killing and punishing us, like you do, whenever they can, as you can be persuaded' (*Apol.* 31.5). To support this claim he asserts that Bar Kochba ordered that '*only* the Christians should be subjected to fearsome tortures if they did not deny that Jesus was the Messiah' (31.6). In Roman ears, when the war was still a living memory, the example would be a persuasive one; no one would be likely to voice the objection that Bar Kochba was acting within the bounds of permitted Jewish self-regulation. In fact, that *only* Christians suffered seems improbable, and it is

---

[15] On Justin's contribution to the development of this legend see M. Müller, 'Graeca sive Hebraica Veritas? The Defense of the Septuagint in the Early Church', *SJOT* 1989/1 (1989) 103–24.

noteworthy that Justin does not make the same claim in the *Dialogue* where it could have served him well.[16]

His second reference, this time only to Jewish hatred of Christians, again comes when Justin appeals to the proper understanding of prophecy which is inspired by the divine *logos* (*Apol.* 36.1–3). Once again the Jews are explicitly those 'who possess the books of the prophets' but who fail to understand them; instead they respond with hatred to Christian demonstration that they crucified the one whose coming the prophets foretold.

Thus Jewish hostility serves an apologetic function in the appeal to fulfilment of prophecy, and so qualifies the necessary recognition of their prior claim to the Scriptures. The competitive element which is implicit here is explicit in the *Dialogue*. As is well known, Justin finds in prophecy the promise of two parousias of Christ, the first in obscurity, the second in glory. In an exegesis of Micah 4.1–7 in these terms (*Dial.* 109–10) he interprets 'I shall make her that is driven out a remnant and her that is oppressed a strong nation' (v. 6) as a reference to the Christians, 'driven out even from the world as far as you and all other people can, not permitting any Christian to live' (110.5). Yet he acknowledges that the Jews, perhaps in the aftermath of the Bar Kochba revolt, interpret this passage of themselves, 'that this has happened to your people'. This he can not allow: *they* suffer deservedly as all the Scriptures testify, *Christians* suffer in company with Christ and in fulfilment of Isa. 57.1 ('See how the righteous one is destroyed . . .'). Thus Jewish involvement in Christian suffering is an important element in delegitimating not only any Jewish appeal to scriptural fulfilment but also Jewish suffering itself.

Scriptural models

The contribution of scriptural exegesis to charges of persecution could also take other forms. Irenaeus uses the well-known theme of brotherly rivalry, Esau representing the Jews, Jacob the Christians: 'Jacob took the blessings of Esau as the latter people has snatched the blessings of

---

[16] Neither does he capitalize on these Christians' failure to support Bar Kochba's own messianic pretensions – as later scholars have done; see also R. Bauckham, 'Jews and Jewish Christians in the Land of Israel at the Time of the Bar Kochba War', in G. N. Stanton and G. G. Stroumsa, eds., *Tolerance and Intolerance in Early Judaism and Christianity* (Cambridge University Press: Cambridge, 1998) 228–38.

the former. For which cause his brother suffered the plots and persecutions of a brother, just as the church suffers this self-same thing from the Jews' (Irenaeus, *adv.Haer.* IV.21.3).[17] For Hippolytus the two elders who spied on Susannah represent 'the two peoples (δύο λάοι), one from the circumcision, the other from the nations', who still seek false witness against Christians in the hope of stirring up destructive persecution (*ad Danielem* I.13–15). The editors of this text for *Sources Chrétiennes* take this as evidence of contemporary Jewish involvement in persecution, citing Harnack in support,[18] but, as always with exegetically rooted assertions, it would be better to ask whether the exegeted text has been more creative than historical experience: modern experience of the use of the Bible easily demonstrates both that suitable texts can be found which mirror reality, but also that reality becomes shaped in its presentation and language by the text. Thus Hippolytus goes on to describe how the action of the elders is fulfilled when on a suitable day 'the two peoples' come into the house of God where all are praying and singing hymns, and drag them out saying, 'worship the gods with us or we will testify against you', and, so saying, drag them for judgement and condemnation (I.20).[19]

Universal witness

The generalizing 'two peoples' and the improbability that Jews would use such terms – 'worship the gods with us' – introduce a further theme. A similar scenario appears in an apparently narrative context in the *Martyrdom of Polycarp*, often seen as guilty of an 'undisguised anti-semitism'.[20] In the initial account of the persecution which broke out at Smyrna no mention is made of the Jews; it is the crowd (τό πλῆθος) who are astounded by the bravery of the earlier martyrs and who cry 'Away with the godless (ἄθεοι); let Polycarp be sought!' (3.2), with no hint that Jewish voices were added to (never mind loudest in) that cry. It is only when the narrative focuses on Polycarp that they appear:

[17] In Jewish exegesis Jacob represents the Jewish people, Esau the Roman (and later Christian) Empire.

[18] G. Bardy and M. Lefèvre, eds., *Hippolyte, COMMENTAIRE SUR DANIEL* (SC 14. Éditions du Cerf: Paris, 1947) 99.

[19] The editors take the specific reference to 'acting against the decree of Caesar' as a reference to Sulpicius Severus's edict according to *Hist.Aug.* XVII against *Jewish* proselytizing and against Christianity (*Hippolyte*, p. 111).

[20] H. Musurillo, *The Acts of the Christian Martyrs* (OECT, Clarendon Press: Oxford, 1972) xiv.

when, after his arrest and refusal to renounce his Christian confession, the herald is sent into the stadium or amphitheatre to announce to those who had been waiting that 'Polycarp has confessed three times that he is a Christian',

> the whole crowd of Gentiles and Jews (ἅπαν τὸ πλῆθος ἐθνῶν τε καὶ Ἰουδαίων) dwelling in Smyrna cried out in uncontrollable anger and with a great shout, 'This is the teacher of Asia [*or* of impiety],[21] the father of the Christians, the destroyer of our gods, the one who teaches many to neither sacrifice nor worship!'. (12.2)

The description fills a number of literary functions, as the drama of the moment betrays. These we cannot pursue except to note that it is irrelevant, albeit true, that the words are unlikely to have been found on Jewish lips – they would not have claimed the city gods as 'theirs' nor ventured to accuse someone else of avoiding their worship without running the risk of having the same charge turned against themselves. It is equally pointless to allocate the cries to the groups involved, so that the Jews contribute only the first two affirmations, or to debate the 'orthodoxy' of the Jews involved or the official nature of their involvement.[22] From the point of view of the narrative, Polycarp's clear testimony must have a universal audience and he himself must stand alone against the gathered forces of the opposition.

This theme of the universality of the audience of the Christian witness – and a martyr is a witness – appears to be a traditional one. It is already there in the promise that the disciples will be 'scourged in their synagogues and led before rulers and kings . . . as a witness to them and the Gentiles' (Matt. 10.17–18 par.), a passage echoed in the delegitimating avowal that none of the Montanists 'had been persecuted by the Jews or killed by the lawless' (Eusebius, *H.E.* V.16.12).[23] In a more neutral context Acts uses similar language to *Mart.Poly.*, when 'all those dwelling in Asia, . . . Jews and Greeks' came to hear Paul's preaching (19.10, 17; cf. 14.1, 5).[24] According to Hegesippus's account of his martyrdom, James,

---

[21] All the Greek manuscripts except M(oscow) read 'teacher of impiety'; 'of Asia' has the support of M, Eusebius and the Latin translation.

[22] Musurillo, *Christian Martyrs*, 11, n. 16 attributes the accusations to different groups in the throng; Parkes, *Church and Synagogue*, 137 ascribes the action to Jewish 'lewd fellows of the baser sort' and denies its official character – however 'official' might be defined.

[23] The passage continues that none had been scourged in the synagogues or stoned; an exegesis of Matt. 10.17 is more probable here than a reference to contemporary Jewish persecution.

[24] Acts 19.10, 17 anticipate the apparently redundant 'dwelling in Smyrna' in *Mart.Poly.*

the brother of Jesus, was invited to persuade those who had come to Jerusalem for the Passover, namely 'all the tribes together with the Gentiles' (Eusebius, *H.E.* II.23.11).[25] After his death and burial James is declared to be a true witness 'to both Jews and Greeks that Jesus is the Christ' (*H.E.* II.23.18):[26] in James's case the focus of the testimony is christological, in *Mart.Poly.* it is Polycarp himself as teacher and as martyr. Although not a martyrdom, Peter is told in his eponymous *Acts* that he will have a 'trial of faith' with Simon Magus before 'many more of the Gentiles and Jews', although in the event those gathered in the forum are addressed only as 'men of Rome' (*Acts of Peter* 16; 30). The third-century *Martyrdom of Pionius*, which both contains much authentic tradition and is explicitly rooted in the theological and literary tradition of *Mart.Poly.*, marks a further development when it identifies the crowd witnessing Pionius's testimony as composed of 'Greeks and Jews and women' (*Mart.Pion.* 3.6). The theme becomes a truism and formulaic: Cyprian speaks about Christian patient hope of vindication in the midst of the changing tumults and persecutions of Jews, Gentiles or heretics (*de Bono Pat.* 21; cf. *Epist.* 59.2); Tertullian declares 'we have as many enemies as there are outsiders . . . Jews from envy, soldiers from extortion, even our own servants from their nature itself. Daily we are besieged . . .' (*Apol.* 7.3). Even Tertullian's much quoted description of the Jewish synagogues as 'fount-heads of persecution' is immediately followed by the 'peoples of the nations with that circus of theirs' (*Scorp.* 10.9).[27]

The cry of these 'peoples of the nations', 'How long the third race? (*usquequo genus tertium*)', serves to underline that this picture of universal opposition is only the obverse of the awareness by Christians that they constitute a new people or even a third race over against Greeks and Jews, an idea already hinted at in Hippolytus's 'two peoples'. The tendency for the Jews to merge into or emerge out of an otherwise undifferentiated crowd of the lawless in *Mart.Poly.* (13.1; 17.2–18.1) and elsewhere is a reflection of the way that this Christian self-identity oscillates between a model of the '*third* race' and a dualist contrast between the righteous and the unrighteous. Thus the charge of Jewish involvement in persecution is deeply implicated in Christian apologetics

---

[25] It is not clear whether 'Gentiles' (ἔθνοι) here are non-Jews or Jews from the Diaspora.

[26] K. Beyschlag, 'Das Jakobsmartyrium und seine Verwandten in der frühchristlichen Literatur', *ZNW* 56 (1965) 149–78, argues for a common tradition underlying the martyrdom of James, that of Polycarp, and other Christian martyr traditions.

[27] On this passage see n. 7 above.

of self-identity; considering the dialectical relationship with Judaism within those apologetics, claiming their antiquity and heritage while denying their legitimacy, we may be surprised that it is not found more frequently.

The activity of the devil

The *Martyrdom of Polycarp* brings us to another ominous theme: the ultimate source of all this opposition is not the proconsul nor the mob nor even the Jews, although we shall return to them, but the devil.[28] Already at the beginning of the account the colourful variety of tortures endured by the earlier martyrs was recognized as the devices of the devil trying by many means to subvert them to denial (*Mart.Poly.* 2.4–3.1). At that point he appears merely as 'the devil',[29] but in the final scenes after Polycarp's death, and in opposition to 'the greatness of Polycarp's martyrdom, his blameless life and the crown of immortality he has now won', his true identity is manifested; as 'the jealous and envious and evil one, the one who opposes the race of the righteous', he determines that the Christians will be deprived at least of the 'poor body' of the martyr. To this end he incites Nicetas, the father of the police-chief Herod and, incidentally, brother of a certain Alce, to request the magistrate that the body not be handed over on request, as was usually possible, 'lest abandoning the crucified one, they begin to worship this man' (17.1–2).

At this point (17.2) 'the Jews' reappear, 'inciting and urging'.[30] Showing his hand ever more clearly, the author continues,

> they[31] also kept watch as we were about to take him from the fire, not realising that we shall never be able to desert the Christ, who, for the sake of the

---

[28] This is a standard theme in martyr accounts, compare the Martyrs of Lyons in Eusebius, *H.E.* V.1.16.

[29] And possibly as 'the tyrant' (ὁ τύραννος) which is read in 2.4 by the majority of Greek MSS (except M). Although often seen as secondary, it is not a common term in Christian martyrologies, while it is used of the earthly opponent and persecutor in Jewish martyr stories (4 Macc. 9.1, 10, etc.), and so perhaps should be preserved.

[30] In 13.1 they had appeared as contributing with customary enthusiasm to the gathering of wood for the fire. The exact connection at 17.2 is obscured by grammatical unevenness (smoothed out in Eusebius *H.E.* IV.15.41), although the general sense is clear. I subject all these passages to a detailed analysis in *Image and Reality. The Jews in the World of the Christians in the Second Century* (T&T Clark: Edinburgh, 1996) 57–102.

[31] Still the Jews, although the motive which follows has just been attributed to Nicetas.

salvation of the whole world of the saved, suffered blameless for sinners, and so to worship some other one . . . At this, the centurion, seeing the contentiousness of the Jews, placed him in public, as is their custom, and burnt him,

– although he first would have had to reignite the fire which a little while ago had been quenched by Polycarp's blood! However, the Christians are not prevented from later gathering 'the precious bones' and putting them in an appropriate place (18.2).

Again, a number of concerns have shaped the text, and have probably contributed to its unevenness in its present form. We may only note and pass by the concern about the veneration of the martyr's remains in relation to the worship of Christ which seems to be reflecting an inner-Christian debate under the guise of objections made by Jews or pagans: it is, after all, improbable that either group would fear that, or be worried whether, Christians desert Jesus in favour of Polycarp; projecting the problem onto them would be a rhetorically effective way of dealing with it. We can also only note the role played by Nicetas who requests the magistrate that the body not be surrendered; we are reminded here for the second time (cf. 8.2) that he is the father of Herod, the police-chief, a piece of information given not just for biographical interest but to recall for us the role played by Herod in the (Lukan) narrative of Jesus' Passion. Polycarp's martyrdom is explicitly 'according to the gospel' (1.1), and at a number of points echoes Jesus' own arrest, trial and death, in which, of course, the Jews inevitably featured. It is unlikely that the imitation theme has created the presence of the Jews entirely – if it had, more explicit verbal echoes could be expected – but that a 'Herod', even if not a Jew, should be closely related to the activity of the Jews should against this background cause no surprise.

For our purposes it is the way the role played by the Jews is presented which is most important. Here they are no longer one group within the crowd, as in the earlier references, but initiators of the attempt to thwart the influence of Polycarp, even after his death. Their activity is explicitly parallel to, or perhaps the earthly counterpart of, that of the 'evil one who opposes the race of the righteous'; just as he 'incited' (ὑπέβαλεν) Nicetas, so too they are all the while 'inciting' (ὑποβαλλόντων) these things.

Blaming persecution on the demons is not an exclusively 'anti-Jewish' theme. Indeed, like other themes we have traced, it may have Jewish roots: in the *Martyrdom of Isaiah* the prophet's suffering at the hands of

Manasseh is attributed to the latter's 'ally' the devil (3.11f.; 5.1).[32] Where martyrdom, or even faithful perseverance, is seen as part of a conflict waged with the devil, it is natural to identify the agents of persecution as in some way doing the work of the devil.

But there are other sources too: in *Apology* 5 Justin argues that it was demons who engineered Socrates's death when he exposed by reason (*logos*) the deception by which the people had come to worship them as gods; the charge against him was atheism. Justin then blames the persecution of Christians on the same demons, for Christians too expose them in the name of the Logos incarnate, Jesus Christ.[33] The theme is repeated in *II Apology* 8 where Justin adds Heraclitus and Musonius to the list of those who lived by reason and suffered the murderous hatred of the demons. He would probably have included also Abraham, Elijah and the Three Young Men of Daniel 3, whom he also lists as 'living by reason' and who were also martyrs or near martyrs (*Apol.* 5).[34] Demons are also responsible for apparent pagan anticipations or imitations of Christian concepts, for heresy, and for disbelief; it is no surprise that they continue their opposition through inciting *pagans* to persecute Christians (57.1), while they had already engineered the death of Jesus 'at the hands of the foolish Jews' (63.10).

A different schema is followed in the *Dialogue*, where, as we have seen, the emphasis is much more on Jewish opposition. The contribution of demonic inspiration to persecution by pagan outsiders is less important (*Dial.* 18; 39), but at a highly significant point Justin speaks of Christian fidelity in the face of the 'punishments even to death which have been inflicted on us by demons and by the host of the devil, through the aid given to them by you' (131.2). This comes in the introduction to his long judgement-history, a sort of inverted salvation-history (131–3); it can not be separated from Justin's assertion that the Jews ('*you*') repeatedly sacrificed their children to demons (133.1; cf. 19; 27; 117), a crime he aligns with the making of the golden calf, the slaying of the prophets, and with their supposed 'mutilation' of the Greek translation of the Scriptures (73.6) – a suggestive juxtaposition of the

---

[32] See T. Baumeister, *Die Anfänge der Theologie des Martyriums* (MBTh 45, Aschendorff: Münster, 1980) 288; 60.
[33] See T. Baumeister, 'Das Martyrium, in der Sicht Justins des Märtyrers', in Livingstone, ed., *Studia Patristica* XVII.2, 631–42, 633.
[34] Baumeister, 'Das Martyrium', 633. On the importance of demons in Justin's scheme see E. Osborn, *Justin Martyr* (BHTh 47, Mohr: Tübingen, 1973) 55–65.

themes that we have already discussed. In telling contrast, Gentile Christians are those who by their conversion have turned away from demons (30; 78). Thus, in the *Dialogue,* blaming the devil for persecution does nothing to alleviate the Jews of responsibility; instead it gives their opposition a more comprehensive character in both creating and defining Jewish identity.

There are, of course, some New Testament roots to this: there it is Judas who is suborned by Satan (Luke 22.3; John 13.2, 27), although John can speak of the Jews as stemming from their father the devil who was 'a murderer from the beginning' (8.44); particularly significant is the letter to the church at Smyrna in Rev. 2.8–11 which speaks of the slanders 'of those who call themselves Jews but are not, being rather the synagogue of Satan' (v. 9), and in the next verse warns of the suffering to come when the 'devil' (διάβολος as in *Mart.Poly.* 3.1) will cast some of them into prison. In Justin these separate elements are being shaped into a more comprehensive, and so rhetorically more persuasive, whole.[35]

Defining by opposition and imitatio Christi

Christians thus share in the experience of Christ, and this too may demand a role for the Jews, at least in Polycarp's martyrdom which is 'a testimony according to the Gospel' by which he becomes a 'partaker of Christ' (*Mart.Poly.* 1.1; 6.2; cf. above, p. 146). Yet also on a broader base, persecution – and here Jewish persecution must play a special role – is but the necessary condition and foil for a Christian response which defines their new identity and values.[36] Already in Justin's *Apology,* Christian readiness to pray for their enemies is a matter of pride, and demonstrates their conversion from past ways, and indeed from enslavement to demons (*Apol.* 14). In the *Dialogue,* the charge of Jewish *cursing* of both Jesus and Christians, which is the regular preliminary to accusations of more active persecution (16.4; 95.4; 96.2; 133.6),[37] plays a

---

[35] Baumeister, 'Das Martyrium', asks whether the motivating force was the tradition from which Justin spoke, the real experience of Jewish opposition, or even his hope that this might bring about repentance; he continues, 'He speaks from the position of the persecuted, not the powerful. It is tragic that the thought developed by him, later, when the former persecuted were in possession of state power, produced such devastating consequences' (638).

[36] Perkins, 'Apocryphal Acts', 222.

[37] 122.2 associates proselytes blaspheming his name with their seeking to kill 'us'.

prominent role in this. The issues raised by this charge are too complex to be treated here in detail, although again they would have to be looked at first not in relation to some supposed external reality,[38] but in relation to the rhetorical reasons why Justin not only claims that it happened but does so repeatedly (16.4; 93.4; 95.4; 96.2; 108.3; 133.2). Thus, for example, Justin's focus on cursing is not to be divorced from his exegesis of the Old Testament, including his long discussion of Deut. 21.23 in *Dial.* 89–96.[39] On the one hand, the scriptural 'cursed be everyone who hangs on a tree' anticipated how the Jews would treat both Christ and Christians, yet, on the other, it also sets into sharp relief the Christian response of steadfastness and forgiveness, as they meet cursing with prayer and forgiveness (96.1–3).

A final passage both draws this out and evokes a number of the themes we have considered. At the end of that reverse judgement-history in *Dial.* 131–3 alluded to earlier, Justin reaches a climax following a quotation of Isa. 3.9–15; 5.18–25:

> For in truth your hand was lifted high to do evil, for even when you had killed the Christ you did not then repent, but you also hate and murder us who believe through him in the God and Father of all, as often as you get the power, and unceasingly you curse both him himself and those of his, while all of us pray for you and for all people, even as we have been taught to do by our Christ and Lord, when he instructed us to pray for our enemies, and to love those who hate us and to bless those who curse [Luke 6.18]. (133.6)

In all these texts we have been listening to rhetoric, even in the deceptively narrative *Martyrdom of Polycarp*. Such rhetoric served to create a persuasive world or symbolic universe for insiders if not for outsiders; the role of the Jews in the persecution of Christians becomes part of that world, but a surprisingly less central part than might have been expected. It is one which must have been rooted in *perceived* experience, although what sort of experience these texts alone can not tell us. We have seen how exegesis could be an interpretative response

---

[38] Most frequently in relation to the *birkat-ha-minim*, although most of Justin's references seem too general for this.

[39] This is why, although Justin also speaks of Jews reviling, blaspheming and profaning, 'cursing' plays such a major role; see further J. Lieu, 'Reading in Canon and Community: Deut. 21.22–23, A Test Case for Dialogue', in D. Carroll, D. Clines and P. Davies, eds., *The Bible in Human Society: Essays in Honour of J. Rogerson* (JSOT.SS 200, Sheffield Academic Press: Sheffield, 1995) 317–34, 326–8 = pp. 151–68, 161–3 below.

to experience, but might in turn create 'reality' for an immediate audience or for subsequent interpreters, thus shaping their 'experience'. This is a process which is an intrinsic part of early Christian – Jewish interaction, and demands of the modern interpreter a path between a simple historicism and a sceptical dismissal of theological fantasy.[40]

---

[40] For a detailed study of literature about martyrdom and the way it shapes Christian identity see below, pp. 211–31.

10

Reading in Canon and Community:
Deut. 21.22–23, A Test Case for Dialogue*

There has over the last twenty years been a significant change in the way the first part of the Christian Bible is thought about in academic study. In 1983 *Beginning Old Testament Study*, edited by John Rogerson, illustrated for students the largely undisputed character of the discipline as they would meet it in academic settings; the editor's initial historical outline and his epilogue on 'Using the Old Testament' acknowledge the anxieties that often arise from such study.[1] In Rogerson's 1990 article on 'Biblical Criticism', while affirming the new pluriformity of methods, he maintains a firm defence of historical critical analysis, again acknowledging the dilemmas it has caused Christian faith communities – sensitivities illustrated by the character of the *Festschrift* in his honour.[2] The tension between the scholarly and the confessional context (here '*the church*') is familiar, but remarkable now appears the earlier 'unproblematic' use of the term 'Old Testament', and the lack of any prescience of the currently pervasive dilemma, 'Hebrew Scriptures' *or* 'Old Testament'.[3]

If we may summarize the contemporary debate by asking, 'To whom do the Scriptures belong?', we are certainly not posing a new question (cf. John 5.39). For Justin Martyr, debating with the Jew Trypho in the second century, the answer was non-negotiable: ' . . . your Scriptures; rather not yours but ours, for we believe them, while when you read

---

* First published in M. D. Carroll, D. J. A. Clines and P. R. Davies, eds., *The Bible in Human Society: Essays in Honour of John Rogerson* (JSOT.SS 200, Sheffield Academic Press: Sheffield, 1995) 317–34. Reprinted by permission of Sheffield Academic Press.

[1] J. Rogerson, ed., *Beginning Old Testament Study* (SPCK: London, 1983) 6–25, 145–52.
[2] J. Rogerson, 'Biblical Criticism', in R. J. Coggins and J. L. Houlden, eds., *A Dictionary of Biblical Interpretation* (SCM Press: London, 1990) 83–6. The 'Festschrift' was the original setting of this essay, and references to it have been retained here.
[3] Other alternatives, 'First' or 'Older' 'Testament', imply a successor, although, even where antiquity is no longer a virtue, perhaps do not so much anticipate their own obsolescence.

you do not understand the sense in them' (*Dial.* 29.2).[4] A century later his anonymous successor elaborated: 'the preservation among the Jews even to the present day of the books which pertain to our worship of God happened by divine providence'.[5] For these writers, of course, the Scriptures they claimed 'as ours' were Greek – the Septuagint – and, to serve their arguments from them, could not be otherwise. The ensuing story is familiar: with the formation of the 'New Testament', the issue became that of the Christian canon; to ask 'To whom do the Scriptures belong?' is now to subject the relationship between Old and New Testaments to scrutiny, for only through being claimed by the church did the Scriptures become 'the *Old* Testament'. The rediscovery of the Hebrew and the abandonment of the Greek Scriptures in the Protestant churches only intensified the problems to come: the Old Testament, now defined as or by the Hebrew Scriptures, is no longer those Scriptures which Justin and his successors valiantly defended against the attacks of Marcion, and thus preserved as 'ours'. We must now add, when we have before us a *Biblica Hebraica Qumranica*, collating the biblical (*which?*) texts among the Dead Sea Scrolls, to whom will it belong: to the Christian church, although it be an 'Old Testament' they may never have known before;[6] to Judaism, although again it may present a text not part of that interpretative tradition; or will it be the preserve only of those other potential owners, the scholarly community, as the 'Scriptures' of a community long dead?

The kaleidoscopic tangle of issues thus becomes clearer. If the severance of the Old Testament from the New made possible the historical critical method,[7] the latter in turn has prompted the renaming of 'the Hebrew Scriptures'. It was the signal contribution of that method to preserve the integrity of the Scriptures against the imperialism of a dogmatically determined interpretation which could only proceed by allegory or typology, and so to establish the neutral ground of the texts'

---

4 Contrast his emphasis in *Apol.* 31 on Jewish possession of the Scriptures, supporting his apologetic appeal to their antiquity and integrity.

5 Ps. Justin, *Cohortatio ad Graecos* 13.5.

6 Although it may sometimes be closer to a text the earliest Christians knew than current editions of the MT or LXX. J. A. Sanders, 'Hebrew Bible *and* Old Testament: Textual Criticism in Service of Biblical Studies', in R. Brooks and J. J. Collins, eds., *Hebrew Bible or Old Testament: Studying the Bible in Judaism and Christianity* (Notre Dame Press: Notre Dame, 1990) 41–68 makes a plea for editions reflecting the actual textual pluriformity.

7 Rogerson, 'Biblical Criticism', 84.

own self-witness where all, regardless of any confessional loyalty, may meet. However, for many the result has been to distance them, imprisoning them among a remote people, time and setting, creating the danger of a new 'Marcionism'.[8] Rediscovered as speaking to their own time, how can they – or do they – speak to ours? Hence the dilemma of the contemporary hermeneutical maze.

Accordingly, choice of the title 'Hebrew Scriptures' deliberately distances them from their Christian adoption or sequestration. Here the term 'Scriptures' mocks 'us' who claim them as Scripture, Scripture being not simply that which is written, but that which, once written, speaks still and cannot be silenced, or rewritten. Already as 'Hebrew', they exclude, if not the Aramaic sections, then the order and additions which come to us via the Greek text, recognized as Christian Scripture from our earliest witnesses, forcing the question in a Christian context, as '*Hebrew* Scriptures' are they *Scriptures*?[9]

More fundamentally, the use of the term 'Hebrew Scriptures' is intended to remind 'us' that they were not 'ours' first: we are to acknowledge that their first owners, even their rightful owners, for they were never willingly ceded, were 'the Hebrews'. We cannot decry such motives; Adolf von Harnack's words no longer ring with triumphant certainty but with relentless accusation: 'Such an injustice as that inflicted by the Gentile Church on Judaism is almost unprecedented in the annals of history. The Gentile Church stripped it of everything; she took away its sacred book.'[10] Historically that assertion is a nonsense; no one can read the writings of rabbinic Judaism, or study the remains of the synagogue at Sardis with its Torah shrine(s), or those at Dura Europos with its painting of an 'ark', no one can share in the service of a modern synagogue, and believe that Judaism has lost, or ever did lose, its sacred book to Christian hands; to claim that is to play into Harnack's hands

---

[8] So J. F. A. Sawyer, *From Moses to Patmos: New Perspectives in Old Testament Study* (SPCK: London, 1977) ix, 2, determines 'to liberate Old Testament study from the grip of archaeologists, philologists, and latter day Marcionites' and to 'concentrate on the Old Testament as part of the Christian Bible'.

[9] H. Hübner, 'Vetus Testamentum und Vetus Testamentum in Novo Receptum. Die Frage nach dem Kanon des Alten Testaments aus neutestamentlicher Sicht', in I. Baldermann et al., eds., *Zum Problem des biblischen Kanons* (*JBTh* 3; Neukirchener Verlag: Neukirchen-Vluyn, 1988) 147–62, argues for the greater theological relevance for the New Testament of the LXX.

[10] *The Expansion of Christianity in the First Three Centuries* (ET Williams & Norgate: London, 1904–5) I, 81.

and to identify Judaism with a sterile and moribund dinosaur. Yet this is not to deny nor to diminish the truth that the Gentile Church did indeed inflict not just an but many an injustice on Judaism, 'unprecedented in the annals of history'. Recognition of this has inspired those who urge us to speak no more of 'Old Testament', with its imperialist and supersessionist overtones: in an age of dialogue, when the recovery of what unites may offer paths to healing and reconciliation, 'the Hebrew Scriptures', it is hoped, may recall us to our common heritage.[11]

The motivation is beyond reproach, but the solution is deceptive. Already in the first and second centuries CE the adjective 'Hebrew' carried an antiquarian note; used of the worthies of old, it was largely sentimental, born out of respect for antiquity and past heroism.[12] The label 'Hebrew' distances the 'Hebrew Scriptures' from *any* living community: they become a curiosity, the relic of the distant past. This is not a quibble about a term whose virtues can still be defended; it prompts the question whether there can be *Scriptures* without a community, and if the Scriptures should properly define the community, does not the community also define the Scriptures?

Here contemporary hermeneutical debate adds its support: the claimed inviolability of an objective historical exegesis has come increasingly under attack, both in principle and as an achievable goal.[13] One element in the contemporary redrawing of the exegetical map is the recognition that the text's post-history, both in the wider textual context and beyond, becomes part of its meaning.[14] If this may be true of any literary text with a long history within a culture, it is particularly so of these writings in virtue both of their canonical shape*s* and of their foundational and authoritative role within each religious community:

[11] A. Lacocque, 'The "Old Testament" in Protestant Tradition', in L. Boadt, H. Croner and L. Klenicki, eds., *Biblical Studies: Meeting Ground of Jews and Christians* (Studies in Judaism and Christianity, Paulist Press: New York, 1980) 120–42, prefers the 'Prime Testament' and claims 'the Bible as a Christian book clearly robs the Jews of their own Scriptures' (121).

[12] See A. Arazy, *The Appellations of the Jews (IOUDAIOS, HEBRAIOS, ISRAEL) in the Literature from Alexander to Justinian* (PhD, New York, 1977; Univ. Microfilms 78–3061).

[13] Rogerson, 'Biblical Criticism', 86.

[14] See F. B. Watson, *Text, Church and World: Biblical Interpretation in Theological Perspective* (T&T Clark: Edinburgh, 1994) 3, 'the Hebrew scriptures . . . can also be read as the Christian Old Testament, distinct from the New Testament but inseparable from it and shaping the way that it is read, *as well as being reciprocally shaped by it*' (my emphasis).

if we must always interpret a text in its context, that context is not the original historical context alone, nor even the immediate literary context, but the context of the canon and/or of the believing community. So too, exegesis of Scripture is an intrinsic and idiosyncratic part both of the study of the two religious traditions and of participation within them.

In this elemental context Jews and Christians do *not* share these Scriptures, for as Jewish or as Christian Scriptures they are essentially different; they cannot be reduced to 'the common ground' as sometimes claimed, merely to be supplemented by the Christians' own further collection (or expanded 'Writings'), or even, more 'ecumenically', to be complemented in one tradition by the 'New Testament', in the other by the rabbinic corpus.

This point is not new, and, significantly, those who defend the 'Old Testament' as part of the Christian Scriptures are not necessarily those who charge 'the Judaism which rejected the Christ event [with having] remarkably enough terminated the formation of the Old Testament'.[15] Claims for 'the common ground', such as those above, may rest on a Christianizing understanding of 'canon'; by contrast, L. B. Wolfenson's argument that if there is a 'canon' in the Jewish context it is not Tanach but Torah, and then the other binding or normative regulations articulated in Mishnah and Gemara, has several modern advocates.[16] Among them Jon Levenson has argued cogently that recovery of the 'Hebrew Bible' through historical criticism has led to the establishment not of 'common' but of 'neutral ground' for Jews and Christians, compelling 'its practitioners to bracket their traditional identities':

> unless historical criticism can learn to interact with other senses of Scripture
> – senses peculiar to the individual traditions and not shared between them –
> it will either fade or prove not to be a meeting ground of Jews and Christians,
> but the burial ground of Judaism and Christianity, as each tradition vanishes
> into the past in which neither had yet emerged.[17]

[15] H. Gese, *Essays on Biblical Theology* (ET Augsburg: Minneapolis, 1981) 13.
[16] L. B. Wolfenson, 'Implications of the Place of the Book of Ruth in Editions, Manuscripts, and Canon of the Old Testament', *HUCA* 1 (1924) 151–78. B. S. Childs, *Introduction to the Old Testament as Scripture* (SCM Press: London, 1979) 670, concedes but sees as outside his scope that 'Wolfenson's point does appear to lend support to those who stress the elements of discontinuity between the two faiths'.
[17] J. D. Levenson, 'Theological Consensus or Historicist Evasion? Jews and Christians in Biblical Studies', in Brooks and Collins, eds., *Hebrew Bible or Old Testament,* 109–45, 144.

In what follows I shall explore from this perspective a text with a potent 'post-history' within the Christian tradition, shaping both Christian Scripture and the way it is read, while also playing a role in the 'meeting of Jews and Christians' in the past, and I shall suggest that, while we cannot repeat, neither can we refuse to engage with, that history.

Deuteronomy 21.22–23 as Old Testament: early Christian interpretation

Deut. 21.22–23 has attracted frequent attention for its impact on the interpretation of Jesus' death both by Paul and within other New Testament traditions; for brevity's sake we shall rely on earlier work for sketching its role as 'Scripture' for the early Christians. An initial translation of the MT reads:

> And if a man has committed a crime punishable by death, and he is put to death, and you hang[18] him on a tree, his corpse shall not remain[19] all night upon the tree, for you shall certainly bury him on that day, for a curse of God is a hanged one and you shall not defile the land which the LORD your God is giving you as an inheritance.

a. Paul

In Gal. 3.10–14, Deut. 21.22–23, intertextually related to other passages, assumes a central role in Paul's own argument, and, through the contribution of Galatians to later reflection, has helped shape subsequent Christian perceptions of the nature and function of Torah:

> For all who rely on the works of the Law are under a curse; for it is written, *'Cursed be everyone who does not abide by all the things written in the book of the law, to do them'* [Deut. 27.26]. Now it is evident that no one is justified before God by the Law; for, *'The righteous one by faith shall live'* [Hab. 2.4]; but the Law is not by faith, for *'The one who does them shall live by them'* [Lev. 18.5]. Christ redeemed us from the curse of the Law, having become a curse for us, for it is written, *'Cursed be everyone who hangs on a tree'* [Deut. 21.23] – that in Christ Jesus the blessing of Abraham might come upon the Gentiles, that we might receive the promise of the spirit through faith.

---

[18] See below, p. 164, n. 46.
[19] Or 'you shall not leave his corpse'.

Paul's argument has been exhaustively analysed and discussed, although the debate is not yet settled. Self-evidently we are not hearing a systematic theologian or exegete dispassionately analysing his texts: Paul is driven by the conclusion that he needs to reach – that all believers, especially here Gentile Christians, are included in God's plan for salvation on the basis of faith alone. The context is polemical, countering those who argued that male converts must be circumcised if they were to claim an inheritance in God's promises to Abraham (Gal. 3.3; 5.2). This is no theoretical discussion provoked by a disinterested attempt to reconcile different parts of Scripture; it is rooted in Paul's prior mission among the Gentiles which he felt to be self-justifying, and in his experience of the Christian communities he founded.[20] It is certainly also shaped by his opponents who could equally appeal to Scripture, although, unfortunately, we can not hear their arguments directly.

Paul's initial text, Deut. 27.26, was perhaps already part of this debate, for its force is disputed and could even undermine Paul's thesis.[21] The repeated 'everyone . . . all' is certainly significant, while for our purposes the intertextuality established with Deut. 21.23 is pivotal. In between these two texts, whatever the details of the logic, Hab. 2.4, set in antithesis to Lev. 18.5, establishes the essential choice: life must be *either* by faith *or* by doing (= by Law), not both. Yet 'it is not the biblical text itself that has made this seeming contradiction self-evident to him. Because of his conversion . . . he now sees faith and law as two different paths'.[22] Paul interprets and combines these different texts not so as to demonstrate how he reached a 'Christian' perspective but from the vantage of already having one. Moreover, it is not his ('rabbinical') hermeneutical technique of resolving apparent contradictions in Scripture which is distinctively 'Christian', but his definition of the contradiction – faith versus Law-obedience – and his solution to it.

Within this framework we should read his appeal to Deut. 21.23, 'Cursed be everyone who hangs on a tree'. Assuming, without demonstration, that this Scripture applies to Jesus, Paul inverts it; it becomes a prophecy – a use of 'Scripture' which becomes pivotal in

---

[20] Among many others see A. Segal, *Paul the Convert* (Yale University Press: New Haven, 1990) 118–25.

[21] On the text see p. 158 below; it may be questioned whether there was such an absolutist and rigorist application of the text, even for converts.

[22] Segal, *Paul the Convert*, 122.

Christian thought. By absorbing this text and its curse into himself, Christ annuls the potential curse against (Gentile) believers.[23]

Paul's argument presupposes, and requires, a text closer to that of the LXX than that of 'the Hebrew Bible'. The critical 'everyone – everything', although found in the Septuagint,[24] is absent from the MT of Deut. 27.26, a problem that Jerome already recognized and readily attributed to the subsequent editing of Paul's original Hebrew text by the Jews, 'so that they should not be seen to be under a curse' (*in Gal.* 3.10 [*PL* 26. 383]). More recently Hans Hübner has drawn from here his conclusion that for the New Testament the Septuagint has a theological significance not possessed by the Hebrew.[25]

In his reading of Deut. 21.23 Paul created the intertextual relationship with Deut. 27.26 by using the same formula that he found there, 'Cursed be everyone . . .' (ἐπικατάρατος πᾶς). This diverges from the MT where the vocabulary and constructions of the two passages are unrelated,[26] but it does develop the LXX of 21.23 which already adds 'everyone', and which replaces the MT's noun, 'a curse', with a verbal form (participle), 'cursed' (κεκατηραμένος).[27] In so doing, however, Paul ignored (i.e. omitted) the ambiguous, and, for him, awkward qualification, 'curse *of God*' (MT), or 'cursed *by God*' (LXX); this Jerome also noted, finding a, for him plausible, explanation in the subsequent addition by Jews 'of God' both in the Hebrew and in 'our texts', 'in order to charge us with the infamy of believing in Christ as cursed by God' (*in Gal.* 3.14 [*PL* 26.387–9]). Jerome's solution will not do, although the long history of belief in Jewish corruption of the Hebrew text suggests the seriousness of the hermeneutical issue.

It is now a commonplace in Pauline scholarship that by 'works of the Law' (eisegeted into Deut. 27.26) Paul was not expressing a 'Lutheran'

---

[23] On Paul's argument see J. D. G. Dunn, *Galatians* (BNTC, A&C Black: London, 1993) 168–80.

[24] The Samaritan Pentateuch also reads 'everything'; neither addition appears in the other Greek versions or the Targumim; see A. Salvesen, *Symmachus in the Pentateuch* (JSS.M. 15, University of Manchester: Manchester, 1991) 158–9. The substitution of 'that has been written' for 'words', and of 'the book of the Law' for 'the [this] Law' probably depends on Deut. 30.10.

[25] Hübner, 'Vetus Testamentum', 148; see n. 9 above.

[26] That is, Deut. 21.23: קללה, a construct noun within a causal clause (כי); Deut. 27.26: ארור, passive participle.

[27] Paul also follows the LXX in reading 'hung *on a tree*' in Deut. 21.23 (but cf. 11QTemple 64.12). On Paul's use of the LXX here see C. Stanley, *Paul and the Language of Scripture* (Cambridge University Press: Cambridge, 1992) 245–8.

rejection of reliance on *doing*, on 'works', over against faith or unmerited grace;[28] the consequences of that 'Lutheran' reading of Paul, which resulted in Judaism being characterized as a religion founded on 'doing', itself often 'illustrated' from rabbinic writings, have been exposed as a travesty – even though they are still to be found, colouring the interpretation also of Deut. 21.22–23.[29] Yet even with this new rereading of Galatians, Paul's selection of texts, his use of Deut. 27.26 linking curse and Law, and his creation of an intertextual bond with the curse on the 'hung' one in Deut. 21.23, still focus soteriology and Christology on the one hand, Torah on the other, fundamentals which must remain part of any dialogue.

b. Preaching and narrative

The wider influence of Deut. 21.22–23 illustrates well the creative impact of Scripture on Christian discourse, although where our predecessors saw fulfilment we may now recognize the dynamic interaction between text and experience.

i. As Max Wilcox has argued persuasively, Deut. 21.22–23 (in a non-LXX Greek version and possibly following a non-MT *Vorlage*), and particularly 'hanging *on a tree*' (v. 22), lies behind the early Christian preaching reflected in Acts 5.30, 'The God of our fathers raised Jesus whom you killed by *hanging him on a tree*' (cf. 10.39), and in 13.28–30, which has a number of echoes of Deut. 21.23, 'And finding no guilt of death, they asked Pilate to kill him so they completed all that had been written about him; then they took him down *from the tree* and placed him in a tomb, but God raised him from the dead.'[30] 'Scripture' has thus provided the language for confession and proclamation, a tradition continued in the 'Martyrs of Lyons and Vienne' where Blandina is '*hung upon a tree*' (Eusebius, *H.E.* V.I.41).

---

[28] Although that meaning is maintained by the REB in Gal. 3.10a, 'Everyone who relies on obedience to the Law'; the REB appears to have read this back into its translation of Deut. 27.26: 'A curse on anyone who does not fulfil this law by doing *all* (= LXX; Gal. 3.10b) that it prescribes.'

[29] The fundamental work is E. P. Sanders, *Paul and Palestinian Judaism* (SCM Press: London, 1977). The debate is not closed and the bibliography is extensive, but attention now focuses on the 'covenant markers', circumcision, sabbath, etc.; see C. E. B. Cranfield, '"The Works of the Law" in the Epistle to the Romans', *JSNT* 43 (1991) 89–101; J. D. G. Dunn, 'Yet once more – "The Works of the Law"; A Response', *JSNT* 46 (1992) 99–117.

[30] M. Wilcox, '"Upon the Tree" – Deut 21:22–23 in the New Testament', *JBL* 96 (1977) 85–99, 90–93; also B. Lindars, *New Testament Apologetic* (SCM Press: London, 1961) 233–4.

ii. John alone among the Gospels describes how Jesus' legs would have been broken, and that his body was taken down, with the purpose that '*the bodies should not remain on the cross* on the sabbath (*NB*)' (19.31), suggesting an echo of Deut. 21.22–23;[31] by contrast, the Synoptic accounts neither demand nor offer an explanation for Jesus' immediate burial. Appeals to external parallels for such action and immediate burial as based on Deut. 21.22–23 are weak;[32] they are probably also inappropriate, since John does not closely link the statement in v. 31 with Jesus' burial (19.38–42), which involves different actors. In typically Johannine fashion, Scripture is shaping the narrative; given the probable allusion in John 19.36 to the Passover Lamb of Exod. 12.10, '*remain*' may also establish an intertextual link with Exod. 12.20, 'You shall leave none of it until morning'. Such a shaping of narrative by Scripture is continued by the *Gospel of Peter* where it serves that Gospel's characteristic hostility towards the Jews: even before the crucifixion Herod confirms their obligation to bury Jesus, 'for it is written in the law that *the sun should not set upon a killed (NB) man*' (2.5); as supernatural darkness falls, provoking general alarm, the same words are repeated, exposing their legalistic hypocrisy (5.15).[33]

iii. Before long Christian exegetes were to interweave other texts into the pattern set by Deut. 21: the '*tree*' or 'wood' carried by Isaac for his 'sacrifice', or the ram '*hanging*', divinely provided as his substitute (Gen. 22.6, 13);[34] the *tree* in the Garden of Gen. 2–3, and 'your life *hanging*' in Deut. 28.66 (LXX).[35]

---

[31] Wilcox, 'Upon the Tree', 94; Wilcox also finds (less persuasive) allusions in 1 Peter and the Lukan Passion Narrative.

[32] R. E. Brown, *The Death of the Messiah* (Doubleday: New York/Chapman: London, 1994) II, 1174 cites Philo, *in Flacc.* 10 [83] (so also R. Schnackenburg, *The Gospel according to St. John* (ET Crossroad: New York, 1968–83) III, 288) suggesting 'that on special days there was greater pressure for observance'; however, here the bodies of the crucified are taken down *in honour of the Emperor's birthday*! Josephus, *B.J.* IV.5.2 [317] says even condemned criminals when crucified are taken down and buried 'before the setting of the sun', but as evidence for Jewish concern for burial; compare *c.Apion* II.29 [211].

[33] The setting of the sun recalls Josh. 8.29; Josephus, *B.J.* IV.5.2 [317] (n. 32); Philo, *de Spec. Leg.* III.28 [152] where Deut. 21.23 again expresses consideration for the dead.

[34] The Isaac allusions within the NT suggested by Wilcox, 'Upon the Tree', 97–9, lack clear linguistic echoes. An allusion to the ram of Gen. 22 as '*hanging*' (not LXX), but not on 'the tree', appears first in Melito, Fragment 12 (S. Hall, *Melito of Sardis On Pascha and Fragments* (Clarendon Press: Oxford, 1979), 76–77); however, Melito does not cite Deut. 21.23.

[35] Irenaeus, *adv.Haer.* IV.10.2, cites Deut. 28.66 (LXX) of the one shown '*as hanging on the tree*'.

c. Justin Martyr

Despite its importance for Paul, Deut. 21.22–23 appears surprisingly infrequently in early Christian writings (before Chrysostom and Cyril of Alexandria). Its first major exponent is Justin Martyr, who, possibly independently of Paul, also associates it with Deut. 27.26. Once again we can only note the main contours of his argument. It is, however, particularly important here, set within Justin's debate with Trypho and his rejection of Jewish rights and ability to interpret Scripture.

Here it is Trypho who introduces the Deuteronomic injunction that *crucifixion* brings or implies a *curse* (from God) (Deut. 21.23) as presenting a far greater obstacle than the mere assertion of a suffering Messiah;[36] he repeats this three times before Justin finally takes it up: 'This so-called Christ of yours was dishonourable and degraded for he fell foul of the ultimate curse (κατάρα) in the law of God for he was crucified' (*Dial.* 32.1); 'For the crucified one is said to be cursed (ἐπικατάρατος: cf. Gal. 3.13; Deut. 27.26) in the law' (89.2); 'he was crucified and died thus shamefully and dishonourably the death which is cursed (κεκατηραμένος: Deut. 21.23 LXX) in the law' (90.1).[37] The touch of realism in Justin's hesitancy to take up the challenge tempts us to forget that he is pulling the strings, or wielding the pen: is this a genuine Jewish reading of the text?

Justin's answer is tortuous: the curse is only 'apparent' (90.3), while 'the cross' is pervasive through Scripture. In the brazen serpent incident (Num. 21.8–9), where God apparently commanded Moses to act (i.e. to make an image) in contradiction to the Law he had given, the people gazed at the serpent Moses lifted up and were freed from the bites of the serpents plaguing them; this serpent, evoking the one *cursed* by God in Genesis 3 which was the source of death, was not itself the means of salvation but was a type of Christ, who brought deliverance from the 'bites of the serpent', fulfilling Isa. 27.1 (*Dial.* 91.4; 94.1–5; 111–112). Only then does Justin cite Deut. 27.26, the curse on all who do not obey the [whole] Law, but he takes it as establishing all people,

[36] For the whole section see W. C. van Unnik, 'Der Fluch der Gekreuzigten: Deuteronomium 21,23 in der Deutung Justinus des Märtyres', in C. Andresen and G. Klein, eds., *Theologia Crucis – Signum Crucis: Festschrift für Erich Dinkler zum 70. Geburtstag* (Mohr: Tübingen, 1979) 483–99; O. Skarsaune, *The Proof from Prophecy: A Study in Justin Martyr's Proof-text Tradition* (NT.S 56, Brill: Leiden, 1987) 216–20.

[37] Note the reversal '*crucified* and died' (cf. n. 64).

Jew and Gentile alike, as 'under a curse'.[38] This alone refutes their right to charge Jesus as 'remaining cursed': rather, he took upon himself the curse which lay upon all humankind (95).

Only now (96.1) can Justin tackle Deut. 21.23: it does not mean that 'God was cursing this crucified one',[39] but foresees the Jewish response to Jesus; the Jewish endeavour to curse Christians and to demonstrate that Christ was crucified as 'cursed and an enemy of God' (cf. 93.4) is an obscene response to what he did in accordance with God's will, and itself fulfils Deut. 21.23 – the curse on the one who hangs upon the cross is the curse the Jews seek to effect (95.2–96.2).[40]

Deut. 21.23 is thus integrated with Justin's repeated charges of extreme Jewish hostility against the Christians, among which 'cursing' is but one, albeit significant, component: they curse in their synagogues those who believe in Jesus (16.14; 93.4; 95.4; 96.2; 108.3; 133.2) and even curse Jesus himself (95.4; 133.6).[41] It is a cursing which sometimes has murderous intent (95.4; 122.2; 133.6; through the Gentiles: 16.4; 96.2). In this the Jews are only acting in continuity with their killing of Jesus, for which they fail to repent (133.6), and with the killing of the prophets before him (16.4).Yet in sharp contrast to their 'ceaseless *cursing* of him and those who belong to him', shines Jesus' injunction that Christians should love those who hate them and 'bless those who *curse* them' (133.6: Luke 6.28; cf. 96.3: Luke 6.35–6).[42]

We need not pursue here the debate as to what, if any, reality lies behind the charges of 'cursing', particularly when given a liturgical context (16.4; 137.2).[43] Arguments for such a malediction and for other

---

[38] His text follows Paul's closely (with the omission of πᾶσιν before τοῖς γεγραμμένοις, although this is added by E. Goodspeed, *Die ältesten Apologeten* (Vandenhoeck & Ruprecht: Göttingen, 1914) 209), but his completely different application leads van Unnik, 'Der Fluch', 498–9 to deny any real dependence.

[39] Although his quotation agrees with Paul's text, his interpretation, using the verb καταράομαι (also 93.4) with God as subject [not said by Trypho!], recalls the Septuagint.

[40] In *Dial.* 97.2 Exod. 17.2 is fulfilled by Jesus' remaining on the cross until evening, suggesting that Deut. 21.23 is still in the background.

[41] They also revile or despise (137.2), reject and dishonour (16.4), blaspheme (35.8; 122.2; 126.1), anathematize (47.4), profane (120.4 from Mal. 1.11).

[42] The quotations are not exact but note καταράσθαι from Luke 6.28. At *Dial.* 35.8 Christians pray for the Jews.

[43] W. Horbury, 'The Benediction of the *Minim* and early Jewish-Christian Controversy', *JTS* 33 (1982) 19–61; R. Kimelman, '*Birkat Ha-Minim* and the Lack of Evidence for an Anti-Christian Jewish Prayer in Late Antiquity', in E. P. Sanders , A. L. Baumgarten and A. Mendelson, eds., *Jewish and Christian Self-Definition*, II. *Aspects of Judaism in the Graeco-Roman Period* (SCM Press: London, 1981) 226–44.

countermeasures, however, have been used by contemporary as well as by ancient writers to make the Jewish response appear far more reprehensible than either Christian provocation or counter-polemic. Yet any assessment of the historical issue must recognize that these biblical models have helped shape Justin's account and his frequent accusation that the Jews *curse* Christ and Christians. More fundamentally, the text of Deuteronomy becomes a locus where blessing belongs to the Christians, curse to the Jews.

Deuteronomy 21.22–23 as Old Testament: translation and interpretation

The continuing 'power' of the text (here Deut. 21.22–23) as refracted through the tradition of its reception – the way it has shaped and been shaped by the self-understanding of the community for whom it is Scripture – is readily illustrated by a survey of recent translations of these verses:

> REB: When someone is convicted of a capital offence and is put to death, and you *hang him on a gibbet,* his body must not remain there overnight; it must be buried on the same day. *Anyone hanged* is <u>accursed</u> *in the sight of God,* and the land which the LORD your God is giving you as your holding must not be polluted. (NEB: '. . . his body shall not remain on the gibbet overnight; you shall bury it on the same day, **for** *a hanged man* is <u>offensive</u> *in the sight of God.* You shall not . . .'.)

> NIV: If a man guilty of a capital offence is put to death and his body is *hung on a tree,* you must not leave his body on the tree overnight. Be sure to bury him that same day, **because** *anyone* who is *hung* <u>on a tree</u> is *under God's curse.* You must not desecrate the land the LORD your God is giving you as an inheritance.

> NRSV: When someone (RSV a man) is convicted of a crime punishable by death, and is executed, and you *hang him on a tree,* his corpse shall not remain all night upon the tree; you shall bury him that same day, **for** *anyone hung* <u>on a tree</u> is *under God's* <u>curse.</u> You must not defile the land that the LORD your God is giving you for possession. (RSV: . . . tree, but you shall bury . . . , **for** *a hanged man* is <u>accursed</u> *by God;* you shall not defile the land which the LORD your God gives you for an inheritance.)

> JPS: If a man is guilty of a capital offence and is put to death, and you *impale* him *on a stake,* you must not let his corpse remain on the stake overnight, but must bury him on the same day. **For** *an impaled body* is *an* <u>affront</u> *to God.*

you shall not defile the land that the LORD your God is giving you to possess.[44]

The interpretative issues involved and reflected in the translations are well known:

a. the different choices of punctuation and sentence-breaks adjudicate the uncertain relationship between the clauses, with significant consequences for the sense achieved.[45]

b. Undoubtedly the passage describes not a form of execution but the subsequent public exposure of the corpse. The JPS translation '*impale*' (rather than '*hang*') reflects later debate regarding the semantic range of this verb (תלה, and also of its Aramaic equivalent, צלב).[46] While this rendering, particularly as 'impaled *body*' in v. 23,[47] tends, whether or not deliberately, to exclude the Christian application, the REB's semi-technical '*gibbet*' (for עץ) in v. 22 (also at Josh. 8.29 and Gal. 3.13) promotes it.[48]

c. More problematic for the translator is the ambiguous description of the hanged one as 'a curse of God' (קללת אלהים). As we shall see, the construct may be objective ('curse to God') or subjective ('cursed by God'). Paul, despite omitting 'of God', implicitly opted for the latter in his interpretation, following, as we have seen, the LXX with its passive participle and agent, 'cursed by God', an interpretation not adopted by the other Greek versions.[49] While the JPS, accompanied only by the NEB, represents the former possibility, namely that the 'hung' one causes God <u>offence</u> or <u>affront</u>, the weight of 'Christian' translation follows Paul. Indeed, in ominous agreement, the REB and RSV adopt the verbal '<u>accursed</u>',[50] anticipating neatly Gal. 3.13 ('cursed'), while the NIV's and NRSV's retention of a noun ('<u>curse</u>') is countered by the unequivocal '*under God's*'. The 'consensus' is illustrated by A. D. Mayes's rejection

---

[44] *The Torah: The Five Books of Moses: A New Translation of the Holy Scriptures according to the Massoretic Text*, First Section (Jewish Publication Society of America: Philadelphia, 1967).

[45] Thus starting a new sentence 'Anyone hanged . . .' (REB) with no causal link with what precedes (i.e. ignoring the MT כי = for, because) supports Paul's use of the verse.

[46] See J. Baumgarten, 'Does *TLH* in the Temple Scroll Refer to Crucifixion?', *JBL* 91 (1972) 472–81, 476; Philo, *de Spec. Leg.* III. 28 [151–2] (ἀνασκολοπίζω), sometimes cited in support of 'impalement', more probably interprets Deut. 21.23 as crucifixion.

[47] Similarly the Good News Bible, 'corpse', although תלוי is masculine (cf. '*man*', '*anyone*').

[48] Similarly, the Good News Bible renders, 'hanging *on a post*', and adds this to v. 23 (so also NRSV and NIV; cf. n. 27).

[49] See above, p. 158.

[50] Also the Jerusalem Bible.

of the objective genitive in his commentary on Deuteronomy: 'However, the latter is not supported by the traditional understanding of the text, represented by LXX and Vulg (cf. also Gal. 3:13)';[51] whose tradition is this?[52]

Deuteronomy 21.23 as Old Testament: history and interpretation

Here, again, we can only indicate major areas of debate. It is widely assumed that Paul was driven to his own (tortuous) reinterpretation of Deut. 21.23 because this text was already used by Jewish opponents, even by the persecutor 'Saul', against the 'blasphemous' preaching of a crucified Messiah.[53] Yet evidence for Jews interpreting Deut. 21.23 to show that one crucified was cursed by God and could not be the Messiah is notoriously thin; in fact it is provided only by Jews who speak through Christian mouths, namely Justin's Trypho, Jews whose objections provoke Tertullian's alternative exegesis, and those later demanded by Jerome's exegetical tradition and argument.[54] On the contrary, efforts to uncover a hidden reference to Jesus as 'the hanged one' in rabbinic texts have proved in vain,[55] while surviving Jewish exegesis offers little further support.[56] The problem was more arguably an internal one: Irenaeus cites Deut. 21.23 in an inner-Christian argument, and Tertullian debates it with Marcion, as perhaps did Justin before him.[57]

---

[51] A. D. Mayes, *Deuteronomy* (NCB, Marshall, Morgan & Scott: London, 1979) 305.
[52] Contrast the extensive support for the objective genitive in Jewish interpretation: M. J. Bernstein 'כי קללת אלהים תלוי (Deut 21:23): A Study in Early Jewish Exegesis', *JQR* 74 (1983) 21–45; see also below.
[53] See U. Wilkens, 'Statements on the Development of Paul's View of the Law', in M. Hooker and S. Wilson, eds., *Paul and Paulinism: Essays in Honour of C. K. Barrett* (SPCK: London, 1982) 17–26; F. F. Bruce, 'The curse of the Law', in Hooker and Wilson, eds., *Paul and Paulinism*, 27–36. H. Räisänen, *Jesus, Paul and Torah* (ET JSNT.SS 43, Sheffield Academic Press: Sheffield, 1992) 42–4 rejects the popular view that reflection on this text provoked Paul's rejection of the Law.
[54] On Trypho's 'Jewish?' objection see above, p. 161; Tertullian, *adv.Jud.* 10 and van Unnik, 'Der Fluch', 484; Jerome, above, p. 158. Jerome's reference to the reading of the lost 'Dialogue of Jason and Papiscus' as 'the one hanged is an insult (λοιδορία) of God' tells us nothing about the context (*in Gal.* 3.13–14. [*PL* 26.387]).
[55] E.g. R. T. Herford, *Christianity in Talmud and Midrash* (Williams & Norgate: London, 1903, reprinted KTAV: New York, n.d.) 86–7, and the critique by J. Maier, *Jesus von Nazareth in der talmudischen Überlieferung* (Wissenschaftliche Buchgesellschaft: Darmstadt, 1978) 235–7, who notes instead the significant failure by rabbinic texts to exploit the potential allusion to Jesus.
[56] Bernstein, 'Study', and below, pp. 167–8; also Salvesen, *Symmachus*, 156.
[57] Irenaeus, *adv.Haer.* III.28.3; IV.20.2; V.18.1; Tertullian, *adv. Marc.* III.18.1; V.3.10.

While Jewish interpretation of Deut. 21.23 *may* yet have light to throw on Jesus' crucifixion and burial,[58] one thing we cannot say is that 'every Jew opposed to Jesus could – indeed had – to say with Deuteronomy 21:22–23: This one who has been hung on the cross has suffered his just punishment; he died "cursed of God!" '[59] In such an assertion the Christian reading of the text has become history, and the necessity of that 'had' excludes all other readings.

Conclusion

These readings of Deut. 21.22–23 illustrate graphically the 'Old Testament' as Christian Scripture. In a Christian context a 'canonical' reading will have to recognize the creative potential of the text, so that new narratives, including the 'theological narrative' of Gal. 3, cannot be told without it or disentangled from it, while, retrospectively, this weight of interpretative history has become part of the signification of these verses.

As an / *the* 'Old Testament' interpretative key, the text locates Jesus' death firmly in a Jewish context – no longer in its Roman political but in a Jewish religious setting, in terms of Torah and curse.[60] Intriguingly, this parallels later Jewish traditions about Jesus, that he was stoned or even hung, although, significantly, these include no appeal to Deut. 21.22–23, although how this development has happened is far from clear.[61] However, the theological consequences have had a long, and well-rehearsed history.

More fundamentally, the text has come to encapsulate the division between Judaism and Christianity. Even when this is not projected onto history,[62] through the interaction between text and community – the community's values and needs shaping the reading of the text, the text contributing to the community's self-understanding – the text has also shaped the perception of 'the other', Judaism. Again, the theological consequences are far-reaching, and the destructive potential of this reading, already visible in Justin's handling, must force the interpreter

---

[58] See Brown, *Death of the Messiah*, I, 532–3, 541; II, 1209–11.
[59] P. Stuhlmacher, *Jesus of Nazareth – Christ of Faith* (ET Hendrikson: Peabody, 1993) 35; he describes this as a 'logical and dreadful interpretation of Jesus' death'.
[60] See W. D. Davies, *Paul and Rabbinic Judaism* (SPCK: London, 1948) 227–8.
[61] Cf. *bSan.* 43a; see Maier, *Jesus von Nazareth*, 219–32, esp. 227 + nn. 464–5.
[62] As it is by M. Hengel, *The Son of God*, reprinted in *The Cross of the Son of God* (SCM Press: London 1986) 1–90, 65–6, who presents this as implicit in the life and death of Jesus from the beginning.

to a judgement on it, and to criteria for that judgement. Only by recognizing this as a contextualized reading can we escape the consequences of absolutism.

The alternative may not only be to return to a supposedly objective, historical-critical reading, in which this text may lose any real creativity.[63] Although sometimes motivated by (for or against) a Christian agenda concerned with crucifixion, Deut. 21.22–23 and its early interpretation has received disproportionate scholarly attention, revealing alternative channels of creative meaning in new contexts in the past and present.[64]

Thus, 11QTemple 64.7–12 and 4QpNah. 3–4 i 6–8 suggest that, contrary to the rabbinic consensus in favour of 'exposure' (mSan. 6.4, etc.), others did find in the text a reference to or even a mandate for crucifixion,[65] a reading that would locate Christian usage within a broader first-century textual and interpretative spectrum. However, as Bernstein has shown, even here there is little parallel to the particular power that the phrase 'curse of God', removed from its proper context, assumes for Paul. Nonetheless, the text does generate a range of interpretations, taking the genitive either as subjective or, more frequently, as objective.[66] So, we may find syntactically unpersuasive but historically suggestive the view that the 'curser of God' is hung (already in Josephus, Ant. IV.8.6 [202]);[67] yet perhaps we should pause longer over the insight that the exposed body is 'a reproach unto God', even because the one

---

[63]   See above, pp. 152–3; G. von Rad, *Deuteronomy* (ET OTL, SCM Press: London, 1966) 138 is remarkably evasive, speaking of 'the maxim explaining the reason for the ordinance' and 'about being cast out into the domain of the curse'; more overtly theological, I. Cairns, *Word and Presence: A Commentary on the Book of Deuteronomy* (Eerdmans: Grand Rapids/ Handsel Press: Edinburgh, 1992) 192–3 sees a real continuity with Gal. 3.13 in 'God's implacable hostility to all the signs of death', but his exegetical justification for this is weak.

[64]   Bernstein, 'Study'; J. Fitzmyer, 'Crucifixion in Ancient Palestine, Qumran Literature and the New Testament', *CBQ* 40 (1978) 493–513.

[65]   Compare Philo (n. 46); the Peshitta's 'is crucified . . . and is put to death' can now be compared to 11QTemple 64.10–11, see M. O. Wise, *A Critical Study of the Temple Scroll from Qumran Cave 11* (University of Chicago: Chicago, 1990) 121–7; also M. P. Horgan, *Pesharim; Qumran Interpretations of Biblical Books* (CBQ.MS 8, Catholic Biblical Association: Washington, 1979) 176–9. Whether the reference is to crucifixion or hanging constitutes a further debate: see E. Levine, *The Aramaic Version of the Bible: Contents and Context* (BZAW 174, de Gruyter: Berlin, 1988) 158–9; Baumgarten, '*TLH* in the Temple Scroll'; D. Halperin, 'Crucifixion, the Nahum Pesher, and the Rabbinic Penalty of Strangulation', *JJS* 32 (1981) 32–46.

[66]   Surveyed by Bernstein, 'Study'.

[67]   Bernstein, 'Study', 26–8; Brown, *Death of the Messiah*, I, 532–3.

hanged is also in the image of God: 'it is a slight to the King because man is made in the divine image'.[68]

While Christianity may not have 'taken away [Judaism's] sacred book', what did happen was the disenfranchisement of Jewish interpretation of that book, a process which played no small part in the 'injustice' to which Harnack pointed.[69] Alternative readings, such as those hinted at above, may be no less contextualized than those which take place in a Christian setting,[70] but they equally merit a hearing. Indeed, in an age of dehumanization as well as of dialogue, they may speak across the boundaries.

[68] J. Hertz, ed., *The Pentateuch and the Haftorahs* (Soncino Press: London, 1950) 842, quoting Rashi with approval.

[69] A. Lacocque, ' "Old Testament" in Protestant Tradition', 124, 'The Jews were disowned of their Scriptures, which, it was taught, had never been understood by their mechanical writers'.

[70] M. Hengel, *Crucifixion*, reprinted in *The Cross of the Son of God*, 93–185, 177 suggests that the countless crucifixions of Jews by the Romans helped shape rabbinic exegesis of the verse.

Part IV

The Shaping of Early 'Christian' Identity

11

The Forging of Christian Identity and the
*Letter to Diognetus**

To speak of 'the forging of Christian identity' is to choose a deliberate ambiguity. 'Forging' sounds both more decisive and more creative than 'formation' or 'development'. Yet 'forging' also suggests other possibilities, and, if one were to abstract any moral judgement implied, it would be interesting to explore the role of pseudonymity, of the preservation and multiplication of favourable imperial rescripts and other documents, and of the late (re-)appearance of 'apostolic' records, bishop lists, and the like in the early Christian discovery of its own history. That is not the task of this essay, although 'forging' will offer a reminder of the often derivative and imitative character of early Christian identity-formation.

This, the creation, at least rhetorically, of a self-conscious and distinctive identity is a remarkable characteristic of early Christianity from our earliest sources; indeed it is inseparable from the appearance of those sources and from Christianity's equally characteristic literary creativity.[1] This itself creates a problem which will provide a thread through this essay. For our period, the first two centuries CE, material remains are not available as markers of Christian identity, or/and, if available, they would not be or perhaps are not distinguishable.[2] What

---

* Given at the 'Fergus Millar Seminar on Identities in the Eastern Mediterranean in Antiquity' held at the Humanities Research Centre, Australian National University, Canberra, November 1997, and reprinted from *Mediterranean Archaeology* 11 (1998) 71–82.

---

[1] See A. Cameron, *Christianity and the Rhetoric of Empire: The Development of Christian Discourse* (Sather Classical Lectures 45, University of California Press: Berkeley, 1991) 21, 'But if ever there was a case of the construction of reality through text, such a case is provided by early Christianity . . . Christians built themselves a new world. They did so partly through practice – the evolution of a mode of living and a communal discipline that carefully distinguished them from their pagan and Jewish neighbours – and partly through a discourse that was itself constantly brought under control and disciplined'; 'As Christ "was" the Word, so Christianity *was* its discourse or discourses' (p. 32).

[2] See R. Kraemer, 'Jewish Tuna and Christian Fish: Identifying Religious Affiliation in Epigraphic Sources', *HTR* 84 (1991) 141–62.

is the relationship between an analysis of identity or ethnicity based on material remains and that based on internal literary sources? How far should literary sources, particularly by a single author, be seen as evidence of a pre-existing identity, how far are they constructive of identity, but only once they become internalized and authorized within the community?

Historical studies have long paid attention to the development of Christian identity, defined traditionally in terms of ecclesiastical authority and of doctrinal formulation, often seeing in it little cause for surprise; more recent emphasis, however, on social history in its various forms has produced an unabating flood of analyses of the formation of Christian identity and its 'difference'. Since the vast majority of those working on 'early Christianity' are trained as and continue to identify themselves as New Testament specialists, the focus has inevitably settled on the New Testament texts.

Three distinct, if overlapping, approaches may be detected in the scholarly literature. Perhaps the first was the observable or external identity of early Christian communities. Eschewing the assumption that 'the church', the *ekklesia*, was *sui generis*, best interpreted through theological categories, what were the models of collective organization known in the Graeco-Roman world to which it most closely conformed? In terms of what known categories would observers, and perhaps adherents, interpret its common life and organization? Initially, Graeco-Roman 'voluntary associations', *collegia* and *thiasoi*, were set over against the Jewish synagogue; cults, particularly mystery cults, and philosophical schools were also brought into the comparison;[3] broadening the range may have served only to demonstrate the limitations of the enterprise as a means of differentiation: for example, synagogues may have been treated as a form of *collegium*, and also may have presented themselves as centres of philosophy.[4] It may be doubted whether more can be achieved along these lines, and there are problems: the apparently dispassionate exercise could, of course, mask or provoke theological

---

[3] R. Wilken, 'Collegia, Philosophical Schools and Theology', in S. Benko and J. J. O'Rourke, eds., *Early Church History: The Roman Empire as the Setting of Primitive Christianity* (Oliphants: London, 1972 [= *The Catacombs and the Colosseum* (1971)]) 268–91; idem, 'Christianity as a Burial Society', in *The Christians as the Romans Saw Them* (Yale University Press: New Haven, 1984) 31–47; W. Meeks, *The First Urban Christians* (Yale University Press: New Haven, 1983) 74–84.

[4] See J. Kloppenborg and S. G. Wilson, eds., *Voluntary Associations in the Graeco-Roman World* (Routledge: London, 1996).

concern. Barton and Horsley's oft-quoted analysis of the Dionysius cult (Ditt. *Syll.* 985) is a case in point: the final paragraph, entitled 'Salvation: Present or Future', claims 'The consequence of this [i.e. Christian belief in the inbreaking of a new age] for their morality (as a response to "grace") and their corporate activity (as sharing of a common experience of "grace") . . . lies at the basis of the differences separating them from a group like Dionysius", and in so saying moves beyond the espoused realm of description.[5] For W. Meeks a decisive distinguishing characteristic of the church, at least in its Pauline manifestation, was its universal or translocal form, something not so easily explained within his descriptive framework.[6] Yet, on the one hand, such a universal self-awareness may not have been unique to Christianity, while, on the other, when and how it develops is an important but problematic question: even in the case of the Pauline churches it may have been mediated more through Paul's own person as founder and traveller than fixed in any primary community consciousness.[7] As important for our purposes is the tension between self-identity and perceived identity. It is arguable that early Christianity as portrayed by Luke–Acts may be described in the language of 'school', yet the terminology that the author prefers is the anomalous ἐκκλησία, primarily of the local community, perhaps germinally of the community of communities, constructing a harmonious unity that was more ideal than real.[8]

An apparently more comprehensive key to Christian identity-formation has been offered by recent exploration of the separation

---

[5] S. C. Barton and G. R. Horsley, 'A Hellenistic Cult Group and the New Testament Churches', *JbAC* 24 (1981) 7–41, 41. J. Kloppenborg, 'Egalitarianism in the Myth and Rhetoric of Pauline Churches', in E. A. Castelli and H. Taussig, eds., *Reimagining Christian Origins: A Colloquium Honoring Burton L. Mack* (Trinity Press International: Valley Forge, 1996) 247–63 is more cautious, warning against an idealism that treats rhetoric as descriptive.

[6] Meeks, *First Urban Christians*, 107.

[7] So rightly R. Ascough, 'Translocal Relationships among Voluntary Associations and Early Christianity', *JECS* 5 (1997) 223–41.

[8] On early Christianity as a school see L. Alexander, 'Acts and Ancient Intellectual Biography', in B. W. Winter and A. D. Clarke, eds., *The Book of Acts in its Ancient Literary Setting* (The Book of Acts in its First Century Setting I, Paternoster: Carlisle/ Eerdmans: Michigan, 1993) 31–63, 32–9; C. K. Barrett, 'School, Conventicle, and Church in the New Testament', in K. Aland and S. Meurer, eds., *Wissenschaft und Kirche: Festschrift für E. Lohse* (Luther-Verlag: Bielfeld, 1989) 96–110, 107–8 emphasizes Luke's own preference for the language of ἐκκλησία. See Wilken, 'Collegia', 269, 'We would expect the self-understanding of the Christians to differ from the impression of them which was held by outsiders. Yet on many points we have, quite uncritically, accepted the Christian view of things and dismissed the views of their contemporaries.'

between Christianity and Judaism, an exploration inspired by two primary factors: first, the rediscovery of the multifaceted richness of first- and second-century Judaism, of which the earliest 'Jesus movement' was a part; secondly, the timely recognition of the shameful heritage of the unreflected repetition of the rhetoric of identity and destiny, both of self and 'other', which accompanied that separation. Contemporary preoccupation with a child's discovery of identity through painful separation from the parent, and the biblical adoption of the folkloric or mythical theme of sibling rivalry, have provided congenial models for understanding the development of Christian identity through distancing from and conflict with Judaism.[9] Christians claimed to be the true heirs of the inheritance, to be 'Israel', children of Abraham and heirs of the promise made to him; to rightly represent the original intention of the founder, of God or of Moses in the giving of the Law; to possess the proper interpretation of the definitive texts, the Scriptures; all these claims, incessantly repeated in early Christian literature, not only in that directed against the Jews but also in apologetics for outsiders, as well as in paraenesis and exegesis for insiders, could readily be paralleled, *mutatis mutandis*, in other sectarian, reformist and breakaway movements. Novelty, particularly but not only in the ancient world, offers only an insecure identity: even gnostic groups, who largely rejected an identity founded on historical continuity with Israel's past, discovered for themselves a new 'history' through the 'myths' of cosmic fall and redemption.

The reverse side of the coin may seem to have a certain inevitability. The 'failure' of most of the Jews to recognize in Jesus and the early Christian movement the true goal of the promises and dynamic of past experience threatened the credibility of Christian claims, both in the eyes of outsiders and also in those of insiders. The solution was to discredit the Jews, not only for their present unbelief, but for a history of wilful disobedience and obtuseness stretching back to the beginning, a history that was authenticated by a rereading of the shared Scriptures. Thus Jewish identity, negatively constructed, came to constitute the necessary foil for the construction of Christian identity. The terms that have been used in the last few sentences, 'inevitability', 'necessary', have come to provoke searching analysis: can Christian identity tolerate the

---

[9] Cf. A. Segal, *Rebecca's Children: Judaism and Christianity in the Roman World* (Harvard University Press: Cambridge, Mass., 1986).

dissolving of the demonized identity of the Jews which accompanied its formation? Was the latter really an integral element or merely a contingent ancillary throughout the process? Recognition of the function of vituperation in ancient rhetoric has given a historical context for the vigour of the polemic; yet it has not wholly stifled the sometimes anguished debate as to whether the responsibility of the historian is to remain distanced from the past or to acknowledge its post-history and continuing power.[10]

Various forms of sociological analysis have refined or at least given a quasi-scientific veneer to the generalized account given above. By applying conflict analysis or by comparing the strategies adopted by groups in the face of the apparent disconfirmation of the core values or principles of their identity, scholars have sought to side-step the long tradition which gave an automatic theological affirmation to the past tradition. Sociological analysis has also been applied to the Christian communities themselves as represented by the surviving literature. Particularly influential has been the emphasis on the symbolic universe by which people organize, make sense of, and rationalize their experience.[11] Thus the subjects of 'theology' become the structural components of a social world; the reversal of values or of status epitomized by Jesus' humiliation in incarnation and death becomes the norm for Christian social experience and its value system. Ritual, specifically baptism and eucharist, legitimates this social world by establishing new patterns of belonging, effecting dramatic separation from past experience, embodying a unity which transcends real difference. Equally important has been the analysis of sectarian formation, definition, legitimation and development. Not only can Christianity's separation from Judaism be explored in terms of sect formation, but the different patterns of relationship towards 'the world' which have been used to categorize nineteenth- and twentieth-century sects can be or have been applied to early Christian communities as accessible through the literature.[12]

Such approaches have become commonplace and need not be further described here. Some features require special emphasis: first, emphasis

[10] On the issues in this paragraph see further J. M. Lieu, *Image and Reality: The Jews in the World of the Christians in the Second Century* (T&T Clark: Edinburgh, 1996).
[11] The influence of P. Berger has been paramount, e.g. *The Social Construction of Reality* (Doubleday: Garden City, 1966).
[12] Here B. Wilson has been most influential, e.g. *Patterns of Sectarianism* (Heinemann: London, 1967).

on internal rhetoric inevitably leads to a strong sense of self-identity, often at odds with other evidence that early Christian groups were more amorphous. Inevitably, the moment of separation provokes much more vigorous rhetoric, enhancing this sense of otherness, which may be less visible to outsiders; the rhetoric of difference may become less urgent precisely when a clearer separate identity becomes more visible to outsiders.

Secondly, a consequence of the concentration on the textual rhetoric of identity has been the increasing difficulty of talking about 'Christian identity'. In part this is in recognition that such terminological precision is lacking in the first century, and that the concept is self-evidently anachronistic. Paul, the Gospel according to Matthew, or the Gospel according to John, each present a different model of the relationship between Judaism and Christianity, reflect a different social context, and betray a different potential both for existing relationships and for future development. The Pauline Epistles have been particularly receptive to the sociological analysis of community formation, if only because in Paul's letters we have open address to a number of such communities.[13] The communities behind the various Gospels, although at times viewed as more accessible to scholarly reconstruction than the so-called historical Jesus, are necessarily more opaque. Yet despite such opacity, each produces a different model of identity and structure. New Testament scholars have found it easier to talk about Pauline, Johannine, or Matthaean Christianity than about first-century Christianity. This is, perhaps, an inevitable consequence of the work of W. Bauer, who, more than sixty years ago, exploded the 'myth' of a pristine Christian 'unity' and 'orthodoxy'; in so doing he paved the way for an emphasis on diversity, free of the value judgements favouring an orthodoxy that was now perceived as the result of political processes.[14] The result is that the questions of cohesive or integrating identity, and of the path to the development of such an identity in the second century are ever more problematic.[15] One answer

[13] Meeks, *First Urban Christians*; G. Theissen, *The Social Setting of Pauline Christianity* (ET T&T Clark: Edinburgh, 1982); idem, *Social Reality and the Early Christians* (ET T&T Clark: Edinburgh, 1993).

[14] W. Bauer, *Orthodoxy and Heresy in Earliest Christianity* (ET Fortress: Philadelphia, 1971) = *Rechtglaubigkeit und Ketzerei im altesten Christentum* (Mohr: Tübingen, 1934 [1965]).

[15] See B. Meyer, *The Early Christians: Their World Mission and Self-Discovery* (Michael Glazier: Wilmington, Delaware, 1986) 53–4 who finds sociological approaches such as that of Meeks inadequate in answering questions as to why the early Christian diversity did not lead to schism.

has been to distinguish 'identity', which is 'what one's allegiance makes one to be', and which has an atemporal quality, from 'self-definition', which is 'identity culturally and historically conditioned'.[16] Another answer would be to come to a better understanding of the still inadequately explained mechanisms of cohesion in the second century: in literary terms, the development of the concept of a fourfold Gospel,[17] and the rapid development of the letter genre, used even for martyrdom accounts which themselves serve to create identity.

Thirdly, these sociological models operate with an oppositional model, leading to a tendency to see early Christian formation exclusively in opposition to Graeco-Roman society: where Christianity adopted contemporary social patterns it is frequently said to have reversed or inverted them. This is surely tendentious: the correlation between social change and religious change may be disputed; yet whereas earlier studies saw Christianity's success as a response to and evidence for Graeco-Roman religion's failure, it might be better to see it rather as a symptom of and a participant in contemporary social change and potential for change.[18]

In this essay it is argued, first, that the construction of Christian identity is much more fragile than much of this contemporary analysis presupposes. Further, that there are a number of variables in the formation of Christian identity, the interplay between which invites exploration. Most obvious are, the second major theme, those inner tensions provided by the Jewish origins of Christianity. Here, it is often said that Judaism represents an ethnic or a particularist identity, Christianity a universalist one. This has been rightly criticized in recent debate, but the comparison continues to require clearer

---

[16] Meyer, *Early Christians*, 174; idem, 'The Church in Earliest Christianity: Identity and Self-Definition', in *Christus Faber: The Master Builder and the House of God* (Pickwick Publications: Allison Park, Pennsylvania, 1992) 149–69. V. Wimbush, '" . . . Not of this World . . . " Early Christianities as Rhetorical and Social Formation', in Castelli and Taussig, eds., *Reimagining Christian Origins*, 23–36 speaks of 'discursive and rhetorical formations ever productive of new social formations' (34).

[17] See G. N. Stanton, 'The Fourfold Gospel', *NTS* 43 (1997) 317–46.

[18] So G. Theissen, 'Christology and Social Experience', in *Social Reality*, 187–201, who argues that the plausibility structures of Christian christological convictions, particularly about the self-humiliation and subsequent exaltation of Christ as a model for all believers, and about the body as a symbol of unity in society, are rooted in social change and ideology of the early Empire; see also Cameron, *Christianity and the Rhetoric of Empire*, 31. (See also above, pp. 97–9 applying this to the position of women.)

analysis.[19] Yet, thirdly, equally clear are the tensions between a discrete local and a common 'universal' identity, and between the language of differentiation from the trends of society and that of reflection of them. Seen within a wider framework, these have been recurrent and perhaps inherent tensions in Christian history: Christian missions have played their part in the articulation of local identities, for example in the development of scripts and the recording of local languages, or in the identification of particular forms of Christianity with particular national groups such as the Arian Goths; yet they have also provoked intense debate about the integrity of indigenous articulations of Christian identity in a post-colonial age and their relationship to any universal identity. Martin Luther's search for an identity established before and by God alone, that is, theoretically independent of local or institutional control, has been seen as resulting both in 'a strong sense of group identity which is closely linked, though not identical with various German regional identities', and in a dualistic negation of other cultures.[20]

In this context two quotations may set the theme for this discussion:

This conviction that they were a *people* – i.e., the transference of all the prerogatives and claims of the Jewish people to the new community viewed as a new creation which exhibited and put into force whatever was old and original in religion – this at once furnished adherents of the new faith with a *political and historical* self-consciousness. Nothing more comprehensive or complete or impressive than this consciousness can be conceived . . . This estimate of themselves rendered Christians impregnable against all attacks and movements of polemical criticism, while it further enabled them to advance in every direction for a war of conquest.[21]

We may contrast with this the claims of the *Epistle to Diognetus*, a perhaps late-second-century apologetic writing whose original authorship, context and audience is now lost to us:

For Christians are distinguished from the rest of humankind not by land nor by language nor by customs. For they do not live in their own cities nor use any corrupted dialect, nor do they practise a distinctive life . . . Dwelling in both

[19] Cf. J. D. Levenson, 'The Universal Horizon of Biblical Particularism', in M. Brett, ed., *Ethnicity and the Bible* (BIS 19, Brill: Leiden, 1996) 143–69; J. Barclay, '"Neither Jew nor Greek": Multiculturalism and the New Perspective on Paul', in Brett, ed., *Ethnicity and the Bible*, 197–214.
[20] See J. Riches, 'Cultural Bias in European and North American Biblical Scholarship', in Brett, ed., *Ethnicity and the Bible*, 431–48, 435–6.
[21] A. von Harnack, *The Expansion of Christianity in the First Three Centuries* (ET Williams & Norgate: London, 1904–5) I, 300–1.

Greek and barbarian cities, as allotted to each, and following the native customs in clothing and life-style and the rest of life . . . (*ad Diognetum* 5.1–2, 4)

The contrast between the two estimates might be seen as the internal self-identity, clearly defined and separate, as represented by Harnack, *versus* the external, observed identity – a lack of visible differentiation – at least as conceived and portrayed by the apologist. It may also be seen as two sides of a common coin: both in effect express the sublimation of any particularist identity in order to claim a highly articulated meta-identity. This claim is already there in *ad Diognetum*: to complete the last sentence –

Dwelling in both Greek and barbarian cities . . . and following native customs . . . they demonstrate that the constitution of their own citizenship (πολιτεία) is both marvellous and self-evidently strange (παράδοξος) . . . To put it shortly, what the soul is for the body so are Christians in the world. (5.4; 6.1)

Although translated 'citizenship', πολιτεία would provide a good equivalent or foundation for 'identity', at least in the present context and in that of the search for and maintenance of identity in Graeco-Roman cities.[22] Yet here it implies a complete relativization of any local loyalty or identity: 'They inhabit their own native lands, but as sojourners; they share everything as citizens, and endure everything as foreigners' (5.5). The language of sojourning and foreignness is already well established in the first century in a variety of New Testament contexts (1 Peter 1.1, 17; 2.11; Eph. 2.19; Heb. 11.13); it is, of course, rooted in the Jewish tradition (cf. Gen. 23.4; Psalm 39.12), a tradition ignored by this author.[23] When its correlative is a citizenship of heaven (cf. Phil. 3.20) it can justify an immunity to social values or pressures. So, here, 'They pass their time on earth, but exercise a citizenship in heaven' (5.9) leads into a celebration of the abuse, persecution and rejection they endure: 'They are dishonoured and are glorified in the dishonour' (5.14). In this way such an ethos serves an internal purpose of reinforcing group solidarity and identity – their heavenly citizenship

---

[22] On πολιτεία and πολιτεύομαι in the Jewish claim for identity see below, nn. 25–7.

[23] H. Meecham, *The Epistle to Diognetus: The Greek Text with Introduction, Translation and Notes* (Manchester University Press: Manchester, 1949) 109 refers to Philo, *de Conf.Ling.* 17 [77f.]. Yet, as noted below, the charge of being 'aliens' in a civic sense is sharply rejected by Josephus when speaking of the Jews of Alexandria (*c.Apion.* II.6 [71]). On the Jewish tradition and its re-use in the New Testament see R. Feldmeier, 'The "Nation" of Strangers: Social Contempt and Its Theological Interpretation in Ancient Judaism and Early Christianity', in Brett, ed., *Ethnicity and the Bible*, 240–70.

explains the abuse, abuse is a confirmation of that citizenship. Yet its external apologetic value would be ambivalent, as, too, would its effectiveness in shaping an alternative social identity. This is particularly clear when we contrast the use in Second-Temple Jewish literature of πολιτεία for a distinctive and ancient way of life. Josephus, rewriting Moses's farewell to the Jews in Deuteronomy, and reinterpreting the significance of the Torah, has him say, 'I have compiled for you, under God's dictation, laws and a πολιτεία, and if you observe it in due fashion, you would be considered by all to be the most fortunate of people.'[24] He also, I would suggest deliberately, uses the same term for the political status guaranteed from the beginning to the Jews in Alexandria and in the cities of Asia Minor, where he likewise vigorously opposes their treatment as 'aliens': Josephus too could say that the Jews have a πολιτεία in other cities but his meaning is very different![25] More particularly, πολιτεία denotes the distinctive Jewish way of life when threatened by suppression: in 2 Maccabees 13.14 Judas Maccabeus urges his fellow combatants to fight to the death 'for the laws, the Temple, the city, their native land, and the πολιτεία'.[26] Similarly, Jewish texts speak of their πατρίοι νόμοι for which they die and by which they are to govern themselves – if this is, as it surely must be, the Torah, it is viewed not as divine revelation but as national tradition: the despotic Antiochus inveigles them, 'Have confidence then and you will receive governing rule over my affairs, once you have denied the ancestral ordinances (θεσμός) of your πολιτεία' (4 Macc. 8.7).[27] Not surprisingly, this phrase is nowhere used by the early Christians.

[24] *Ant.* IV.8.2 [193]. J. R. Bartlett, *Jews in the Hellenistic World: Josephus, Aristeas, The Sibylline Oracles, Eupolemus* (Cambridge Commentaries on the Writings of the Jewish and Christian World 200 BC to AD 200, Cambridge University Press: Cambridge, 1985) 161–2 sees Josephus as setting the Mosaic Law in a new context here.

[25] *c. Apion.* I.22 [189]; II.4 [39], 6 [71]; *Ant.* XII.3.1–2 [119–128].

[26] 2 Macc. 4.11; 8.17; 3 Macc. 3.21, 23; 4 Macc. 3.20; 8.7; 17.9; cf. Josephus, *Ant.* XII.6.3 [280]; XIII.1.1 [2]. Philo uses πολιτεία of Jewish life (*de Spec.Leg.* I.9 [51], 11 [63], 57 [314], 59 [319] ; II. 25 [123] etc.); in *de Spec.Leg.* II.17 [74] he implies the potential universalization of πολιτεία in 'the *politeia* which is wholly on virtues and laws which alone propound the common good'. Yet the characterization by common laws remains its chief characteristic: *de Spec.Leg.* III.9 [51], 'the *politeia* according to Moses does not permit any harlot . . .'.

[27] Cf. Josephus, *Ant.* XII.5.1 [240]; 2 Macc. 6.1; 7.2, 8, 24, 27, 37; 4 Macc. 4.23; 5.33; 9.1; 16.16. However, see J. van der Klaauw, 'Diskussion', in J. W. van Henten, B. Dehandschutter and J. van der Klaauw, eds., *Die Entstehung der Jüdischen Martyrologie* (SPB, 38, Brill: Leiden, 1989) 220–61, 222 for debate as to whether the reference is to the Torah.

This difference is underlined by the *ad Diognetum* when the author adds to his New Testament models, 'Every foreign country is their native land, and every native land foreign' (5.5). This may point to a 'citizenship of the world', and might suggest the adoption of the ideals of some contemporary thought; Epictetus spoke of the world as a city, and held up the example of Heracles 'who had the power to live happily in every place', for all are citizens of Zeus.[28] Philo, perhaps more realistically, sees the world as a 'megalopolis', governed by a single πολιτεία which is reason, although it is constituted by individual cities with their own, additional laws, necessitated by the inability of Greeks and barbarians, and divisions within these, to get on with each other.[29] The dilemma Christian identity faced in claiming to incarnate such an ideal may be seen in Lucian's *Hermotimus*, more or less contemporary with the *ad Diognetum*. Hermotimus, an adherent of Stoicism, is slowly and insidiously weaned from his philosophical commitment by Lycinus, who starts by purportedly sharing his friend's idealism. An old man had once told him about a city where 'all were aliens and foreigners, and no-one was a native, but even many barbarians and slaves and cripples and dwarfs and impoverished were citizens . . . There neither was nor was named in the city inferior or superior, noble or ignoble, slave or free.' Yet citizenship of such a city would mean abandoning native country, children and parents. At the end of the dialogue Lycinus persuades Hermotimus to abandon his quest and to join the common life, 'and share in citizenship with others'.[30]

So does such an apparent disinterest towards specific loyalty invite the charge of disloyalty? – a charge, ironically, which might also be laid against Jewish communities: so Tacitus, 'Converts to their customs observe the same practice. The first thing they learn is to scorn the gods, to cast off their native country, to hold cheap fathers, children, brothers' (*Hist.* V.2). The answer given by the *ad Diognetum* is emphatic: 'They obey the ordained laws, and in their own lives surpass the laws' (5.10). Yet any practical content to this is surprisingly thin and hardly able to create an alternative community: 'They marry as do all, they

---

[28] Epictetus, *Disc.* III.24.9–21.

[29] *de Ios.* 6 [29–31]; but see *de Opif.* 49–50 [142–44] for citizens of the world. Celsus wishes, but gives up on the wish, 'that it were possible to unite under one Law inhabitants of Asia, Europe and Libya, both Greeks and barbarians, even at the farthest limits' (Origen, *c.Cels.* VIII.72).

[30] Lucian, *Hermotimus* 22–4; 84. The parallel is noted by Meecham, *Diognetus*, 108.

have children, but they do not expose their offspring. They provide a shared table, but not a shared bed' (5.7). Other apologists will add to these values, but barely trespass beyond their bounds; they are, ironically, the values already established by Jewish communities in the Diaspora and by Jewish apologetic writings.[31]

Earlier, the author of 1 Peter had taken a different track but only to reach a similar impasse; it has been argued that the 'sojourners' to whom that letter is addressed – 'Peter, apostle of Jesus Christ to the elect sojourners of the diaspora of Pontus, Galatia, Cappadocia, Asia and Bithynia' (1 Peter 1.1) – are not those exiled from heaven, as assumed by most modern translations, but those who socio-politically had no secure place in the city structures. Within the Christian community such alienation might continue to be their lot but it would be compensated for by a new belonging and identity within the household of God.[32] Yet when the author of 1 Peter comes to articulate the rules of the new household he says little that would shock contemporary moralists – 'Be subject to every human institution . . . whether the Emperor . . . or governors . . . Slaves be subject in all fear to your masters, not only to the good and gentle but also to the harsh . . . Likewise, let wives be subject to their own husbands' (1 Peter 2.13–14, 18; 3.1). Reassurance may, of course, have been part of his intention, and was an important part of early apologetic – Christians do not subvert the established *mores*, indeed they surpass them;[33] the need for such reassurance may betray the existence of very different patterns of behaviour and principle in early communities – and some recent study has preferred to focus on that implied world, a world of egalitarian freedom from social convention, rather than on the constructed world of the exhortation. But for the moment we may stay with that constructed identity, even while viewing it with due suspicion.

If identity-formation is a process of differentiation, the social identity of the Christians here appears remarkably opaque. To return to the *ad*

---

[31] On the coherence between Christian and Jewish apologetic values see Aristides, *Apology*, and Lieu, *Image and Reality*, 173–5.

[32] So J. H. Elliott, *A Home for the Homeless: A Sociological Exegesis of 1 Peter, Its Situation and Strategy* (SCM Press: London, 1982).

[33] See D. Balch, *Let Wives be Submissive: The Domestic Code in 1 Peter* (SBL.MS 26, Scholars Press: Atlanta, 1981); G. Theissen, 'Some Ideas about a Sociological Theory of Early Christianity', in idem, *Social Reality*, 257–87, 285, 'Where rules of conduct and values were shared with the world around the difference took the form of an outbidding of the consensus. Christians were not merely citizens like everyone else; they were "better citizens".'

Diognetum, the analogy the author develops between Christians in the world and the soul within the body (6) only reinforces this opacity: it implies symbiosis and invisibility, not differentiation. This is surely deliberate. One of the anomolies of the *ad Diognetum* is its silence about the Jewish heritage of Christianity and about the need to respond to contemporary Judaism's claim to that heritage. Yet when the author says that Christians are not distinguished by land, language or customs, we may wonder whether there is an implied apologetic contrast with the Jews who, notoriously, were, at least in popular polemic, so distinguished.[34] Although Jews were scattered around the then known world, Josephus could assert 'Our race is one and the same everywhere . . . why should you be surprised if those who came to Alexandria from elsewhere remained within the laws established from the beginning'? (*c.Apion.* II.6 [66–67]).[35] Tacitus expresses the view from the other side: 'With them all is profane that among us is sacred. Again, acts with them are permissible that for us are incestuous' (*Hist.* V.2). The Christian apologist Justin Martyr's Jewish dialogue partner, Trypho, sees the Christian 'difference' from another – Jewish – point of view: 'although you claim to be pious and consider yourselves different from other people, you do not separate yourselves from them at all, neither do you distinguish your way of life from that of the gentiles' (*Dial.* 10.3); although Trypho speaks only with Justin's permission and through his pen, his objection is never seriously addressed. Social separation is not a Christian characteristic.

In contrast to this 'invisibility', the opening chapter of the *ad Diognetum* introduces a further model which will be equally problematic – rhetorically effective but practically tenuous:

> Since I see, most excellent Diognetus, that you are particularly enthusiastic to about learn the piety (θεοσέβεια) of the Christians and are clearly and diligently inquiring about them, . . . and why this 'γένος' or practice has entered life as a new thing now and not before . . . ' (1)

Here the Christians represent a new 'γένος' and practice (ἐπιτήδευμα) in contrast to the Greeks and the Jews. γένος is ambiguous; in other

---

[34] So also Meecham, *Diognetus*, 108. Cassius Dio interprets the recent Bar Kochba revolt as inspired by Jewish rejection of 'another people' or 'alien rites' being established in their city (*Hist.Rom.* LXIX.12). This would be particularly significant if the *ad Diognetum* was written while this was still a vivid memory.

[35] Cf. Philo, *Legatio* 29 [194] which contrasts the πολιτεία of the Jews throughout the world with being Alexandrians.

writers, including the apologist Aristides, perhaps writing earlier than the *ad Diognetum*, it may be translated 'race' and is explicitly prefixed 'third', contrasted with Jews and Greeks.[36] There is some debate as to whether that idea originates in the polemic of observers, for which we may recall Suetonius's description of the Christians as a '*genus* of men given to a new and wicked superstition' (*Nero* 16.2) as well as Tertullian's cameo of the 'peoples of the nations' crying out 'Whence the third race?' (*Scorp.* 10.10);[37] or whether its source is Christian self-consciousness, for which we may appeal already to Paul in the middle of the first century, 'There is neither Greek nor Jew, circumcision nor uncircumcision' (Col. 3.11). The alternatives illustrate the ambivalence of the claim: on the one hand a 'fifth column', subverting the proper and accepted structuring of the world which underlies the organization of all society – so Celsus who speaks of the Christians as a 'people who . . . wall themselves off and break away from the rest of humankind' (Origen, *c. Cels.* VIII.2);[38] on the other, a new category, superseding and embracing within it the existing dichotomies.[39]

The latter – a new inclusive category – is Paul's theoretical construct and so he speaks of a new ἄνθρωπος, whose ultimate pattern and goal is 'the image of the creator' (Col. 3.10), that is, humankind as first created before the various forms of polarization and opposition which, according to this reading of the Genesis narrative, eventuated. This is not the place to explore the theological roots and ramifications of Paul's concept, but his letters bear eloquent testimony to the practical context, the creation of new communities both out of individuals and out of existing networks or households of both Jewish and non-Jewish background without, theoretically, giving priority to either.[40] The fragility of the construct, both practically and theoretically, is equally clear. Thus Paul's

---

[36] Aristides, *Apol.* 2; the Syriac speaks of four races and has some claim to originality, see Lieu, *Image and Reality*, 165–9.

[37] See also *ad Nat.* I.8 where Tertullian objects that every race has its Christians, and then admits that as third 'genus' it is a matter of religion (*superstitio*) and not of nation (*natio*); 20.4.

[38] See A. Schneider, *Le Premier Livre* Ad Nationes *de Tertullien* (Inst. Suisse de Rome: Neuchâtel, 1968) 187–91.

[39] See J. Z. Smith, 'Fences and Neighbours: Some Contours of Early Judaism', in W. S. Green, ed., *Approaches to Ancient Judaism* II (BJS 9, Scholars Press: Chico, 1980) 1–26, 12–13.

[40] On the importance of networks in the spread of early Christianity see L. M. White, ed., *Social Networks in the Early Christian Movement: Issues and Methods for Social History* (*Semeia* 56, Scholars Press: Atlanta, 1992).

letters also bear eloquent testimony to what has been seen as a tension between identity and ethos, understanding ethos as that which ensures the continuity of a social system, particularly when it is a minority within a wider culture.[41] In practice, what we see in the Pauline communities is a spectrum of ethos, even to the point of potential conflict, between those whose background was Jewish and those who were Gentile, or between those who favoured affirmation of or continuity with the majority society, and those who rejected it, for example in the heated debate as to the permissibility of continuing to participate in meals which might involve eating 'meat offered to idols' (1 Cor. 8; 10.14–33).

Such tensions were not, of course, new with Christian communities. Jewish communities, which also espoused a degree of exclusive self-identity, faced similar dilemmas in balancing the equation between identity and integration. Indeed, it is arguable that the sharpening rhetoric of self-identity characteristic of the late Second-Temple period is as much a function of internal conflicts over the issue as of external attempts to suppress identity.[42] Philo condemns those who, on the grounds of an allegorical interpretation of circumcision and sabbath which he shares, treat their literal observance lightly: 'As if they were living alone by themselves in a desert land or had become disembodied souls and knew neither city, nor village, nor house, nor any form of human association'; for Philo due observance is an expression of recognition of our bodily existence and the careful concern for the πάτριος πολιτεία (*de Migr.Abr.* 16 [88–93]). Yet while recognizing that Jewish communities maintained sufficiently separate identity over the centuries both to survive and to be recognized and reviled for the distinctiveness by observers, recent attempts to describe the core of that identity have found themselves speaking of Judaism*s*, and asking 'Who was a Jew?' or 'How would you know a Jew?'.[43] We may summarize the problem as 'How broad a range or spectrum is possible without fracturing identity?'

---

[41] See M. Wolter, 'Ethos und Identität in Paulinischen Gemeinden', *NTS* 43 (1997) 430–44.

[42] As is well illustrated by the debate over the interpretation of the Maccabean revolt and the question of hellenism.

[43] J. Neusner, W. S. Green and E. S. Frerichs, eds., *Judaisms and their Messiahs at the Turn of the Christian Era* (Cambridge University Press: Cambridge, 1987); M. Goodman, *Who was a Jew?* (Yarnton Trust for Oxford Centre for Postgraduate Hebrew Studies: Oxford, 1989); S. Cohen, 'Those who say they are Jews and are not', in S. Cohen and E. Frerichs, eds, *Diasporas in Antiquity* (BJS 288, Scholars Press: Atlanta, 1993) 1–47.

In proclaiming a new identity in which the contrasted identities of Jew and Greek, itself a Jewish polarity, had no place, Paul was not solving but compounding the Jewish dilemma. John Barclay has recently attempted to analyse different Jewish patterns of response to the majority society along three scales, accommodation, acculturation and assimilation.[44] However useful that may prove, it cannot be applied to early Christianity. If the problem about the 'Judaism and Hellenism' debate is that we do not have the evidence to describe Judaism before Hellenism,[45] – we cannot measure acculturation if we do not know what is being acculturated – there is no Christianity to be described prior to its interaction with the majority society. Jew and Greek remained as much as did slave and free, male and female (Gal. 3.28) – or if they did not so remain what did they become?[46]

The practical problem, therefore, is what is a third race without an identity? Again, Christian self-designation as a race, which in the second century we also find in the *Martyrdom of Polycarp* and in Melito of Sardis, as well as in the *Kerygma Petri* excerpted by Clement of Alexandria, is paralleled by and perhaps dependent on the Jewish self-ascription common in the Maccabean literature.[47] Yet this only underscores the contrast and the dilemma, for what constitutes a 'race'? Is an identity which subsumes and so obviates the identity of Jew or Greek a possibility?

The theoretical problem is closely related. Identity, so we are told, is constructed by opposition; it involves self-awareness in relation to the other: 'us' demands 'them'. It is the assertion of a collective self and the simultaneous negation of collective others.[48] Indeed, if such a binary mode of thought is fundamental to human thinking and identity, this

---

[44] J. Barclay, *Jews in the Mediterranean Diaspora* (T&T Clark: Edinburgh, 1995); also, 'Paul among Diaspora Jews: Anomaly or Apostate', *JSNT* 60 (1995) 89–120.

[45] So A. Momigliano, 'Review of M. Hengel, *Judentum und Hellenismus: Studien zu ihrer Begegnung unter besondere Berüksichtigung Palästinas bis zur Mitte des 2. Jh. v. Chr.*, (J.C.B. Mohr: Tübingen, 1969)', *JTS* 21 (1970) 149–53.

[46] In this context Pauline Christianity cannot only be seen in relation to its 'separation' from Judaism. Thus L. Michael White distinguishes the Matthaean sectarian (= separatist/revolutionary) pattern from the Pauline 'cult' pattern which represents the attempt to import 'an essentially novel world view into a dominant culture': L. M. White, 'Shifting Sectarian Boundaries in Early Christianity', *BJRL* 70 (1988) 7–24, 23.

[47] See Lieu, *Image and Reality*, 166–9; eadem, 'The Race of the Godfearers', *JTS* 46 (1995) 483–501 = pp. 49–68 above.

[48] See G. Porton, *GOYIM: Gentiles and Israelites in Mishnah-Tosefta* (BJS 155, Scholars Press: Atlanta, 1988) 288–9.

is why 'third race' is perceived as subversive. In practice this is also how the rhetoric of the third or new race or kind works in early Christian writers; it is characterized not by its inclusiveness of earlier dichotomies but by its exclusiveness. Christians share in the errors of neither Greeks nor Jews. In practice for Diognetus this can be limited to the nature and worship of God: 'they do not reckon the gods so-considered by the Greeks, neither do they observe the superstition of the Jews' (1). Both Greeks and Jews are thus identified not by a broad spectrum of social and cultural practice, but purely by what is now a conventional exposé of idolatry and of Jewish praxis, both drawn more from a polemical tradition than from any genuine social experience: he even treats the Jerusalem sacrificial system as still in place. This is not to deny the enormous and fundamental consequences of Christian rejection of what is so blithely described as the worship of wood, stone and metal work (2.2); it is to wonder, rather, at the failure to exploit this for identity: how can the author still say that Christians live in Greek and barbarian cities and follow local customs; even that the Christian θεουέβεια remains invisible (6.4)?

Again dependence on Jewish models is both self-evident and paradoxical; Jewish Hellenistic texts abound in the condemnation of idolatry, and in isolating it as the characteristic marker of non-Jewish versus Jewish identity.[49] For the *Letter of Aristeas* the rest of humankind think there are many gods and this is why God 'hedged us in to prevent our being perverted by contact with others or by mixing with bad influences' (§§ 134; 142); yet such Jewish texts seem to see avoidance of idolatry as a virtue available to all people.[50] For Christian writers it is a matter of exclusive self-definition, and when they extend the differentiation to include the Jews as 'other', Jewish worship of God and observance of the law are brought under the same rubric of idolatry: for the *ad Diognetum* 'they seem to me to differ not at all from those who show the same honour to what are deaf' (3.5).[51] In practice, however, Christian avoidance of involvement in idolatry differed from Jewish by

---

[49] See John J. Collins, *Between Athens and Jerusalem: Jewish Identity in the Hellenistic Diaspora* (Crossroad: New York, 1983); e.g. *III Sibyll.* ll. 545–55; *V Sibyll.* ll. 75–85; 353–60; 403–5; *Joseph and Asenath* 8.5. Even in Rabbinic Judaism the Gentile as 'Other' is the Gentile as idolater, cf. Porton, *GOYIM*. Christians took over this definition of Gentile otherness from the beginning, cf. 1 Thess. 4.3f.

[50] See Collins, *Athens and Jerusalem*, 167–8, 180–1.

[51] On the presentation of the Jews as idolatrous see Lieu, *Image and Reality*, 145.

being less marked – although it is only at the beginning of the third century that we find this seriously discussed.[52]

The persistence of a binary model of self-identity is thus self-evident in this as in all early Christian writings, including those which speak of a third race or kind. It is also there when this author speaks of the soul and the world: 'the world hates the Christians although it has not been wronged by them' (6.5). Such an affirmation sits oddly with the more integrative comments a little earlier. It is the use of 'the world' which makes this possible. Although it has its roots in the Jewish eschatological contrast between 'this world' and 'the world to come', this opposition to 'the world' is characteristically, although not exclusively, Christian.[53] Within the New Testament it is most developed in the Johannine literature where it has often been dubbed 'sectarian', yet in principle it may become a fundamental organizing point for Christian self-identity, capable of multiple expressions.[54] This is the language of internal identity-formation, not of external visible perception. Its effectiveness in maintaining cohesion, in legitimating ascetic life-styles, and in explaining hostility, is self-evident: the latter is no longer rejection by former family and friends, or by the state to which one claimed loyalty, but by a universalized and impersonalized opposition.

Thus, while a binary opposition may be endemic to all identity-formation, it is particularly attractive in a context of persecution. The interplay between persecution and identity for both Jews and Christians is not unexpected, and the development of 'citizenship' language in this context has already been noted above. Similarly, it is also in the literature associated with the persecution and ensuing revolt under the Maccabees in the early second century BCE that Hellenistic Jewish literature develops the language of 'race' as well as the term 'Judaism'. 'Christianity'/ 'Christianismos' and 'Christian' also seem first to seed and flower in that context.[55] Paradigmatically, towards the end of the second century (?) in Pergamum, the 'martyr' responds to the question, 'What is your name?', 'My first and most distinctive name is Christian, but if you

---

[52] The practical ambiguities are illustrated by Tertullian, *de Idolatria* who describes idolatry as 'the chief crime of the human race' (1.1) but carefully has to allow for Christians in general and for slaves to participate in family festivals involving idolatry so long as they do not share in the act itself (16–17).
[53] A rare Jewish example is *Test. Job.* 48–9.
[54] See Wimbush, '". . . Not of this World" . . .', 32–4.
[55] See Lieu, *Image and Reality*, 29–31; 85–6.

seek that in the world, Carpus'.[56] It is a reflection of the ambiguities which this essay has explored that Jewish literature does not develop the opposition from or to 'the world' in the persecution context.[57] Christian self-identity, however, because of, or in spite of, its non-differentiation, demanded the alternative identity of 'the world' so that, as Celsus perceptively commented, 'If all men could be Christians, the Christians would no longer want them' (*c. Cels.* III.9).

Finally, there is one further route to self-identity: the discovery of a past. It is a common argument that a major component of identity is a common history, ancestry or descent, which may but need not be conceived in biological terms.[58] Such a history might seem intrinsically problematic for a third or new race, as also for a *politeia* without a native land. Yet while in terms of individual history, at least initially, Christian literature spoke of a separation from the past, a model that was to become paradigmatic, in terms of corporate history it found a history either in the Scriptures – as when Christians called Abraham 'our father' (*1 Clement* 31) – or in the Christian story – as when the *Martyrdom of Polycarp* becomes a literary mimesis of the Gospel narrative (*Mart. Poly.* 19.1). The *ad Diognetum* is unusual in the second century in not finding any such history;[59] consistent this may be, yet ultimately it was to prove unsatisfactory, and the denial of history, as implied by Marcion's rejection of the Creator God of the Jews, was excluded as heretical. This may bring us back to the beginning and the 'forging' of Christian identity – 'Without [that] historical continuity any answer to the identity question can only be invented rather than discovered'.[60]

---

[56] See the *Martyrdom of Carpus, Papylus, and Agathonice* 2–3 in H. Musurillo, *The Acts of the Christian Martyrs* (OECT, Clarendon Press: Oxford, 1972) xv–xvi; 22–37. See further below, pp. 211–31.

[57] Ctr. 4 Macc. 17.14, 'Eleazar was the first contestant, the mother of the seven sons entered the contest, and the brothers contended. The tyrant was the antagonist; the world and the life of humankind were watching'.

[58] See Porton, *GOYIM*, 291–3.

[59] It mentions nothing of Israel's history, shows no knowledge of the Hebrew Scriptures, and little of the 'Jesus' story; it knows only the past 'time of unrighteousness' now overtaken by the 'time of righteousness' (9.1).

[60] D. Novak, *The Election of Israel: The Idea of the Chosen People* (Cambridge University Press: Cambridge, 1995) 2.

12

The New Testament and Early Christian Identity*

My title may well appear unsurprising and straightforward: unsurprising because my responsibility is after all to 'profess' the New Testament, while in my previous appointments it was 'early Christianity and Judaism'; straightforward because if the New Testament is about anything it is, presumably, about early Christianity, and in practice it has served as definitive in constructions of 'true' Christian identity – a paradigm of the symbolic uses of the past for the present. Such an opening should immediately warn an audience that what we are to explore is neither straightforward nor unsurprising. To begin with, each one of the terms within that title invites contestation. 'Identity' is, as is often noted, a modern term, first entering the English language towards the end of the sixteenth century, and with no obvious equivalent in the languages of the first-century Mediterranean basin. It probably evokes ideas of sameness and difference, of commonalities and boundaries, and of individual and/or group. Yet, as has frequently been remarked, it has only been in the last forty years, as the intrinsic ideas of sameness and essence have been radically called into question, that in social and political life as well as in academic discourse, identity has come to play a focal, often determinative role.[1] What we are doing when we speak about identity in relation to the past, and in particular when we retroject thereon our own bounded ideas of identity, is by no means self-evident – which does not stop a good many people doing it, myself included.

* Inaugural lecture, King's College London, October 1999. Since this was originally conceived as an oral presentation, only basic footnotes have been added, identifying references or pointing to the wider debate.

---

[1] The bibliography on this is vast, and I intend to explore it in a forthcoming monograph. For the problem noted in this sentence see R. Handler, 'Is "Identity" a Useful Cross-cultural Concept?', in J. Gillis, ed., *Commemorations: The Politics of National Identity* (Princeton University Press: Princeton, 1994) 27–40.

'Early Christian' is also more problematic than may at first seem the case. I leave on one side the term 'early', remarking only that what was once tendentiously labelled – by Christian scholars – *late* Judaism has more recently been reinstated as 'early', for the justifiable reason that 'late' leaves little room for two thousand years more of history; but at what stage 'early' becomes 'middle', not to speak of 'late', seems to be beyond solution while we are as yet *in medias res*. 'Christian', however, offers us more of a challenge. Although students and teachers, even Professors, of the New Testament find it extraordinarily difficult to speak of those who populate and stand behind its pages without using the term, 'Christian' appears but three times therein, twice in Acts (11.26; 26.28), once in 1 Peter (4.16), arguably each time on the mouths of detractors. To speak of the group established by Paul in Corinth as 'the first urban Christians' – the title of a deservedly influential monograph[2] – is self-evidently an anachronism, for apparently neither he nor they knew the term; or if Paul did, as Acts 11.26 might lead us to expect, his silence is no less telling – Acts 11.26 reports that the disciples were first called Christians at Antioch just as Saul *aka* Paul first arrives there. Yet at what stage 'Christian' ceases to be an anachronism is less evident. This is not simply a matter of deciding the still disputed question of how and where the term originated, whether as a denigrating political label on the mouths of outsiders and opponents or as a proud self-designation; nor is it only a case of noting how many authors even in the second century manage to speak about 'Christians' without using the term – Clement, Polycarp, Hermas, Barnabas . . . 'Christianity' (*Christianismos*), is nowhere to be found in the New Testament, it appears first in the early second century, and it remains a rare term for another century and more. Yet behind and more important than the semantic problem lie more intractable ones. Ignatius, the first to speak of *Christianismos*, uses it, and perhaps coined it himself, in conscious opposition to *Ioudaismos*/Judaism: Christianism, he claims, did not set its faith in Judaism but Judaism in Christianism – a claim difficult both to translate and to justify (*Magn.* 10.3); yet *Ioudaismos*, exclusively a Greek term, is also highly circumscribed in use and probably equally tendentious; it first appears in the literature of the Maccabean revolt, where it is used to create new boundaries, insiders against outsiders,

[2] W. A. Meeks, *The First Urban Christians: The Social World of the Apostle Paul* (Yale University Press: New Haven, 1983).

boundaries which, as the polemic betrays, not all recognized;[3] it too remains rare and has no obvious contemporary equivalent in Hebrew or Aramaic. Most Jews of this period would not have filled in the gap on the form requesting 'religion' with the word 'Judaism' – although the point is, of course, that even had there been forms to fill in, they would not have had a heading 'religion'. The apparently monolithic 'early Judaism' of my former job description is no less insubstantial, resisting simple classification, as the recent increasingly sophisticated analyses of Jewish identity have all too clearly demonstrated. All this points us to the question of what often, but, as I have suggested elsewhere, unhelpfully, has been labelled 'the parting of the ways':[4] at what stage did 'Christianity' emerge as separate from its parent 'Judaism'? And if we cannot use either substantive, 'Christianity' or 'Judaism', because both are anachronistic, can we, or how can we, rephrase that question? If – and I stress that 'if' – the Jesus movement, a superficially less tendentious label but in fact equally value-laden, was in its earliest stages one among a number of movements among first-century Jews – comparable to the community of the Dead Sea Scrolls – how did it become increasingly differentiated, and how should we speak of it at any particular stage? An observation meriting reflection is that the Good News Bible, or Today's English Version, of the New Testament uses the word 'Christian' fifty-nine times; the effect on readers is likely to be quite different from that of the 'more restrained' NRSV which uses the term only where the Greek form appears.

Working back through our title, we shall pass over the apparently innocuous 'and', although perhaps everything here is about the nature of the correlation implied therein. And so to 'the New Testament'. Once again, it would be possible to pre-empt further extending this intro-duction by demonstrating the facticity of the latest edition of the Greek New Testament – which at least circumvents debates about the potential distortions inherent in any particular translation.[5] Yet this is an eclectic text, drawing from numerous manuscripts, every one of which contains numerous scribal variants, whether minor or more far-reaching; the result is in intention a text which exhibits as little as possible such

[3] 2 Macc. 2.21; 8.1; 14.38; 4 Macc. 4.26. On this see further p. 59 above.
[4] See J. M. Lieu, '"The Parting of the Ways": Theological Construct or Historical Reality', *JSNT* 56 (1994) 101–19 = pp. 11–29 above.
[5] I.e. 'Nestle-Aland': *Novum Testamentum Graece* (27th edition, Deutsche Bibelgesellschaft: Stuttgart, 1993).

deviations from a theorized and confessedly unattainable 'original text'. In practice it is a text which conforms to no text which has functioned as the New Testament for any Christian, early or otherwise; as printed text it promises a fixity and homogeneity which it itself – with its numerous footnoted variants – undermines. It is an academic construct – no less useful, indeed, but liable to hide from us both the diversity and the dynamism which will have characterized the experience of its earlier constituency, a diversity we can either ignore in pursuit of a mythical 'original' or explore in all its richness.

Yet even in recognizing that diversity we have leap-frogged a prior conundrum. A Professor of New Testament Studies is bound to 'profess' something which, within the period of her expertise, did not exist. Although we may, and do, choose to read other texts, the 'identity' of a 'New Testament scholar' is predicated upon the closure of this body of texts, a closure determined not by date nor by authorship, but by a process which extends, even achieves momentum, outside and beyond the limits of our responsibilities (i.e. into and beyond the fourth century CE). Here we encounter the problem of 'the canon', a problem which has generated a vigorous debate in other literary studies, but is here enshrined within the title of the discipline and Chair. Much could be said here about the history and proper location of that discipline, but that would take me down paths I do not today intend to pursue.

If, then, the apparently clear terms with which we started have become increasingly problematic, this is also hardly surprising. It has been a premiss and a consequence of more than a century of historical-critical study that the Old and New Testaments are to be seen as historical phenomena, and this means that today we can no longer – if we ever did – suppose that the text is 'merely' a window through which we can trace the 'men and movements' which produced it. In the study of the Old Testament/Hebrew Bible[6] the effect of this has lead to searching questions. Does the formation of Tanak/Scripture during the Second Temple period, however achieved, give rise to Judaism – for the most part, as we have seen, our term? So understood, Judaism becomes the system predicated upon and made possible by the formation of the text as a source of identity and interpretation. Or is the production of this body of Scriptures itself the work of just one group from amongst the rich heterogeneity of those who shared a common but more extensive

---

[6] On the problem of labelling see pp. 151–5 above.

resource of traditions, memory and practice? and as such, more importantly, is its production a claim for power by that group to the exclusion of others, the power to determine the authoritative inter-pretation of past, present and future? a claim, moreover, although once more arising in the Maccabean tradition, in no way beyond contestation still by the time of the New Testament. That debate has been a politically explosive one within Hebrew Bible/Old Testament studies.[7] Ours has yet to be fully explored.

Our exploration of the dynamic between New Testament and early Christian identity, will take the form of a series of journeys, journeys that will show that although the problem in some ways sounds a very modern one, it is also ancient. And it is with the ancient that we shall start. For on the surface, the case of the New Testament is very different from that of the 'Old'. Contrary to some popular presentations, Tanak/ the Old Testament did not owe its existence to the decisions of councils nor to the decree of influential individuals; yet for the New Testament our starting point will be Athanasius, bishop of Alexandria. His *39th Festal Letter*, written in 367 CE, has become a classic in the 'History of the Canon', the tracing of the process by which this collection of texts became reified as 'the Bible'; in this letter Athanasius declares how he has decided to set out 'the books which are canonized and handed down and believed to be divine'. Much has been written about the use of the term *kanôn* (κανών), rule or measure: does it emphasize that these books are a measure of true belief or that they have been measured? It seems to have been Athanasius who first used the term in this context, and who also used the denominative verb, *kanonizô* (κανονίζω), 'canonized' (transitive), and so settled for the second meaning: thus that which is measured presupposes those who measure, and suggests a picture of harmony, consensus.

The list of books that Athanasius offers, often cited out of context, betrays a more tangled tale.[8] Athanasius seems concerned, perhaps the first to be so, not only to lay out the names of the books, but also their order. Here, for the New Testament, the four Gospels, Matthew, Mark,

---

7 See T. L. Thompson, *The Bible in History: How Writers Create a Past* (Cape: London, 1999).

8 For the Greek text see T. Zahn, *Grundiss der Geschichte des neutestamentlichen Kanons* (Deichert: Leipzig, 1904) 86–92; translation in A. Robertson, *Select Writings and Letters of Athanasius, Bishop of Alexandria* (The Nicene and Post-Nicene Fathers, T&T Clark: Edinburgh, repr. 1991 [1891]) 551–2.

Luke and John, take first place, followed by the Acts of the Apostles, then follow the seven Epistles known as 'Catholic' – James, Peter (2), John (3) and Jude. Following these are the fourteen letters of Paul 'in order', first to churches – to the Romans, the Corinthians (2), Galatians, Ephesians, Philippians, Colossians and Thessalonians (2), and that to the Hebrews; and then immediately those to Timothy (2), Titus, Philemon, all individuals, and finally the Apocalypse of John. This, at any rate, is the account of the surviving Greek and Syriac versions of Athanasius's letter; but the Coptic, which preserves much more of it, places, also 'in order', Hebrews after 2 Corinthians and before Galatians.[9] The divergence witnesses to the contested history of Hebrews, whose author, according to Origen, 'God only knows'; its relocation in the Coptic version is not a scribal error but a reflection of that church's own independent tradition. Theologically, the change may appear of little account; yet it bespeaks a dynamic reciprocity, still being exercised at the time of the translation of Athanasius's writings, and long after, between New Testament and Christian identity, the one shaping and maintaining the other. This example could be repeated again and again through different manuscript traditions and different churches and confessions. It reminds us again that texts are constructs, and construct identity; to translate, to preserve, to read, and to determine reading are acts of power. And the assertion of difference, however apparently minor, of how 'we' do it, is not to be summarily dismissed as either error or curiosity.

Yet whatever we decide about the origins of the term and of the concept of canon, Athanasius is engaged not so much in an act of inclusion as in an act of exclusion. He is, he declares, afraid for the innocent who are deceived by apocryphal books, especially by those bearing the same names at the genuine Scriptures. Such books are to be ignored even if they have something of value in them – an ecumenical concession which opens no doors. Even where they appear to be ancient, they are recent, the work of heretics, bent on sowing discord within the church. All identity is, of course, about exclusion; the erection of boundaries against 'the other', and so at the same time the labelling, the rhetorical construction of, the other. The labelling of 'the heretic' is peculiarly characteristic of early – and not just early – Christianity, and

9 S. Athanase, *Lettres festales et pastorales en Copte*, L.-Th. Lefort, ed. (CSCO Copt. 19, 20, Dubecq: Louvain, 1955).

the manifold exercise of power evidenced therein was pointed out by Walter Bauer sixty years ago, while we continue to wrestle with the consequences.[10]

It was, ironically, the dry sands of Athanasius's Egypt which were eventually to defeat his best intentions, and ensure that the discord was not hidden under some higher harmony. While a series of earlier discoveries began to hint at what might yet be to come, little would remain the same after 1945 which saw the unearthing of the thirteen codices which have come to be known as the Nag Hammadi Library – contemporary with Athanasius himself and containing a range of texts from part of Plato's *Republic* to the *Trimorphic Protennoia* with its provocative evocation of the prologue to John's Gospel or to the *Apocalypse of Adam* which lacks anything distinctively 'Christian'.[11] Never again would we be able to think of Jewish-Christianity, of gnosticism, or of orthodoxy as self-evident and hermetically sealed categories, nor of gnosticism as a falling away from the pure virgin church of the New Testament. From among these texts students of the New Testament are now accustomed to pay particular attention to the *Gospel of Thomas*, 114 sayings set in the mouth of 'the Living Jesus'. The debate as to whether this 'Gospel' is entirely derivative from those other Gospel traditions already known to us and enshrined in Athanasius's canon, or whether in part or in whole it preserves independent Jesus traditions, is as yet unresolved. This is not a purely technical source-critical issue: for here we encounter another remembered Jesus – just as the 'canonical' Gospels also present us with 'remembered Jesus-es', not 'historical Jesus-es' – another attempt to re-speak what he was all about, another way of conceptualizing the formative moment. Therefore, another piece in the jigsaw of early Christian identity, a jigsaw which is becoming so much more perplexing than the twenty-seven pieces we thought we knew where to place.

Also from the fourth-century Egypt of Athanasius but hidden by its sands until this century is a papyrus codex known as part of the Bodmer collection.[12] Students of the text of the New Testament will encounter

---

10 W. Bauer, *Rechtgläubigkeit und Ketzerei im ältesten Christentum* (Mohr/Siebeck: Tübingen, 1934); it was only translated into English nearly 40 years later: *Orthodoxy and Heresy in Earliest Christianity* (ET Fortress Press: Philadelphia, 1971).

11 In English translation conveniently available as J. M. Robinson, ed., *The Nag Hammadi Library in English* (Brill: Leiden, 1977).

12 Published as *Papyrus Bodmer V–XII* (Bibliotheca Bodmeriana, Cologny–Genève, 1958–64). Jude and 1–2 Peter constitute *P.Bodmer* VII–VIII.

seven pages from the middle of this codex and its final thirty-six pages under the symbol 𝔓72, an important witness for the text of Jude and 1 and 2 Peter which these pages contain. Although Athanasius lists 2 Peter without question as part of the New Testament, there is little early evidence for anyone knowing or using the letter much before him; 𝔓72, therefore, has been welcomed as securing 2 Peter for the pre-Nicene/pre-Constantine New Testament, and as evidence that despite the otherwise deafening silence it was surely at least on its way to being 'Scripture'. Yet in removing these pages of Jude and 1 and 2 Peter from their original location and in putting them in the Greek New Testament as 𝔓72 we are being deceived; although *we* may read these as canonical texts, this codex does not so recognize or differentiate them. They are combined without distinguishing marks of honour in a heterogenous collection of writings, including not just an (the 11th) *Ode of Solomon* – not by Solomon – but also the *Birth of Mary*, here described as the 'Revelation of James', which it certainly cannot be, and the – as we would call it, 'apocryphal' – correspondence between Paul and the Corinthians which is not by the Corinthians nor by Paul; all these, the last two aggressively 'orthodox', falling firmly under Athanasius's strictures against texts falsely claiming scriptural authorship. To ask what this combination of texts in a single codex means may be to ask the unanswerable; yet for the student of early Christian identity and of these texts, 1 and 2 Peter and Jude do not only belong in the New Testament; they belong as part of this curious conjunction of writings, because it was as such that they were read and valued; in that context they point to other patterns of experience, other pieties. The boundaries around and the correlation between New Testament and early Christianity are perhaps not so predictable after all.

This provides a link to a further observation: 2 Peter is remarkable for the number of textual variants it exhibits, evidence of that unsteady path to authoritative status. One remarkable variant is found at 2 Peter 2.10 where Nestle-Aland's text reads (from v. 9) 'the Lord knows how to keep the unrighteous under punishment until the day of judgement, and especially those who adhere to the flesh in polluting [𝔓72 reads 'fleshly'] lust and despise authority. Bold and wilful, they do not hesitate to revile the glorious ones' (perhaps meaning angels). One manuscript, however, the minuscule (cursive) 2138, according to the critical apparatus, concludes instead, 'Bold and wilful, they do not hesitate to revile the divine powers or the ecclesiastical authorities.' That was no scribal slip but was intended for the audience; it is no accident that this manuscript was written at the behest of the beleagured Michael VII Dukas, Emperor from 1071 to 1078, who, ironically but unknown to the scribe, was before long to abdicate, to join a monastery, and later to be named metropolitan of Ephesus.[13] We should remember not just the power of literacy but also the coercive potential of possessing Scriptures, and their political uses. This creates a nice irony when Luther, unaware of this reading, which was probably almost immediately consigned to oblivion, interprets the 'reviling of the glorious ones' in 2 Peter 2.10 of the Pope's attempts to excommunicate and to reject the appropriate authority of secular powers.

Recognition of this exercise of power in possession and interpretation also belongs to the study of the New Testament; belongs to it, perhaps, in more ways than one: this idiosyncratic variant seems to have attracted no attention in earlier analyses of this manuscript nor in commentaries, and so it is natural to wonder whether the editors included it 'tongue in cheek'. Power continues to be exercised by those – including Professors – with control over the text, and even the mask of dispassionate objectivity worn by 'lower criticism' cannot be left untouched by our postmodern sensitivities. In this way the text continues to tell a story and to participate in a story of conflicting identities.

Yet MS2138's defence of ecclesiastical authorities has not been included here merely for light relief, but to point to the next stage. This section of 2 Peter, 2.1–11, begins with a warning against 'false-teachers': here the letter coins a new word, *pseudodidaskaloi* (ψευδοδιδάσκαλοι), perhaps – since it does not otherwise refer to teachers or teaching – so defining all teachers. This brings us back to Athanasius who offers one more challenge to a Professor of New Testament Studies. For while his *39th Letter* is targetted against those who made much of the apocryphal books, it also aims a number of side-swipes against those yet more dangerous – teachers. It has been suggested that what Athanasius was doing in this letter was using the concept of Canon to take authority from the teachers and to locate it firmly within the ecclesiastical and liturgical context. The true teacher, he avers, is Christ alone: 'For the nature of everyone who is of the created order is to be taught, but our Lord and Craftsman is by nature a teacher.' Scripture, Athanasius

---

[13] On this manuscript see K. Treu, *Die griechische Handschriften des neuen Testaments in der UdSSR* (*TU* 91, Akademie Verlag: Berlin, 1966) 328–31.

suggests, is self-sufficient; in it alone is to be found the teaching of piety; to be satisfied with Scripture is to purge the church of defilement; to celebrate the feast is to celebrate it with Scripture; yet even so there are obscure texts in Scripture and these are to be kept away from new learners, the catechumens. Athanasius uncovers a dilemma in a Professor's obligations; for to profess (*profiteor*) is to confess; yet already from the so-called New Testament period *profiteor* was also to teach.

Athanasius was not the first to perceive a tension between teaching and confession, just as he did not initiate the use of Scripture to include and to exclude. Already at the conjunction of the second and third centuries Tertullian had responded to the appeal to Scripture by those *he* labelled heretics with two fateful claims: first, with the assertion that the crucial question is who has the right to possess the Scriptures; that rhetorical question played an equally important role in the church's polemic against the Jews – the rejection of other claims to revere and to interpret the same text is to assert identity by exclusion, by negation. Tertullian's second conclusion may prove to be yet more disturbing: to ask questions is not to hold on, not to hold on is not to believe, and not to believe is not to be a Christian (*de Praes.Haer.* 14.10). To reject Tertullian's conclusions, as here I must, is to embrace the unknown potential of the text.

Before exploring this, we may make a further significant observation to join the others that have punctuated this essay: it was Tertullian who also dismissed the *Acts of Paul* whose heroine, Thecla, both baptizes – herself – and goes round teaching. 'How', he protests 'could we believe that Paul should give a female power to teach and baptize?' (*de Bapt.* 16). Yet in recent years Thecla has won a place in the academic and popular imagination as a counter-voice to the canonical (New Testament) injunction of 1 Timothy, 'I permit no woman to teach or to have authority over men' (2.12); perhaps this was her original role, at least within the *Acts of Paul*, for, although outside the New Testament, Thecla belongs within the far from harmonious voices of the post-Pauline legacy and of early Christian experience. Certainly, in recent writing she has become a symbolic source from the past in a contemporary search for Christian identity.[14]

---

[14] For example, F. Cardman, 'Women, Ministry, and Church Order in Early Christianity', in R. S. Kraemer and M. R. d'Angelou, eds., *Women and Christian Origins* (Oxford University Press: New York, 1999) 300–29.

Each point of this first journey of exploration could have been illustrated at length: the diversity of belief, organization and practice which hides both behind and beyond this text; the uses and experiences of these texts which disrupt our conception of them; the exercise of power and the strategies of exclusion which may seek to silence the alternative voices; the way the texts both shape and are shaped by the dynamic of identity; the dynamic of the text which refutes any, now unfashionable, essentialist ideas of identity, unchanging over time and space; and so, as ever, the tension in which we as 'professors' are all involved between affirmation and challenge.

These will direct us towards our second journey; and, if in the first the ancient texts pointed us to contemporary dilemmas, in this second one, modern debates will lead us towards earlier quandaries. For, in particular over the last century, the history of biblical scholarship has been a history of tension if not of conflict between professor *qua* confessor and professor *qua* teacher; it has also been a history of changing configurations between the New Testament and early Christian identity. The development of the historical-critical method which has dominated the scholarship of much of the twentieth century was to a large extent the wresting of the Bible out of the grip of the controls of church doctrine, tradition, or other needs. The affirmation of the integrity of the text in its 'otherness', the prioritizing of the question 'What did it mean in its context?', the recognition of the text and of its development as historical phenomena, these provide the ground on which a Chair in New Testament stands. The determination to preserve that 'otherness' has engendered a radical criticism more rigorous than in any other ancillary discipline, prompting charges of scepticism both from believers and from teachers whose focal texts lie elsewhere in the ancient world. Understanding 'what it meant' has demanded – even if sometimes regrettably at second hand – journeying into other territory: both classical and semitic languages; the world of the Graeco-Roman Mediterranean; Judaism of the Second-Temple and early rabbinic periods; and, more recently, the social sciences, classical rhetoric, literary theory . . . The training of the historical critic, when properly pursued, is second to none, and for that I am grateful to my teachers. Too often those who have rejected it as a method have been fleeing from its intellectual demands. I suspect that even if we become convinced that the pursuit of objectivity is chasing after a mirage, it may save all of us from the more dangerous pursuit of our own shadows. But that is also to anticipate.

So, for example, to understand Paul's first letter to Corinth, with its convoluted arguments about food sacrificed to idols, is to ask about the nature of the meat sold in the market-place of the Graeco-Roman city, and the social function of both temples and meals. The interpretation of Paul's letter to the Romans, according to some, may be determined by the Emperor Claudius's expulsion from Rome of Jewish-Christians in 49 CE which would have effectively re-shaped the identity of the Christian community there; but what are we to do if, as some would argue, the expulsion was in 41 CE and was provoked only by the partisans of a Jewish slave, Chrestus? How are New Testament specialists to adjudicate between our sources for that event, Suetonius, Orosius and Cassius Dio?[15] Again, was there indeed a 'benediction' devised by an authoritative meeting of the new Jewish establishment in the mid-90s directed against Christians or at least Christians of Jewish descent – the so-called *birkath-hamminim* or heretic benediction? Can this, as commonly argued, explain the hostility against 'the Jews' in the Fourth Gospel as but a reaction to the hostility already experienced? Is it this, lying outside the pages and remit of the New Testament, which was in fact most decisive for the formation of the identity of one group whose face we seek to uncover through its pages? Yet how are New Testament specialists to assess the peculiar character of our Jewish sources for the period, and the various hypotheses regarding the nature of Jewish organization and control in Israel-Palestine as well as in the Diaspora in the decades following the destruction of the Temple in 70 CE.[16]

To profess the New Testament is, then, to profess its incompleteness, and our inadequacy: its incompleteness to tell us all there is to be told about the 'early Christians'; our inadequacy to hear the full story without

[15] On 1 Corinthians see G. Theissen, *The Social Setting of Pauline Christianity* (ET T&T Clark: Edinburgh, 1982). Most commentaries on Romans discuss the relevance of the expulsion of Jews by Claudius; for the issues see R. Brändle and E. Stegemann, 'The Formation of the First "Christian Congregations" in Rome in the Context of Jewish Congregations', in K. Donfried and P. Richardson, eds., *Judaism and Christianity in First-Century Rome* (Eerdmans: Grand Rapids, Mich., 1998) 117–27, and a counter-argument by H. D. Slingerland, *Claudian Policymaking and Early Repression of Judaism at Rome* (S. Florida Studies in the History of Judaism 160, Scholars Press: Atlanta, 1997).

[16] The classic presentation of the argument is in J. L. Martyn, *History and Theology in the Fourth Gospel* (2nd edn Abingdon: Nashville, 1979 [1968]); for the problems see R. Kimelman, '*Birkat Ha Minim* and the Lack of Evidence for an Anti-Christian Jewish Prayer in Late Antiquity', in E. P. Sanders, A. L. Baumgarten and A. Mendelson, eds., *Jewish and Christian Self-Definition* II, *Aspects of Judaism in the Graeco-Roman Period* (SCM Press: London, 1981) 226–44. See above, pp. 25–6.

the aid of others. It is also to acknowledge that the boundaries around the discipline are not high fences to keep us in and others out, but are points of trade and negotiation. The same is also true of identity; boundedness and the maintenance of boundaries are often seen as the *sine qua non* of identity. Yet whatever the rhetoric of the fixity and givenness of boundaries, they are in practice both unstable and negotiable. And what we have just explored demonstrates this all too clearly for early Christian identity. For 'the early Christians' – who are not, as we have noted, 'Christians' – belong not just in the pages of the 'New Testament', but in those other economic, political, social and religious worlds. Yet, realization of this has not been without its tensions.

To consider this we can turn once again to the discovery of papyri in the sand of Egypt, which in their very ordinariness – most are not as dramatic as the Nag Hammadi or Bodmer codices – fed a fascination with the *realia* of life which breathed new life into historical and social analysis. Publication of papyri letters in their mundane triviality gave a sharp jolt to the study of the various letters of the New Testament – witnessed in the 1960s by the number of North American PhD theses from divinity departments on epistolographical conventions. Suddenly the New Testament Epistles – so called still in liturgical contexts to indicate 'otherness' – became the Pauline, Petrine or Johannine letters, no longer strange specimens in the New Testament zoo, but at home in the forest of Graeco-Roman social life.[17] But, of course, not even all sixty-four volumes of Oxyrrhynchi papyri will provide a total explanatory commentary on the dense argument of the sixteen chapters of Paul's letter to the Romans.

Similarly, when we turn to Gospel research, are the Gospels best understood in the light of Graeco-Roman literary genres such as the *bios*, or are they without any convincing parallel? Is the term 'Gospel'/ *euangelion* with which Mark, whether consciously or not, fatefully prefaces his 'Gospel', drawn from the world of the Roman imperial cult, or is it a new creation, perhaps even a Pauline creation, modelled on Paul's own personal convictions which were rooted in his deepest experience of the meaning of Isaiah 52, 'How beautiful are the feet of those who gospel good things' (Isa. 52.7: Rom. 10.15)?[18] In these examples

---

[17] See S. K. Stowers, *Letter Writing in Greco-Roman Antiquity* (Westminster Press: Philadelphia, 1986).
[18] See G. N. Stanton, *The Gospels and Jesus* (Oxford University Press: Oxford, 1989) 14–33.

I am referring, as specialists will well know, to topics of deeply held conviction and warm debate. The issues are not merely technical ones of vocabulary, literary form or genre. They have become touchstones of the debate how far early Christian identity participated in that of the wider society, how far it was something new, different, revelatory – even, some would still say, unique.

Or yet another example: initially, in the new enthusiasm for 'women's studies', the early Christian, better Jesus', attitude to women was presented as different, radical, liberated and liberationary. The Jewish male might thank God daily that he was not created a woman; Aristotle might label 'woman' a 'misbegotten male', but 'in Christ there is not male and female' (Gal. 3.28). We have moved on from such utopian naivety, and, wherever we are now headed, it has now become clear that Christian women have to be seen alongside their Jewish and pagan contemporaries, no less imperfectly glimpsed through the distorting prism of male rhetoric and imagined potential; that the tangled web of early Christian attitudes to sexuality and to asceticism must be understood within, if also against, the social dynamic of Roman society.[19]

Yet this problem – namely, are we to articulate early Christian identity as part of its Graeco-Roman context or as counter to and unique within that society? – is again no new problem, but one repeated countless times within early Christian literature itself. Tertullian again: 'We live with you, the same food, clothing, education, necessities of life. We are not Brahmans or Indian naked sages, woodland-folk or exiles from life' (*Apol.* 42.1); and yet elsewhere he avers, 'We are trained by God to castigate and to castrate the world'. It is, of course, not insignificant that the first, 'open-doors', quotation comes from Tertullian's *Apology*, ostensibly directed to outsiders, the second, more isolationist, one from a work for insiders – and not just any insiders. It will – although, perhaps only at first glance – appear startlingly anomolous that Tertullian's exhortation to 'castrate the world' comes from his work *On the Apparel of Women* (II.9.8), and is illustrated by, among other things, the evils of dyeing one's hair with saffron. For women play a rhetorically loaded symbolic role in these ambiguities in the discourse of Christian identity within 'the world' – and hair embodies this (still) and the ever-present threat of sexuality in a particular way – with well-known New Testament

[19] See already P. Brown, *The Body and Society: Men, Women, and Sexual Renunciation in Early Christianity* (Columbia University Press: New York, 1988).

roots. 1 Peter addresses its readers as aliens and exiles (1.1; 2.11), apparently not 'at home' in the world; at the same time it exhorts slaves to be subject to their masters, wives to their husbands – encouragement at which few masters or husbands 'in the world' would cavil. 1 Peter here echoes a tradition of the proper binary relations of subordination and superordination which had a long history in Greek political thought concerning the ordering of household and the state; so is this a compromise with society, undermining the 'unique' 'Christian' ethos of differentiation ('In Christ there is neither . . .')? Or is it an attempt to create room for those who necessarily remained 'in the world' to be separate from it?[20] 1 Peter anticipates and compounds the dilemma – the subordination of a woman to her husband, congenial to society's expectations, is surely visible; her holiness which he urges – her 'otherness', separation – is to be marked not by the outward braiding of hair but by the inner meekness of spirit (3.3–4). Where, we might ask, would be the distinguishing symbols of her identity? Thecla, however, whom we discussed earlier, adopts a more provocative and visible stance, for to pursue her teaching career she not only abandons fiancé, but also proposes to cut off her hair and dons male clothing (*Act.Paul.* 25, 40–41). And yet Thecla inhabits a literary genre, the apocryphal Acts (here the *Acts of Paul*), which shares much with the newly emerging Hellenistic romances of the day – part of a trend in Graeco-Roman culture.

Yet these problems of belonging and not belonging, of visibility and invisibility, are always part of the construction and maintenance of identity. How are both continuity and differentness to be configured or articulated – continuity and differentness through the passage of time but also in relationship with those outside, the 'other' who in reality is not simply 'other'. This problem was not, of course, new with or peculiar to early Christianity. Particularly but not only in the Diaspora, Jewish communities had long had to struggle with the same dilemmas of continuity and difference. Inspired in particular by pagan denigration of Jewish practice, much modern scholarship has tended to focus on the differentness, on separation, on the boundaries of the Jewish communities and their markers – forgetting that, as I have indicated, boundaries are not merely nor primarily means of exclusion. More recent study has not only stressed the contingency and negotiability of those boundaries, but also sought to explore the continuities – to

---

[20] See above, p. 182.

explore the Jews within, as part of and so as evidence for, the wider society.[21]

The early 'Christians' inherited as part of their 'Jewishness' this ambivalence, but by forswearing the differentiation of sabbath, male circumcision and dietary rules, they compounded it. Yet the boundaries between them and their Jewish peers were even more complex; given time we could explore how the Christian polemic against the Jews seeks to construct an identity of separation or alienation, to build impermeable boundaries, but how there is much, even within the pages of polemic, which denies that, witnessing to intersecting lives, a shared identity of monotheistic worship, ethical code and textual interpretation.[22] And, also given time, ironically we could return to historical-critical scholarship's judgement on Athanasius's attempt to relegate discord to the purveyors of other, safely excluded texts; and here we would find the New Testament not standing over against the discordant voices of the church, early or not so early, meting judgement against them, but itself witnessing to and participating in their discord. It does not enshrine some pure or core identity understood in now unfashionably essentialist terms; rather it preserves for us a story of convictions and life-styles which at the time appeared and perhaps still appear incompatible with each other. Where we thought to find boundaries, they resist our drawing them, and where we thought to find cohesion we find divisions.

Instead, this final stage of our exploration will be guided by what has seemed like a major wind-change in New Testament scholarship. I need not repeat here the wider setting – the evidence for the seeming collapse of New Testament Studies from unity into multiplicity; the discordant voices, conflicting methods, dissipated goals, no longer a shared journey towards a common understanding. The failure to agree 'what it meant', the ease with which we can see how the preconceptions of those with whom we disagree have clouded their judgement, the disenchantment in the search for the past behind the text, the return to the textuality of the text, disputes about whether meaning lies in text or in reader, an epistemology which recognizes the social location and construction of all knowledge and so can no longer speak of absolutes – all this is a well-known story and not one followed by New Testament Studies

---

[21] See M. Goodman, 'Jews, Greeks, and Romans', in idem, ed., *Jews in a Graeco-Roman World* (Clarendon Press: Oxford, 1998) 3–14.
[22] J. M. Lieu, *Image and Reality: The Jews in the World of the Christians in the Second Century* (T&T Clark: Edinburgh, 1996).

alone.[23] Within my context, the historical-critical approach may have provoked severe hermeneutical challenges particularly when we recognize the religious claims of this text, both inherent and those ascribed by its preservation, but the nature of the challenges to historical analysis and imagination appeared to be more easily defined and perhaps more easily met. Yet this has always been a mirage: the 'observations' within this essay have signalled what we have all come to know – the many threads of preconception, commitment, rhetoric and the exercise of power which are woven into the text – both the text created by the scholar alone or in community and the text with which we deal, our 'primary' or 'secondary' sources.

In coming to know that, and our own implication in it, we have come to be much more aware of the uses of the past, particularly of and as constructed by this text (*viz.* the Old and New Testaments), and its interpretation. It is this which has inspired, as it must, the current often vitriolic debate about whether there can be outside of the text a 'history of Israel', never mind the relationship of such a construct with any subsequent geographical or national entity. Similarly inspired and necessary are the richly varied and often discordant voices of feminist analysis which unite at least to exclude naive repetitions of the role of women 'in' Israel, in the Old Testament, in the New Testament, in the early church, and in Judaism, as if these could be both descriptive and prescriptive. So also the urgent task of addressing the problem of anti-Judaism/anti-Semitism in the New Testament as well as its *Wirkungsgeschichte*, its unfolding in the history not only of the church but of all those societies where the church has spread; all these have, necessarily, developed, particularly as we come to recognize that the history of reception and of interpretation and application is implicated in the 'meaning of the text'.[24] It is not just that all interpretation is positional or perspectival but that all interpretation is also responsible. We who profess the New Testament are not alone; those concerned with Australian history, who must address the questions, 'when does

[23] For the problems posed by contemporary pluralism see U. Luz, 'Kann die Bibel heute noch grudlage für die Kirche sein?' *NTS* 44 (1998) 317–39.

[24] On the problem of 'Israel' see above n. 7; the bibliography on the role of women is extensive, but see Kraemer and d'Angelou, eds., *Women and Christian Origins* for early Christianity; on anti-Judaism and the *Wirkungsgeschichte* see J. M. Lieu, 'Anti-Judaism in the Fourth Gospel: Explanation and Hermeneutics', in R. Bieringer, D. Pollefeyt and F. Vandecasteele-Vanneuville, eds., *Anti-Judaism and the Fourth Gospel* (Van Gorcum: Assen, 2001) 126–43.

this history begin?'; 'How do we tell the story of "settlement"?', and 'Whose history is it?', know that the task is necessarily a 'political' one through which existing power relations may be reinscribed or challenged, even given the opportunity for re-configuration. Within this discipline, 'political', 'a political task', here means 'theological'.

With this argument we have again reverted to identity. For identity is to do with 'the invention of tradition',[25] the discovery of a past for the sake of the present. It is, as the latter half of the twentieth century has demonstrated, a dangerous activity. As indicated in the opening paragraph, even while scholarly analysis has come to recognize such 'memory' as invention or construction, in post-war and post-colonial history it has in case after case become reified, often couched in supra-historical, mythopoetic terms, albeit with appeal to (a supposed) historical verification. 'Old' identities have been rediscovered, often enshrined – sanctified – by the remembered acts of violence and endurance in un-examined continuity between past and present. In her disturbing book, *The Curse of Cain*, Regina Schwartz has explored what she calls 'the violent legacy of monotheism', the way that within the biblical tradition itself as well as in its influence on later theories of nationalism, a collective identity is constructed by the negation of or by violence to 'the other'; yet she also shows how there are within the biblical tradition traces of alternative models which recognize the permeability of boundaries, the fragility of reified concepts of exclusion, the rejection of the denial of the other, the potential for self-criticism – all the seeds of subversion of the dominating voice.[26] And this attuning to the seeds of self-subversion is again familiar to many feminist scholars, often alone keeping them within the community, particularly of ecclesiastically-shaped biblical scholarship. More – our rediscovery of the religious literary character of this text has engendered other ways of reading; the midrashic interpretation of Tanak, the Hebrew Bible, perhaps contemporary with the birth of the New Testament, already knew that the gaps in the narrative may be as important as what is there on the page, for they open the text to continually new questions, new responses.[27] In this

---

[25] E. Hobsbawm and T. Ranger, eds., *The Invention of Tradition* (Cambridge University Press: Cambridge, 1983).

[26] R. Schwartz, *The Curse of Cain: The Violent Legacy of Monotheism* (University of Chicago Press: Chicago, 1997).

[27] See D. Boyarin, *Intertextuality and the Reading of Midrash* (Indiana University Press: Bloomington, 1990).

experience of the biblical text's resistance of the control of those who seek to claim possession of it may we perhaps understand the meaning of the doctrine of the Holy Spirit's work within the text and its interpretation?

We have traced a story in this essay, of unresolved ambiguities, of porous and shifting boundaries, of the dangers of exclusion and the dangerous potential even of this text if it is treated as closed and not open, but most of all of a multiplicity of voices, some of which have been marginalized or silenced in the telling. As a biblical and especially a New Testament scholar, a scholar of early Christianity, I am under multiple obligation to attend to this story. For even if the doctrine of incarnation as later formulated is but one among a number of potential models within the New Testament, it demands that we must exercise particular vigilance against the inclination to submerge the New Testament's contingency in mythopoesis. If the danger of all identity-construction is its tendency to 'demonize' the other, a tendency the Christian tradition has not avoided, then the importance of the often apparent chaos of the study of early Christianity is its demonstration of the shifting identity of the other, now you, now me.

Predicated upon an illusion, and intent upon exposing it as such, the illusion of something that is bounded, complete, self-sufficient, univocal, authoritative, the study of the New Testament carries a very particular obligation to and challenge to Theology and Religious Studies, to the University, and to society.

13

'I am a Christian': Martyrdom and the Beginning of 'Christian' Identity*

> What is your name?
> My first and most distinctive name is Christian, but if
> you seek that in the world, Carpus.[1]

So, the soon-to be-martyr at Pergamum, ostensibly in the late second century.[2]

The cameo of interrogator and victim, the former demanding explanation, conformity, concession, the latter responding only 'I am a Christian', is a familiar one from early Christian martyr literature.[3] If for the historian it embodies the debate concerning the charges brought against Christians – obstinacy (*contumacia*), shameful acts (*flagitia*), or *merely* 'the name'[4] – it no less sets the martyrs and the memorializing of their deaths at the centre of the construction of Christian identity. Martyrdom and identity are in many ways cross-referential terms: to be willing to die for a cause is to acknowledge that it is determinative of one's being, the 'here' where 'I stand', paradigmatically even if now no longer exclusively conceived of in religious or quasi-religious terms.[5]

---

* Invited general lecture given at the Society of Biblical Literature Annual Meeting, Boston, 1999.

[1] *The Martyrdom of Carpus, Papylus, and Agathonice*, 2–3, in H. Musurillo, ed., *The Acts of the Christian Martyrs* (OECT, Clarendon Press: Oxford, 1972) xv–xvi; 22–37.

[2] Eusebius sets this martyrdom in the time of Marcus Aurelius; T. D. Barnes, 'Pre-Decian *Acta Martyrum*', *JTS* 19 (1968) 509–31 considers the Greek recension, in which this exchange occurs, earlier than the Latin, and tentatively dates it to the third century.

[3] *Mart.Poly.* 10.1; 12; Eusebius, *H.E.* V.1.19, 20, 26, 50; *Pass.Perpetua* 2; *Pass.Scill.* 9–13; cf. Justin, *Apol.* 4.5, 7; Tertullian, *Apol.* 2.

[4] For the problem of charges see the classic debate reprinted in M. I. Finley, ed., *Studies in Ancient Society* (Routledge & Kegan Paul: London, 1974) between G. M. de Ste Croix, 'Why were the Early Christians Persecuted?' (210–49) and 'Why were the Early Christians Persecuted? A Rejoinder' (256–62), and A. N. Sherwin-White, 'Why were the Early Christians Persecuted? An Amendment' (250–5); see also T. D. Barnes, 'Legislation against the Christians', *JRS* 58 (1968) 32–50.

[5] As witnessed by the changing definitions of 'martyr' in English dictionaries. Thus B. Anderson, *Imagined Communities: Reflections on the Origins and Spread of Nationalism* (Verso: London, 1991 [1983]) 10 sees nations as something to die for, and recognizes this as symptomatic of the religious roots of many aspects of nationalism.

And, out of the struggle of the few a collective memory can be shaped that will continue to inspire a culture of resistance, with ever new potential applications. Tertullian famously described 'the blood of the martyrs [as] seed' (*Apol.* 50), the source of the church's growth as well as the true carrier of its genetic stamp, and subsequent scholars have agreed that, paradoxically, it was the persecutions which ensured the growth and the survival of the church. Outsiders too remarked, albeit not always as sympathetically, on the Christians' readiness to die; Marcus Aurelius, no less famously, derided the wilful obstinacy on which it was based (*Medit.* 11.3), while for Galen it was a matter of daily experience.[6]

Such comments, at least in popular format, can hardly have been unknown to the early Christians, and like any ascription of identity by others would have been both internalized and transformed in the process – as indeed was the epithet 'Christian', probably initially a term of denigration and abuse, and yet adopted and inverted, redefined to become a mark of honour (1 Peter 4.15–16; cf. Ignatius, *Rom.* 3.2).[7] Thus Apologists not only defended Christians against the charges brought against them, but also affirmed and explained why 'they all disregard the world and disdain death' (*ad. Diog.* 1); their readiness to suffer could thus become a testimony to their conviction, and a provocation for others to be struck by how 'fearless they were in the face of death and all the other things considered terrifying' (Justin, *II Apol.* 12.1).

Yet it is the textualizing and memorializing of the trials, the often extended suffering, and the deaths of believers which becomes determinative not only of the idea of 'the martyr' and martyrdom, but also of what it is to be among those who can say, 'I am a Christian'. The idea of Christian martyrdom is inseparable from the so-called *Acts of Martyrs*, so that the still contested question of the conceptual origins of the former can hardly be separated from that of the literary sources of the latter.[8]

---

[6] Galen in R. Walzer, *Galen on Jews and Christians* (Oxford University Press: Oxford, 1948) 15.

[7] For this view see H. Mattingley, 'The Origin of the name *Christiani*', *JTS* 9 (1958) 26–37; D.van Damme, 'ΜΑΡΤΥΣ – ΧΡΙΣΤΙΑΝΟΣ: Überlegungen zur ursprünglichen Bedeutung des altkirchlichen Märtyretitels', *Freiburger Zeitschrift für Philosophie und Theologie* 23 (1976) 286–303; the alternative view, that the label was initiated by the Christians themselves, is taken by E. Bickermann, 'The Name of the Christians', *HTR* 42 (1949) 109–24.

[8] On the origins of the idea of the 'martyr' see T. Baumeister, *Die Anfänge der Theologie des Martyriums* (Münsterische Beiträge zur Theologie 45, Aschendorff: Münster, 1980); W. H. C. Frend, *Martyrdom and Persecution in the Early Church* (Blackwell: Oxford, 1965).

The question of origins is of less importance here than that of how these *Acts* create a world in which those who go to their deaths are not victims but the central actors in a drama through which a new way of understanding is created and maintained. Yet within this drama the determinative moment is not the death, however extended or graphic, nor even the preceding torture; rather it is the declaration χριστιανός εἰμι, *Christiana sum*, although this is no less the moment the choice is made for death; the individual identity of Christian belongs to the martyr.[9] It is, moreover, emphatically a public moment, and a public identity.[10]

Should we then see the martyr's affirmation as not merely descriptive but as in some sense performative? Does the 'I am', the 'εἰμι', *sum*, itself constitute the speaker as 'Christian', the present tense expressing both intention and achievement?[11] We might think again of Ignatius as he anticipates his death, 'Now I am beginning to be a disciple' (*Rom.* 5.3). In one way this is inevitably the case, for it is when confronted with the choice of confession or denial that the true commitment for or against identity is made, and so, implicitly, until that moment there is only potential. Those who 'fail' have miscarried or failed to attain their birth (Eusebius, *H.E.* V.1.11; cf. 45), whereas others only here achieve their true identity. Thus it becomes a *topos* repeated again and again that bystanders – at Lyons and Vienne, a certain Vettius Epagathos and later Alexander from Phrygia (*H.E.* V.1.9–10; 49–51), at Rome Lucius and another unnamed (Justin, *II Apol.* 2) – only declare, perhaps discover, 'I am a Christian' at the moment of judgement itself.[12] The fortuitously named Agathonike sees in Carpus's death a 'call from heaven'; she throws

---

[9] Thus J. Perkins, *The Suffering Self: Pain and Narrative Representation in the Early Christian Era* (Routledge: London, 1995) 112 calls the *Pass.Perpet.* 'a narrative of Christian self-realization'.

[10] Cf. *Mart.Poly.* 12.2 where Polycarp's reported confession incurs the wrath of 'the entire mass of Gentiles and Jews living in Smyrna'; on this see J. M. Lieu, *Image and Reality: The Jews in the World of the Christians in the Second Century* (T&T Clark: Edinburgh, 1996) 61–2.

[11] It has to be admitted that this is not consistent: in the long version of the *Acts of Justin* Hierax uses past, present and future tense – 'I have been, I am, I shall be Christian' (3.3– 5), although Musurillo adds a footnote 'A melodramatic outburst quite unique in the *acta martyrum*' (p. 57, n. 18). In the middle recension Hierax still says, 'I was a Christian and I shall be' (4.5), and in the short recension, merely, 'I have been a Christian from of old' (4.5).

[12] Clement of Alexandria, *Strom.* IV.9.1f. (a reference I owe to A. J. Droge and J. D. Tabor, *A Noble Death: Suicide and Martyrdom among Christians and Jews in Antiquity* (Harper: San Fransisco, 1992) 142) affirms this possibility.

herself upon the stake and cries ἐγὼ δὲ ἐφ' ὃ πάρειμι. 'That for which I am here!' The converting power of Christian identity is there embodied – a *topos*, incidentally, which is shared with some rabbinic accounts, and so illustrates the patterns of continuity and discontinuity which constitute a thread through this exploration.[13] Moreover, this self-chosen identity is effective: 'Certainly, if I so wish, I am a Christian', says Tertullian, 'Then indeed you may condemn me, if I wish to be condemned; since, then, that which you are able to do against me, you are not able to do, unless I wish, what you are able to do belongs to my will, not to your power' (*Apol.* 49.5).[14]

Yet there is another side to this power of choice – so Perpetua says to her father: 'I cannot say that I am anything other than what I am, a Christian' (*Pass.Perpet.* 3.2). Perpetua's baptism only comes after this encounter (3.5), while Polycarp claims to have served Christ for eighty-six years already (*Mart.Poly.* 9.3), but for both of them the constitutive moment is the moment of martyrological confession: indeed martyrdom becomes not merely 'a second baptism' as for Tertullian and Perpetua (Tertullian, *de Bapt.* 1.6.1; *Pass.Perpet.* 18.3; 21.2), but for some the only 'baptism' they will know.[15]

To explore the potency of this declaration we need to refer back to our opening dialogue; there the name 'Christian' is primary, that 'in the world', 'Carpus', given only as a concession to the interrogator. Similarly, at Lyons the Latin-speaking Sanctus replies '*Christianus*' 'instead of name and instead of city and instead of race and instead of everything else' (Eusebius, *H.E.* V.1.20–21).[16] Perpetua's insistence to her father on this name can also be seen as a deliberate rejection of any other name, not least that he gave her.[17] The subversive implications in this are manifested by the response of those who hear: Perpetua's

---

[13] *Mart.Carp.* (Greek rec.) 42–4. H. Workman, *Persecution in the Early Church* (Epworth: London, 1960 [1906]) 152 speaks of such events as guaranteed by the 'records too numerous to be later inventions'. For the theme of identification with the martyr at the moment of death in rabbinic traditions see *bTaan.* 29a; *bAbZ.* 18a–b.

[14] *Certe, si velim, Christianus sum. Tunc ergo me damnabis, si damnari velim; cum vero quod in me potes, nisi velim, non potes, iam meae voluntatis est quod potes, non tuae potestatis.*

[15] Cf. Thecla, who baptizes herself by leaping into the pool of seals (*Acta Pauli* 34), and the bystanders referred to above.

[16] In the middle recension of *Mart.Iust.*, Hierax, when asked as to his parents, replies, 'Our true father is Christ, and faith in him, mother' (4.8).

[17] See P. C. Miller, *Dreams in Late Antiquity: Studies in the Imaginations of a Culture* (Princeton University Press: Princeton, 1994) 167.

father comes near to attacking his daughter and gouging out her eyes, while Sanctus is rewarded by the renewed and exhaustive efforts of the torturers. 'Christian' has thus become not merely a statement of allegiance, comparable to other patterns of allegiance, and possibly even compatible with some; it does not function as one among a number of, or even within a hierarchy of, identities, in the way that we have come to think of most experience and construction of identity. 'Christian' serves as a total and ultimate, an exclusive act of definition and so of redefinition;[18] it affirms a new, all-encompassing, non-negotiable, and even non-communicable identity. Small wonder that the representatives of the state react with such baffled frustration: 'Who is the God of the Christians?', asks the governor at Lyons; 'If you are worthy, you shall know', obfuscates the aged Potheinos (*H.E.* V.1.31). When the proconsul Saturninus decrees that the six Scillitan martyrs had 'persevered in their obstinacy' (*Pass.Scill.* 14), we should not necessarily cite this as evidence that the 'crime' of the Christians was *contumacia*; rather it bespeaks the total lack of communication between the two sides, the incompatible languages or discourses at work.

Martyrdom and 'the other'

Implicit here, of course, is that the claiming of this identity involves the denial of other alternatives. While historically it may be valid to ask whether the persecutions would have been possible without those willing to be martyred,[19] the reverse is self-evidently true: martyrdom pre-supposes persecution. Despite the initiative claimed by at least some of the martyrs in declaring their identity before being charged or challenged, that declaration is only possible or meaningful because of the threat of annihilation that hangs over it. Ignatius again: 'Christianity (*Christianismos*) is not a work of persuasion but it is [one] of greatness when it is hated by the world' (*Rom.* 3.3); it is in opposition that Christianity gains its true identity. So all identity becomes articulated,

---

[18] Somewhat later, Conon, when asked 'Where do you come from and of what race?', engages in a deliberate act of self-renaming in which the story of Jesus replaces any personal family history – 'I am of the city of Nazareth of Galilee and my kinship is with Christ' (*Mart.Conon* IV.1). Thus I would not take this literally, as if Conon belonged to the *desposynoi*; contra R. Bauckham, *Jude and the Relatives of Jesus in the Early Church* (T&T Clark: Edinburgh, 1990) 123–5.

[19] See G. de Ste Croix, 'Why were the Early Christians Persecuted?'.

perhaps for the first time, in face of the 'other', as well as in the face of attempts by the 'other' to deny its existence. Conversely, the uncompromising affirmation of identity constructs the boundary against 'the other': while the manner of Polycarp's death convinces the crowd that 'there was such a difference between the unbelievers and the elect', the terminology used is, of course, not theirs but that of the martyrological perspective (*Mart.Poly.* 16.1).

Here 'the other' is constituted as 'the unbelievers', but the opposition is for the most part much more sharply delineated than this. At Lyons Sanctus is the object of the overwhelming onrush of the wrath of the crowd and of the prefect and the soldiers, while not only the soldiers but even the civic authorities and the whole mob bring Pothinus to the tribunal (Eusebius, *H.E.* V.1.17, 30). In their violent behaviour the crowd make a mockery of their own treatment of the martyrs as barbarians and 'enemies' (*H.E.* V.1.7), while the governor, too, succumbs to fits of rage which in the contemporary discourse of self-control undermine any claims to true statesmanship (*H.E.* V.1.50).[20] Behind the cover of such irrational violence, the actual causes of the conflict, and the, perhaps more authentic, glimpses of a governor seeking as far as possible to deflect those apparently determined on their own death-course (*Mart.Poly.* 9), are more easily forgotten. As the scholarly debate about the causes and the course of persecution reveals, the precise contours of the oppositional alternative are absorbed by the mythopoetic tendencies to which I shall return. Thus, if from the authorities' point of view Christians effectively opposed and sought to undermine the proper structures of state and society, the martyrs side-step any such portrayal: they may recognize God alone as true sovereign but that does not diminish either Polycarp's acknowledgement of the 'authorities and powers ordained by God' nor Speratus's declaration that he has paid tax on everything he has bought (*Mart.Poly.* 10.2; *Pass.Scill.* 6).[21]

Yet when Ignatius speaks of *Christianismos* he implies a different 'other', for elsewhere he deliberately sets this term, probably his own coinage, against 'Judaism' (*Ioudaismos*): 'For Christianity did not commit itself to', or perhaps 'ground its faith (ἐπίστευσεν) in Judaism, but Judaism in Christianity' (*Magn.* 10.3; cf. 8.1; *Philad.* 6.1).

---

[20] In *H.E.* V.1.57 the crowds at Lyons are described as 'wild and barbarous tribes', i.e. as outsiders to the civilization of the Empire. For the uncontrollable wrath of the persecutor as a topos cf. 4 Macc. 8.2; 9.10; 10.17.

[21] For the importance of this in apologetics see Tertullian, *Apol.* 30.1–5; 32.1; 33.1.

Terminologically, Ignatius's denial of any priority for 'Judaism' will not do. *Ioudaismos* appears first, and when it does so it also is in a martyrological context, in 2 Maccabees and then in 4 Maccabees; there too it affirms a positive choice against its negation, traditionally represented as *hellenismos*,[22] although as we all now know, the dynamics, even on the literary not to speak of on the historical and cultural levels, are much more complex.

This could, and perhaps should, supply the provocation to explore the rich continuities and discontinuities between Christian and Jewish self-understanding as articulated through the experience and through the textualization of martyrdom; and our subject will be incomplete without such. But here I can but refer to what I have explored elsewhere in greater detail, and also to Daniel Boyarin's recent studies on 'Martyrdom and the Making of Christianity and Judaism'.[23] As well as the implicit tale told by the continuing interaction between those traditions, there are other hints of the potential for a conflict over martyrological identity: so Justin Martyr refuses the Jewish appeal to Micah 4.6, 'And it shall be that in that day, I shall gather she who is oppressed, and I shall muster she who is thrust out, even whom I have harmed, and I shall make the oppressed one a remnant and the squeezed out a strong nation' (*Dial.* 110.5).[24] Equally telling may be the fact that while the apologists are well aware of the pagan antecedents to martyrdom, and seek to deconstruct them (Justin, *Apol.* 5.3-4; Athenagoras, *Suppl.* 31; Tertullian, *ad Mart.* 4), they are silent about any Jewish precedents, even about the Maccabean tradition, consigning it to the oblivion of silence. It is only later that the three in the fiery furnace of Daniel 3 become witnesses for the Christian cause, as in Jewish sources they do for the Jewish cause.[25] Yet more importantly, we have, particularly in recent years, become accustomed to thinking of

---

[22] ἰουδαισμός: 2 Macc. 2.21; 8.1; 14.38; 4 Macc. 4.26; ἑλληνισμός: 2 Macc. 4.13; cf. also ἀλλοφυλισμός: 2 Macc. 4.13; 6.25 (ἀλλοφυλεῖν: 4 Macc. 18.5). On this see now above, p. 59.

[23] D. Boyarin, 'Martyrdom and the Making of Christianity and Judaism', *JECS* 6 (1998) 577–627; also now, idem, *Dying for God: Martyrdom and the Making of Christianity and Judaism* (Stanford University Press: Stanford, 1999) which appeared too late to be taken into consideration in this essay. See also J. M. Lieu, *Image and Reality*, 57–102.

[24] See above, p. 141. Compare the question asked of the potential convert in *bYeb.* 47a, 'Do you not know that Israel at this time is pained, oppressed, harrassed, and torn, and that afflictions come upon them'?; cf. *Gerim* 1.1.

[25] *Pass.Mont.* 3.4; *Pass.Fruct.* 4.2; *Eccl.Rabb.* 3.20; *Lam.Rabb.* 131.

Christian identity as shaped by its construction of the Jews as the defining 'Other'. It is, then, the more remarkable that the early martyrdom accounts give little support to Justin's (and others') polemical and apologetic claim that Jews are particularly implicated in the persecution of Christians (*Dial.* 110.5; 122.2), a claim too readily believed by past scholars.[26] Even the one apparent exception, the *Martyrdom of Polycarp*, where the Jews do play a role, does not use the martyr's confession and consequential death as a Christian to draw the boundaries which will position the Jew as the 'Other'. To our puzzlement, at this point, the Jew is not the problem, nor yet the non-problem; the problem is not perceived.

Text and audience

Implicit in all I have said so far is that the martyrs as I have been speaking of them, and as they construct Christian identity, are themselves constructs, constructed by the texts which tell their story and by the survival of those texts. If the martyr represents absolute commitment, the embodiment of the ultimate significance of the values she holds, it is as her story is told and retold that it becomes effective for those who share the same values, the same commitment. Imperiously plagiarizing the prologue of 1 John, the author of the *Passio Perpetuae* declares:

> And so now that which we have heard and have touched, we proclaim also to you, brothers and little children, so that you also who took part may recall the glory of the Lord, and you who now learn through hearing may have fellowship with the holy martyrs and through them with our Lord Jesus Christ (*Pass.Perpet.* 1.6).

The martyrs there act as mediators of Christian identity for a new audience, but they do so only through their textualization.

There are in fact multiple audiences for the martyr's confession: first, within the narrative world, the governor and the mob who watch without perception, according to the *Letter of the Churches at Vienne and Lyons* 'magnifying their idols and ascribing to them the punishments of these' (Eusebius, *H.E.* V.1.60); they often become caricatures, the governor

---

[26] On this see J. M. Lieu, 'Accusations of Jewish Persecution in Christian Sources', in G. N. Stanton and G. Stroumsa, eds., *Tolerance and Intolerance in Early Judaism and Christianity* (Cambridge University Press: Cambridge, 1998) 279–98 = pp. 135–50 above. In later martyrdom acts Jews become regular antagonists.

generalized as ὁ ἄρχων, but labelled 'accursed' or 'wicked', the crowd engaging in unbridled violence, hostile and yet also moved to wonder.[27] Next are those who tell the story, who have privileged access, able at the trial of Polycarp to hear the heavenly voice of encouragement (*Mart.Poly.* 9.1), and yet also, as those who watch with impunity, free from the harrassment which befalls other bystanders such as Alexander and Vettius Epagathos; seeing and yet not seen, omniscient and yet implicated.[28] Then, outside that narrative world, the recipients of the letter, the church at Philomelium, or the brethren in Asia and Phrygia – believers, for these accounts are clearly not meant for an outside audience. They watch those who watch, provided by the text with the key to the true meaning of what lies before them; although ostensibly they are invited to affirm or to deny, to choose the latter would be to choose meaninglessness. Then, beyond them other readers, for these texts are self-consciously catholic in their claim: 'all the sojourning churches of the holy and catholic church in every place' is the ultimate address of the *Martyrdom of Polycarp* (Praes.).[29] For those in the outermost circle the confession, 'χριστιανός εἰμι', no longer challenges and subverts their present reality; it provides it with content, and invites them to embrace this new reality. It offers both authentication and challenge, at the same time forging a unity between the scattered observers whose focus is the martyrs and a shared interpretation of their death.

In one sense these concentric circles of witness to the martyr's confession expand outwards and move from the limited and constrained to the universal, the catholic. On the outermost circle of the arena the readers of the text look down to observe both martyr and persecutors, At the same time, the universal is already present at the very hub: while Polycarp included in his prayer, 'all who had ever encountered him, small and great, noble and ignoble, and the whole catholic church throughout the world', those who demanded Polycarp's death were 'the whole crowd of Gentiles and Jews at Smyrna' (*Mart.Poly.* 8.1; 12.2); at Lyons the crowd constituted 'a multitude from all the nations', and Maturus, Sanctus, Blandina and Attalus are not only led out into the

---

[27] On the caricaturing of the crowd see above; on the governor see *Mart.Justin* C 1.1; 5; *Mart.Conon* 6.6.

[28] The narrator's circle also includes those whose determination may be less firm than the narrator hopes.

[29] But in Eusebius, *H.E.* IV.15.1 a number of manuscripts describe the letter as to the sojourning [churches] throughout Pontus (πόντον instead of τόπον).

'public spectacle of the inhumanity of the Gentiles', but even 'become a spectacle to the world' (Eusebius, *H.E.* V.1.37, 40, 47).[30] The opposition played out is a foundational one, 'the wrath of the Gentiles against the saints' (*H.E.* V.1.4); the mob are also archetypically 'the lawless' (ἄνόμοι), again perhaps an inversion of the charges brought against the martyrs (*Mart.Poly.* 9.2; 16; *H.E.*V.1.10, 24): they, as we have seen, are the real barabarians. Beyond and greater than this, at Lyons, the narrative declares, 'the adversary launched in with full strength, already preluding his future coming which shall inevitably be', only to be opposed by 'the grace of God' or by Christ himself (*H.E.* V.1.5–6; cf. 23, 27; cf. *Mart.Poly.* 2.4 – 3.1; 17.1).[31] The conflict in which the martyr engages is of cosmic and eschatological significance, most vividly captured by Perpetua's visions of treading upon the dragon or battling with the 'Egyptian of terrible appearance', which assured her that her fight was 'not with the beasts but with the devil' (*Pass.Perpet.* 4; 10).[32] Thus the trials and death are endowed with a mythopoetic quality which coexists with the contingent and mundane – as exemplified most starkly by the 'dating' of Polycarp's martyrdom 'on the second day of the month Xanthicus according to the Romans 7 days before the Kalends of March on a great sabbath at the 8th hour; arrested under Herod while Philip of Tralles was High Priest and Statius Quadratus governor, and Jesus Christ our Lord reigning for eternity' (*Mart.Poly.* 21). Here, then, the reader can but observe, caught in passivity, dwarfed by the drama played out before her, whose outcome is both held in suspense and then assured. The narrative becomes no longer an account of a conflict in the arena, but itself participates in and ensures the victory of the martyr's cause.[33]

Within these texts the martyr is alone, separated from those who watch and from those who read; yet the martyr also represents. Conon's interrogator tells him, 'You must answer (ἀπολογησάσθαι) on behalf of all the Christians' (*Mart.Conon* 3.1); in Eusebius's version of Polycarp's

---

[30] Cf. Origen, *Exhort. ad Mart.* 18 where angels join the world and men as spectators. However, Perpetua resists the crowd's gaze, *Pass.Perpet.* 18.2; on this as an act of resistance of a gendered role, see Perkins, *Suffering Self,* 112.

[31] Cf. also 19.2 where 'the unjust ruler' is probably the devil, not the governor. Justin, *Apol.* 10.6; 57.1; *Dial.* 131.2 ascribes persecution to the demons (see above, pp. 145–8) but does not set this is in an eschatological framework.

[32] On this theme see F. Dölger, 'Das Kampf mit der Ägypter in der Perpetua-Vision: Das Martyrium als Kampf mit dem Teufel', *Antike und Christentum* 3 (Aschendorff: Münster, 1932) 177–88.

[33] See J. Perkins, *The Suffering Self,* 104–23.

martyrdom, Germanicus's death leads the whole watching crowd to wonder at 'the virtue of the whole race of Christians' (*H.E.* IV.15.6). This represents a dilemma within the martyrdom narratives themselves; are the martyrs to be imitated or not? Polycarp, whose initial flight from Smyrna might cause some embarrassment, apparently 'waited so that he might be betrayed, as indeed was the Lord, so that we too might become imitators of him, looking not only to our own needs but also to those of our neighbour' (*Mart.Poly.* 1.2; cf. 19.1). Polycarp's relationship with the whole church is emphasized at precisely the same time as is his 'uniqueness' (*Mart.Poly.* 1.1; 5.2; 8.1; 16.2; 19.2). Yet the martyr is also separated from the rest: they form a special 'portion' (κλῆρος) (*H.E.* V.1.10, 26, 48), and can claim a discipleship and a degree of imitation of Christ denied to others (*H.E.* V.1.10, 23); they are chosen 'by the Lord' (*H.E.* V.1.27; 2.3; *Mart.Poly.* 20.1); they are 'worthy', particularly, but not only, in contrast to those who fail through fear (*H.E.* V.1.13); for Hermas they alone are entitled to sit on the right (*Vis.* I.1.9–2.2);[34] repeatedly the language of 'fulfilment' is used of them (*H.E.* V.1.11, 13, 15). Most important is the developing tendency to reserve for those who die the title 'martyr', witness (*H.E.* V.2.2–3). The anxiety about those who put themselves forward is inspired not only by their potential failure of the nerve at the supreme test but by this sense that if the number of martyrs is limited, then it is by divine election – the 'divine call' to which Agathonice responded.[35] By contrast, it is those who fail to confess when faced with the challenge who are condemned, not those whom the narrative assumes by its silence continue unscathed to watch and wait. This, then, takes us back to what we have already seen: that the label 'Christian' belongs pre-eminently to the martyrs, to the rest only in a shadowy and derivative sense.

Text and intertextuality

Despite all that leads to the isolating of the martyrs, there are multiple intertextual threads which combine in their depiction. That which we might expect to be most important is perhaps the most ambivalent, the relationship between martyr and Christ. Polycarp's martyrdom is,

---

[34] Cf. Hermas, *Sim.* VIII.3 where the martyrs are distinguished even from those who suffered but did not die.

[35] On the ambivalence towards 'voluntary martyrdom' and the continuities with Plato's distinction about self-death as dependent on responding to the divine call see Droge and Tabor, *The Noble Death*.

notoriously, 'according to the Gospel of Christ' (*Mart.Poly.* 19.1), and this extends to the involvement of a Herod, to the heavenly voice, to treachery by those close to him, and perhaps to the problematic dating of his death – but this, a literary mimesis, is as far as it extends.[36] The *Letter of the Churches of Lyons and Vienne* quotes Phil. 2.6, but only of the refusal by those who though much tortured were yet alive, to claim for themselves the coveted title of 'martyr' (Eusebius, *H.E.* V.2.2). Blandina, spreadeagled on the stake, becomes the means through which those also under torture see 'him who was crucified for them' (*H.E.* V.1.41), but even this hardly amounts to an *imitatio Christi*. Yet beyond the 'biblical canvas' on which the martyrdoms are painted, explicit quotations of or appeals to the Gospel narratives are rare in the Martyr Acts.[37] Although it is often said that Christian martyrdom is in direct continuity with the suffering of Jesus, and of Jesus' call to his disciples to follow, even 'taking up their cross', it is remarkable how little is made of this.[38] Certainly Christ suffers in Sanctus, defeating the adversary, as he also does in Felicitas, but there is little consistent theological development of the potential of such language.[39]

There is a different level of intertextuality with the city within which the narrative is located. Polycarp is not a criminal but one whose πολιτεία has from the beginning been unblemished, while of Vettius Epagathos it can be said that his πολιτεία had reached such a pinnacle as to merit a similar testimony to that given Zechariah in Luke 1.6 (*Mart.Poly.* 17.1; Eusebius, *H.E.* V.1.9). The development of the language of citizenship – and we probably should add here that of 'race'/γένος – in a martyrological context is again familiar from the Maccabean tradition and invites another exploration of the inter-nexus of relationships between these texts.[40] But for the Christian texts it is in

---

[36] See Lieu, *Image and Reality*, 61.
[37] For the 'Biblical canvas' see V. Saxer, *Bible et Hagiographie: Textes et thèmes bibliques dans les actes martyres authentiques des premiers siècles* (P.Lang: Berne, 1986) 16; on the paucity of explicit appeals to the model of Christ, *Bible et Hagiographie*, 221–3; B. Dehandschutter, 'Le Martyre de Polycarpe et le développment de la conception du martyre au deuxième siècle', in E. Livingstone, ed., *Studia Patristica* 17.2 (Blackwell: Oxford, 1982) 659–68.
[38] The call to 'take up the cross' (Matt. 10.38; 16.24; Mark 8.34; Luke 9.23; 14.27) is rarely interpreted of martyrdom: even in Tertullian (*de Idol.* 12.2) it is spiritualized. However, Origen, *Exhort.ad Mart.* 12 does refer to Matt. 16.24 as ἡ κατὰ τὸ εὐαγγέλιον πολιτεία and associates it with living κατὰ χριστιανισμόν.
[39] Felicitas's words are remarkable: 'there will be another in me who suffers for (*pro*) me because I shall also suffer for (*pro*) him' (*Pass.Perpet.* 15.6).
[40] See Lieu, *Image and Reality*, 82–6. I would now be a little more nuanced.

the ambiguity as to where and how this 'citizenship' was exercised that the power of the text is located.[41] More overtly, as often noted, the imagery of the games into which the martyrs are thrust as 'victims' is subverted; they become protagonists, the noble athletes in a contest, deservedly winning the crown or prize (*H.E.* V.1.36; *Mart.Poly.* 17.1); their death is not defeat but victory, both for themselves and as an offering to God. Blandina, untouched by the beasts to which she is exposed, is brought back to prison, 'preserved (τηρουμένη) for another contest (ἀγῶνα), so that she might conquer through yet more exercises (γυμνασμάτα)' (*H.E.* V.1.42).[42] Such adoption of athletic and agonistic imagery is now new: we find it already in the philosophical tradition as also in the Jewish martyrological literature, as well as, with more general reference, in the New Testament – thus exhibiting multiple lines of continuity and discontinuity.[43] Its affirmation and subversion of contemporary values acknowledges and reinterprets the significance of the moment and the perceptions of those who watch.

The third level of intertextuality is the one to which we have repeatedly referred, that with earlier tradition, particularly as shared with the Jewish experience and representation of martyrdom. It is this about which most could be said, which is arguably the most significant, and which nonetheless remains the most elusive – not least because, as we have seen, the texts refuse to acknowledge it. The continuities of literary and theological narrative and interpretative *topoi* have often been demonstrated, but the differences are no less significant, and these perhaps are too easily obscured when, as so often, the Jewish sources have been viewed through the terminological and ideological spectacles of Christian martyrology.[44] Razi's determined suicide contrasts markedly

---

[41] The relationship with C. Tiberius Polycharmos at Stobi in *CIJ* 694 who πολιτευσάμενος κατὰ ἰουδαισμόν is not straightforward; see M. Hengel, 'Die Synagogeinschrift von Stobi' *ZNW* 57 (1966) 145–83; T. Rajak, 'Jews and Christians as Groups in a Pagan World', in J. Neusner and E. Frerichs, eds., '*To See Ourselves as Others See Us'. Christians, Jews, 'Others' in Late Antiquity* (Scholars Press: Chico, 1985) 247–62.

[42] Musurillo wrongly translates ἀγῶνα as 'ordeal', but it is positive – contest.

[43] See Z. Stewart, 'Greek Crowns and Christian Martyrs', in E. Lucchesi and H. D. Saffrey, eds., *Antiquité Païenne et Chrétienne: Mémorial A. J. Festugière* (Cramer: Geneva, 1984) 119–24; R. Merkelbach, 'Der griechische Wortschatz und die Christen', *ZPE* 18 (1975) 101–48.

[44] On the 'shared subculture' see D. Boyarin, 'Martyrdom'; also J. W. van Henten, 'Zum Einfluss jüdischer Martyrien auf die Literatur des frühen Christentums, II. Die apostolischen Väter', *ANRW* II.27.1 (1993) 700–23; on the need to analyse the Jewish sources in their own distinctive terms see T. Rajak, 'Dying for the Law: The Martyr's

with the 'Christian' martyrs: he repeatedly and finally successfully seeks his own death in order to avoid arrest, 'wishing to die nobly rather than be made subject to the sinful, and to be disgracefully abused of his own nobility' (2 Macc. 14.42); the charge brought against him is *ioudaismos*, but his death is no different from that of Eleazar who seeks to show 'how to die well for the revered and holy laws' (2 Macc. 6.28) – and that phrase alone could provoke an extended discussion of the very different conceptions which underlie these Jewish and the Christian martyrological accounts. Through a range of different 'Jewish' texts the language of transgression or exchange of the law/s *versus* steadfastness to them acts as a common thread and interpretative framework.[45] Perhaps most significantly, it is within the Jewish accounts that the language of national and citizen identity develops; Jan Willem van Henten has spoken of the 'Maccabean martyrs as saviours of the Jewish people', and whatever we feel about the term 'saviours', the intensification of the language of *ethnos, genos, politeia, Ioudaioi, patrioi nomoi* provides the key to these writings;[46] such language signals the synergy of political conceptions with the theological power of martyrdom, as well as being symptomatic of their double attitude to Greek values.[47] Similar language is not absent from the Christian accounts, and contributes to our theme – Germanicus's death at Smyrna leads the crowd to marvel at 'the nobility of the God-loving and God-fearing race of the Christians', while Polycarp has been characterized by his *agathe politeia* even before his martyrdom (*Mart.Poly.* 3.2; 13.1; cf. Eusebius, *H.E.* V.1.9) – but it does not carry the political resonances of its use in 2 Maccabees: for the Christians it is perhaps both their problem and their virtue that they have no *patrioi*

Portrait in Jewish-Greek Literature', in M. J. Edwards and S. Swain, eds., *Portraits: Biographical Representation in the Greek and Latin Literature of the Roman Empire* (Clarendon Press: Oxford, 1997) 39–67.

[45] 1 Macc. 2. 37; 2 Macc. 6; 7.2; 4 Macc. 5. 22–38; Josephus, *B.J.* I.7.5 [150–51]; *c.Apion.* II.32 [233–35]; Philo, *Leg.* 32 [233–36]. Thus J. W. van Henten is probably right to say 'Eleasar kann sein Judentum nur durch das Martyrium bewahren' ('Das jüdische Selbstverständnis', 139).

[46] J. W. van Henten, *The Maccabean Martyrs as Saviours of the Jewish people, A Study of 2 and 4 Maccabees* (Leiden: Brill, 1997).

[47] On the coalescence of theological and political conceptions see van Henten, *Maccabean Martyrs*; H. Kippenberg, 'Die jüdische Überlieferungen als "patrioi nomoi"', in R. Faber and R. Schlesier, eds., *Die Restauration der Götter: Antike Religion und Neo-Paganismus* (Königshausen & Neumann: Würzburg, 1986) 45–60. On the use and transformation of aspects of Greek culture see M. Himmelfarb, 'Judaism and Hellenism in 2 Maccabees', *Poetics Today* 19 (1998) 19–40.

nomoi for which to die. There is no equivalent to the claim of 4 Macc.
1.11 that 'their native land was purified through them'. Instead – and
remember we are speaking not of absolute contrasts but of different
patterns – the Christian martyr is always an individual even when part
of a group, and the single confession 'χριστιανή εἰμι' *Christianus sum*
overshadows, even obliterates, any specific act of resistance.[48] Neither
Polycarp nor the other martyrs die *for Christianismos* – that idea will
wait for Origen, who, of course, knows and uses 2 and 4 Maccabees.[49]

Remembering and forgetting

Finally, if the martyr literature is an act of 'remembering' it must
necessarily also be an act of 'forgetting': in all such narrative and construction of identity we have learned to ask for whom it speaks and
whom it silences. Those who, when given the chance to confess, fail to
do so, are the most harshly denied an existence. They have miscarried
or were stillborn; they are more dead than the martyrs who face death;
their only hope for life is if they are once again conceived and quickened,
rekindled for the church, the virgin mother; those who fail even this are
retrospectively condemned as 'never even having a trace of faith . . .
offspring of destruction' (Eusebius, *H.E.* V.1.45–48).[50] The narrative
permits the reader no other construction of the events, although the
later heated debate in the church about the lapsed suggests a more
contentious reality.[51] Similarly, in his *Dialogue with Trypho* Justin denies
the name 'Christian' to those who did so identify themselves but who
participated in idol sacrifices or ate food sacrificed to idols, perhaps in a
persecution context (*Dial.* 35). Yet others too are excluded by the
martyrological boundary: Eusebius reports that the account of Polycarp's
martyrdom included others too, not least that of Metrodorus, a

---

[48] 2 Macc. 6.6 is the exception that proves the rule; here it 'was not [possible] either to
observe sabbath or to keep the ancestral feasts or, in a word, (ἁπλῶς) to confess [oneself]
to be a Jew'; S. Cohen, *The Beginnings of Jewishness: Boundaries, Varieties, Uncertainties*
(University of California Press: Berkeley, 1999) 90–1 equates this with the prohibition of
circumcision in v. 10, but I take the ἁπλῶς as summing up what precedes – i.e. it is a
definition of observance.

[49] Origen, *Exhort. ad Mart.* does use χριστιανισμός as that for which the martyrs struggle
(e.g. 18; 29).

[50] I assume from context that this last named group are not the 'pagans' but 'failed
Christians'.

[51] See Cyprian, *de Lapsis*; Justin, *II Apol.* 2.14 asserts that neither denial nor avoidance of
confession are possible for 'the true Christian'.

Marcionite presbyter (*H.E.* IV.15.46): the loss of the account serves the same end of denying an existence, while also colluding with Justin's assertion that all such heretics fail the 'test' of a readiness to face martyrdom (*Apol.* 26.7).[52] Yet those who offered themselves, perhaps Montanists, are equally summarily dismissed (*Mart.Poly.* 4), while the celebration of Polycarp as prophet may also undermine Montanist claims to that charisma.[53] Thus Ignatius uses his readiness to die to refute the beliefs of those others whose Christology took such suffering less than seriously (*Trall.* 10; *Smyrn.* 4.2); while the tally of martyrs can be used in defence of the Quartodeciman position.[54] Martyrdom thus comes to function as a means for asserting and defining orthodoxy, and so for exercising control.[55] Saturus, the companion of Perpetua, has a vision in which the bickering bishop and presbyters are made to seek reconciliation from the martyrs, and perhaps face exclusion from the heavenly garden reserved for the latter (*Pass.Perpet.* 13). The stage is set for a struggle for power, not least over the atoning and intercessory power of the martyrs both before and after their actual death – and, it should be added, over women's access to such authority. By the creative commitment of them to writing, by their circulation, and by their preservation, the Martyr Acts become vehicles of power.

Martyrdom, text and Christian identity

This essay was not scheduled as a discussion of the martyr literature, but as exploring 'the beginning of "Christian" identity'. 'Christian' was deliberately in inverted commas, an acknowledgement of the problem that lies within the title. When and of whom may we use the label 'Christian'? The New Testament, notoriously, is far more sparing with the term than most of those who teach or write about it. And our problem is born out of the tension between, on the one hand, a literature which either does address, or which we have been schooled into reading

---

[52] The Syriac of Eusebius, *H.E.* IV.15.46 downplays the significance of Metrodorus's death; it is possible that there is also a covert 'discrediting' of Montanism in the *Martyrdom of Polycarp*: see Lieu, *Image and Reality*, 283.

[53] So G. Buschmann, *Martyrium Polycarpi – Eine formkritische Studie* (BZNW 70, de Gruyter: Berlin, 1994) 24–32, 181.

[54] See Lieu, *Image and Reality*, 77.

[55] For the continuing use of martyr stories to define and exclude, see M. Tilley, 'Scripture as an Element of Social Control: Two Martyr Stories of Christian North Africa', *HTR* 83 (1990) 383–97.

as if it did address, both individuals and communities as self-consciously involved in the creation of 'a new people', and, on the other, a growing historical and social sensitivity which drives us towards seeing both the non-communicating diversity within and beyond the 'New Testament churches', and the capacity to encompass diversity, perhaps even that diversity, within first- and early second-century 'Judaism'. It is in this world of bewildering diversity, whose structural shape is for the most part hidden from us, that we can no longer confidently plot the growth of 'Christian' ministry, doctrine or practice, as if in so doing we were telling the story of the origins of Christianity – a term yet even more rare in our earliest sources. Both 'Judaism' and 'Christianity' have come to elude our conceptual grasp; we feel sure that they are there, and can quote those 'others', outsiders, who were no less sure. How else are we to understand the *fiscus iudaicus*, how else to make sense of the death, if not of the myriads of whom Eusebius speaks, at least of some who would not let go of their conviction about Jesus, as they understood it? Yet when we try to describe, when we seek to draw the boundaries which will define our subject for us, we lack the tools, both conceptual and material. It seems to me equally justifiable to 'construct' 'Christianity' in opposition to 'Judaism' at the moment when Jesus 'cleansed the Temple', at least in the literary representation of that event, and to think of that separation only in the fourth century, stimulated by dramatic changes in access to power – and I could call to my defence advocates of both positions, no doubt determined by their own starting-points and definitional frameworks.

Our problem is, as I have just indicated, the literature. What we think of as 'early Christian literature', particularly but not only that enshrined within the New Testament – but what makes it non-Jewish? – constructs for us, and we suspect for its readers, an identity. We find ourselves torn between seeking to discern the as yet unformed hidden world behind the text, and recognizing that there is no such world, or at least not as accessible to us. If we try to describe the development of early Christianity as independent of, albeit witnessed to, by our texts, we are doomed to failure. When we look to the story of Jesus we are left with unanswered questions as to how the line is to be drawn between him and subsequent Christian self-understanding – something re-inforced by the paucity of explicit appeals to that story in the early literature, inspite of, or perhaps alongside, the attempts to use his story for communal legitimation in the Gospels. Certainly, we cannot imagine that first Jesus, the apostles, or Paul founded a religion, that the threefold ministry 'emerged', that certain doctrinal formulations were formulated, and that then the literature testified to these developments; even less can we conceive of some core essence, the true 'identity', independent of and prior to the diverse cultural manifestations of self-definition.[56] Rather, the literature participates in the attempt to give shape and content to the inchoate experiences and conflicting currents of practice which *we* label early Christianity.

The Martyr Acts offer us a glimpse into this process; perhaps more, because they are so highly rhetorically constructed, they invite us into it. We have become accustomed to construing all identity through such verbs as constructed, imagined, invented, remembered; I do not have to justify speaking of the drawing of boundaries, boundaries which exclude as well as include, while also providing points of trade, negotiation; of the building of a world or world-view which is assumed to be normative and which will eventually become normative; of the exploration of the symbols which constitute a shared culture. If all this is the recognizable stuff of identity-formation it is also the stuff of the martyr literature; not of that literature alone – the sword Perpetua drags to her throat is not the one which will slice open the Gordian knot of what makes a Christian a Christian – although she, or the text which constructs her, might think so. There is no single answer to our problem. I have been selective in choosing this literature, and selective again in what I have chosen from it – and not from reasons of the pressure of time alone. Yet again, this is not an *ad hoc* selectivity, for the Martyr Acts supply memory, commemoration, definition, a rationale for unity, and of course 'the Name', all of which is so poorly developed in earlier literature.

So what I want to draw from our exploration is a series of nodal points around which Christian identity is configured; and I leave to further discussion as to how these should be positioned.

Central is the act of public affirmation: we might suppose this implicitly conveys allegiance – to Christ; association – with others who claim the same allegiance; adherence – to articles of belief and behaviour. Yet, for the most part these implications are not exploited, except perhaps

---

[56] As attempted by B. Meyer, 'The Church in Earliest Christianity: Identity and Self-Definition', in *Christus Faber: The Master Builder and the House of God* (Pickwick: Allison Park, 1992) 149–69.

in the refusal to sacrifice which is conceived more as a refusal to negate that affirmation than as part of a articulated system of belief.[57] The association with others is ambiguous: they – the churches, the readers – draw their identity from the martyrs, not vice versa; the martyrs do not die for Christianity or for the church;[58] neither, as in the Jewish tradition, do they represent the restoration of a way of life against those who sought, even from within, to mutate it. The expanding concentric circles from local to universal are united only by their common gaze and by the refusal to allow any alternative construction of what they see; their unity is ensured by the unadorned *christianus/ christiana sum*. And, again, the derivation of 'Christian' from 'Christ' is all but ignored. The common sociological contrast between personal emotive and ideological transformation, and social conversion does not help us here.[59]

Perhaps what is crucial is the self-recognition and the determination involved in the resolute rejection of other possible identities. As we have seen, the balance between ascription and inscription is tipped decisively towards inscription: the freely chosen affirmation of an identity that, it is felt, cannot be otherwise. The exclusivity built into the martyr's confession and its consequences coalesces with the opposition to society and to the world. It is an opposition which subverts the social reality within which it perforce exists by refiguring both of them. We have seen the construction of an alternative set of values, a diametrically opposed interpretation of experience, a pattern of symbols which invert those that are familiar. Such a construction draws boundaries which are unmistakeable and indisputable – against the lawless, the violent, those bent on and destined for destruction. The boundaries are reinforced by a legitimation of cosmic dimensions. On the one hand this may be interpreted as a rationalization of experience: although it is difficult to know to what degree the sense of alienation from their pagan neighbours was the cause – Tacitus's *odium humani generis*[60] – or the consequence

---

[57] Contrast the defence of their refusal to obey the King by the seven brothers in 2 Macc. 7; 4 Macc. 8–14; *Lam.Rabb.* I. 50. The *Acts of Phileas* (= *P.Bodm.* XX) are most unusual in including a lengthy doctrinal discussion.

[58] But see above, p. 225 n. 48.

[59] Sociologically, this also invites some discussion as to the relationship between public explanatory speech and actual choices: see B. R. Slugowski and G. P. Ginsburg, 'Ego Identity and Explanatory Speech', in J. Shotter and K. Gergen, eds., *Texts of Identity* (Sage: London, 1989) 36–55.

[60] Tacitus, *Ann.* XV.44.

of the persecution; it also provided a justification for the maintenance of a world-view no longer sustained by an immediate eschatological expectancy. Yet the boundaries perhaps have to be mythicized precisely because for the most part there were few more tangible markers – as remarked by Trypho the Jew in his complaint to Justin that 'you do not distinguish your way of life from that of the Gentiles' (*Dial.* 10.3), the point at which, of course, the Jew could appeal to his or her own martyrological tradition.[61] Yet this is not to deny the continuities: the symbols are inverted because they are shared symbols – citizenship, nobility, vigour, a contest, the athletic prize, the crown. These continuities are important for perhaps they help us trace the transformation of a culture. Yet there are also other continuities in the cultural language through which these tales can be told, and so which shapes the experiences themselves as they enter memory – a language drawn from the Scriptures and from Jewish tradition. Such continuities have to be set both against and alongside that world-view which conceives of experience as the arena of a conflict with cosmological dimensions, encompassing powers both earthly and heavenly. The sociological function of such a world-view has often been described, but we should not be concerned with function alone, for this reconceived world-view will also lead to a transformation of the perception of the self.

We know all too well that what the literature offers us is self-evidently the voice of a minority, a minority which assumes the mantle of a majority; its writing is an act of power, and as such will silence others. Our danger always in listening to such voices is that we shall reinscribe their power, and their power to silence others. Some of those other voices I have referred to, voices no less belonging to the diversity of Christian experience in the early centuries, but with a less articulate role in the building of a collective memory. The picture I have drawn is itself easily subverted both by the texts themselves when more closely read, as well as by other literature. Where are the Jews whose traditions have helped shape these narratives, whose own narratives and conceptions of martyrdom perhaps continued to interact with those of the Christians in a common subculture, and, most important, the Jews against whom so many other texts would suggest Christian self-definition was achieved? And again, the Apologists offer alternative constructions

---

[61] Hence the importance of dietary rules in the Maccabean literature; see Rajak, 'Dying for the Law', 64–7.

of the continuities and discontinuities with so-called 'pagan' values, and alternative attempts to address the dilemmas of belonging to 'the world', attempts which claim a common discourse, inviting dialogue not annihilation. And in the intersticies of these texts we glimpse the lives of those others, even perhaps of the majority, for whom boundaries were also crossing points – between different groups of those who claimed the name 'Christian', between synagogue and church, between church and offerings to emperor and to *dis manibus*, or between all of these.

Bibliography

Alexander, L. 'Acts and Ancient Intellectual Biography', in B. W. Winter and A. D. Clarke, eds., *The Book of Acts in its Ancient Literary Setting* (The Book of Acts in its First Century Setting I, Paternoster: Carlisle/ Eerdmans: Grand Rapids, 1993) 31–63.

Alexander, P. '"The Parting of the Ways" from the Perspective of Rabbinic Judaism', in Dunn, ed., *Jews and Christians*, 1–25.

Amir, Y. 'The Term Ἰουδαισμός (*IOUDAISMOS*); A Study in Jewish-Hellenistic Self-Definition', *Immanuel* 14 (1982) 34–41.

Anderson, B. *Imagined Communities: Reflections on the Origins and Spread of Nationalism* (Verso: London and New York, 1991 [1983]).

Arazy, A. *The Appellations of the Jews (IOUDAIOS, HEBRAIOS, ISRAEL) in the Literature from Alexander to Justinian* (PhD, New York, 1977; Univ. Microfilms 78–3061).

Archer, L. 'Bound by Blood: Circumcision and Menstrual Taboo in Post-Exilic Judaism', in J. M. Soskice, ed., *After Eve: Women, Theology and the Christian Tradition* (Marshall Pickering: London, 1990) 38–61.

Archer, L. '"In thy blood live": Gender and Ritual in the Judaeo-Christian Tradition', in A. Joseph, ed., *Through the Devil's Gateway: Women, Religion and Taboo* (SPCK: London, 1990) 22–49.

Archer, L. *Her Price is Beyond Rubies* (JSOT.SS 60, JSOT Press: Sheffield, 1990).

Ascough, R. 'Translocal Relationships among Voluntary Associations and Early Christianity', *JECS* 5 (1997) 223–41.

Aspects du Judéo-Christianisme (Colloque de Strasbourg 23–5 avril 1964) (Presses Universitaires de France: Paris, 1965).

Babcock, W. S. 'MacMullen On Conversion: A Response', *The Second Century* 5 (1985/6) 82–9.

Baeck, L. 'Das dritte Geschlecht', in S. Baron and A. Marx, eds., *Jewish Studies in Memory of G. A. Kohut* (A. Kohut Memorial Foundation: New York, 1935) 40–6.

Balch, D. *Let Wives be Submissive: The Domestic Code in 1 Peter* (SBL.MS 26, Scholars Press: Atlanta, 1981).

Bamberger, B. J. *Proselytism in the Talmudic Period* (KTAV: New York, 1968 [1939]).

Barclay, J. '"Neither Jew nor Greek": Multiculturalism and the New Perspective on Paul', in Brett, ed., *Ethnicity and the Bible*, 197–214.

Barclay, J. 'Paul among Diaspora Jews: Anomaly or Apostate', *JSNT* 60 (1995) 89–120.

Barclay, J. *Jews in the Mediterranean Diaspora* (T&T Clark: Edinburgh, 1995).

Bardy, G. and Lefèvre, M., eds., *Hippolyte, COMMENTAIRE SUR DANIEL* (SC 14, Éditions du Cerf: Paris, 1947).

Bardy, G. *La Conversion au Christianisme durant les premiers siècles* (Théologie 15, Aubier: Paris, 1949).

Barnes, T. D. 'Legislation against the Christians', *JRS* 58 (1968) 32–50.

Barnes, T. D. 'Pre-Decian *Acta Martyrum*', *JTS* 19 (1968) 509–31.

Barnes, T. D. 'Tertullian's "*Scorpiae*"', *JTS* 20 (1969) 105–32.

Barrett, C. K. 'School, Conventicle, and Church in the New Testament', in K. Aland and S. Meurer, eds., *Wissenschaft und Kirche: Festschrift für E. Lohse* (Luther-Verlag: Bielfeld, 1989) 96–110.

Bartlett, J. R. *Jews in the Hellenistic World: Josephus, Aristeas, The Sibylline Oracles, Eupolemus* (Cambridge Commentaries on the Writings of the Jewish and Christian World 200 BC to AD 200. Cambridge University Press: Cambridge, 1985).

Barton, S. and Horsley, G. H. R., 'A Hellenistic Cult Group and the New Testament Churches', *JbAC* 24 (1981) 7–41.

Bauckham, R. 'Jews and Jewish Christians in the land of Israel at the time of the Bar Kochba war', in Stanton and Stroumsa, eds., *Tolerance and Intolerance*, 228–38.

Bauckham, R. *Jude and the Relatives of Jesus in the Early Church* (T&T Clark: Edinburgh, 1990).

Bauer, W. *Orthodoxy and Heresy in Earliest Christianity* (ET Fortress Press: Philadelphia, 1971) = *Rechtglaubigkeit und Ketzerei im ältesten Christentum* (Mohr: Tübingen, 1934 [1965]).

Baumeister, T. *Die Anfänge der Theologie des Martyriums* (MBTh 45, Aschendorff: Münster, 1980).

Baumeister, T. 'Das Martyrium in der Sicht Justins des Märtyrers', in E. Livingstone, ed., *Studia Patristica* XVII.2 (Blackwell: Oxford, 1982) 631–42.

Baumgarten, J. 'Does *TLH* in the Temple Scroll Refer to Crucifixion?', *JBL* 91 (1972) 472–81.

Benko, S. 'Pagan Criticism of Christianity during the First Two Centuries AD', *ANRW* II. 23. 2, 1055–188.

Benko, S. *Pagan Rome and the Early Christians* (Batsford: London, 1985).

Berger, P. *The Social Construction of Reality* (Doubleday: Garden City, 1966).

Bernstein, M. J. 'תלוי אלהים קללת כי (Deut 21:23): A Study in Early Jewish Exegesis', *JQR* 74 (1983) 21–45.

Bertram, G. 'Der Begriff "Religion" in der Septuaginta', *ZDMG* 12 (1934) 1–5.

Bertram, G. 'θεοσεβής, θεοσέβεια', *TDNT* III, 123–8.

Beyschlag, K. 'Das Jakobsmartyrium und seine Verwandten in der frühchristlichen Literatur', *ZNW* 56 (1965) 149–78.

Bibb, J. Field. *Women Towards Priesthood* (Cambridge University Press: Cambridge, 1991).

Bickermann, E. 'The Name of the Christians', *HTR* 42 (1949) 109–24.

Bieringer, R., Pollefeyt, D. and Vandecasteele-Vanneuville, F., eds., *Anti-Judaism and the Gospel of John* (Van Gorcum: Assen, 2000).

Bird, P. 'Images of Women in the Old Testament', in N. Gottwald, ed., *The Bible and Liberation* (Orbis: Maryknoll, 1983) 252–88.

Blumenkranz, B. 'Augustin et les Juifs – Augustin et le judaïsme', *Rech.Aug.* 1 (1958) 225–41.

Blumenkranz, B. 'Die christlich-jüdische Missionskonkurrenz (3. bis 6. Jahrhundert)', in *Juifs et Chrétiens, Patristique et Moyen Age* (Variorum: London, 1977) ch. 10 (reprinted from *Klio* 39 (1961) 227–33).

Bokser, B. *The Origins of the Seder* (University of California Press: Berkeley, 1984).

Bommes, K. *Weizen Gottes* (Theophaneia 27, P. Hanstein: Köln, 1976).

Boyarin, D. 'Martyrdom and the Making of Christianity and Judaism', *JECS* 6 (1998) 577–627.

Boyarin, D. 'Reading Androcentrism against the Grain: Women, Sex and Torah Study', *Poetics Today* 12 (1991) 29–53.

Boyarin, D. *Dying for God: Martyrdom and the Making of Christianity and Judaism* (Stanford University Press: Stanford, 1999).

Boyarin, D. *Intertextuality and the Reading of Midrash* (Indiana University Press: Bloomington, 1990).

Brändle, R. and Stegemann, E. 'The Formation of the First "Christian Congregations" in Rome in the Context of Jewish Congregations', in K. Donfried and P. Richardson, eds., *Judaism and Christianity in First-Century Rome* (Eerdmans: Grand Rapids, 1998) 117–27.

Bremmer, J. 'Why Did Early Christianity Attract Upper-Class Women?', in A. A. R. Bastiaensen, A. Hilhorst and C. H. Kneepkens, eds. *Fructus Centesimus: Mélanges offerts à Gerard J. M. Bartelink à l'occasion de son soixante-cinquième anniversaire* (Instr.Pat. XIX, Kluwer Academic: Dordrecht/Steenbrugis: Abbey of S. Peter, 1989) 35–47.

Brett, M., ed., *Ethnicity and the Bible* (BIS 19, Brill: Leiden, 1996).

Bronner, Leila L. *From Eve to Esther: Rabbinic Reconstructions of Biblical Women* (Gender and the Biblical Tradition, Westminster/John Knox: Louisville, 1994).

Brooks, R. and Collins, J. J., eds., *Hebrew Bible or Old Testament: Studying the Bible in Judaism and Christianity* (Notre Dame Press: Notre Dame, 1990).

Brooten, B. 'Judinnen zur Zeit Jesu', *ThQ* 161 (1981) 281–5.

Brooten, B. *Women Leaders in the Ancient Synagogue* (Scholars Press: Chico, 1982).

Brown, P. *The Body and Society: Men, Women, and Sexual Renunciation in Early Christianity* (Columbia University Press: New York, 1988).

Brown, R. E. *The Death of the Messiah* (Doubleday: New York/Chapman: London, 1994).

Bruce, F. F. 'The curse of the Law', in Hooker and Wilson, eds., *Paul and Paulinism*, 27–36.

Burchard, C. *Untersuchungen zu Joseph und Asenath* (WUNT 8, Mohr: Tübingen, 1965) .

Burrus, V. 'Word and Flesh: The Bodies and Sexuality of Ascetic Women in Christian Antiquity', *JFSR* 10 (1994) 27–51.

Buschmann, G. *Martyrium Polycarpi – Eine formkritische Studie* (BZNW 70, de Gruyter: Berlin, 1994).

Cairns, I. *Word and Presence: A Commentary on the Book of Deuteronomy* (Eerdmans: Grand Rapids/Handsel Press: Edinburgh, 1992).

Cameron, A. *Christianity and the Rhetoric of Empire: The Development of Christian Discourse* (Sather Classical Lectures 45, University of California Press: Berkeley, 1991) .

Castelli, E. A. and Taussig, H., eds., *Reimagining Christian Origins: A Colloquium Honoring Burton L. Mack* (Trinity Press International: Valley Forge, 1996).

Chadwick, H. *The Early Church* (Penguin: Harmondsworth, 1967).

Childs, B. S. *Introduction to the Old Testament as Scripture* (SCM Press: London, 1979).

Cohen, S. 'Crossing the Boundary and becoming a Jew', *HTR* 82 (1989) 13–33 (reprinted in *Beginnings of Jewishness*, 140–74).

Cohen, S. 'Menstruants and the Sacred in Judaism and Christianity', in S. Pomeroy, ed., *Women's History and Ancient History* (University of North Carolina Press: Chapel Hill, 1991) 273–99.

Cohen, S. 'Pagan and Christian Evidence on the Ancient Synagogue' in L. Levine, ed., *The Synagogue in Late Antiquity* (ASOR: Philadelphia, 1987) 159–81.

Cohen, S. 'Respect for Judaism by Gentiles according to Josephus', *HTR* 80 (1987) 409–30.

Cohen, S. 'The Origins of the Matrilineal Principle in Rabbinic Law', *AJSR* 10 (1985) 19–53 (reprinted in *Beginnings of Jewishness*, 263–307).

Cohen, S. 'The Rabbinic Conversion Ceremony', *JJS* 41 (1990) 177–203 (reprinted in *Beginnings of Jewishness*, 198–238).

Cohen, S. 'Those who say they are Jews and are not', in S. Cohen and E. Frerichs, eds, *Diasporas in Antiquity* (BJS 288, Scholars Press: Atlanta, 1993) 1–47 (reprinted in *Beginnings of Jewishness*, 25–68).

Cohen, S. *The Beginnings of Jewishness: Boundaries, Varieties, Uncertainties* (University of California Press: Berkeley, 1999).

Collins, J. J. *Between Athens and Jerusalem: Jewish Identity in the Hellenistic Diaspora* (Crossroad: New York, 1983).

Corrington, G. 'The "Divine Woman"? Propaganda and the Power of Chastity in the New Testament Apocrypha', *Helios* 13 (1987) 151–62.

Cranfield, C. E. B. ' "The Works of the Law" in the Epistle to the Romans', *JSNT* 43 (1991) 89–101.

Currey, G. *Tertulliani Libri Tres, De Spectaculis, De Idololatria, et De Corona Militis* (Cambridge University Press: Cambridge, n.d.).

d'Angelou, M. '*Abba* and "Father": Imperial Theology and the Jesus Traditions', *JBL* 111 (1992) 611–30.

Davidman, L. and Jacobs, J. 'Feminist Perspectives on New Religious Movements', in *Religion and the Social Order: The Handbook on Cults and Sects in America* 3B (JAIPress Inc.: Greenwich, 1993) 173–90.

Davies, A. T., ed., *AntiSemitism and the Foundations of Christianity* (Paulist Press: New York, 1979).

Davies, S. L. *The Revolt of the Widows: The Social World of the Apocryphal Acts* (Southern Illinois University Press: Carbondale, 1980).

Davies, W. D. *Paul and Rabbinic Judaism* (SPCK: London, 1948).

Dawson, L. L. 'Who Joins New Religious Movements and Why: Twenty Years of Research and What We Have Learned', *SR* 25 (1996) 141–61.

de Lange, N. *Origen and the Jews. Studies in Jewish Christian Relations in Third Century Palestine* (Cambridge University Press: Cambridge, 1976).

de Ste Croix, G. M. 'Why were Early Christians Persecuted?', reprinted in Finley, ed., *Studies in Ancient Society*, 210–49.

de Ste Croix, G. M. 'Why were Early Christians Persecuted? A Rejoinder', reprinted in Finley, *Studies in Ancient Society*, 256–62.

Dehandschutter, B. 'Le Martyre de Polycarpe et le développment de la conception du martyre au deuxième siècle', in E. Livingstone, ed., *Studia Patristica* 17.2 (Blackwell: Oxford, 1982) 659–68.

Dehandschutter, B. *Martyrium Polycarpi: Een literair-kritische Studie* (BETL 52, University of Leuven: Leuven, 1979).

Delaney, C. 'The Legacy of Abraham', in M. Bal, ed., *Anti-Covenant: Counter-Reading Women's Lives in the Hebrew Bible* (Almond Press: Sheffield, 1989) 27–41.

Dexinger, F. 'Beschneidung: III. Nachtalmudisches Judentum', *TRE* V. 722–4.

Dodds, E. R. *Pagan and Christian in an Age of Anxiety* (Cambridge University Press: Cambridge, 1965).

Dölger, F. 'Das Kampf mit dem Ägypter in der Perpetua-Vision. Das Martyrium als Kampf mit dem Teufel', *Antike und Christentum* 3 (Aschendorff: Münster, 1932) 177–88.

Droge, A. J., and Tabor, J. D. *A Noble Death: Suicide and Martyrdom among Christians and Jews in Antiquity* (Harper: San Francisco, 1992).

Dunn, J. D. G. 'Yet once more – "The Works of the Law"; A Response', *JSNT* 46 (1992) 99–117.

Dunn, J. D. G. *Galatians* (BNTC, A&C Black: London, 1993).

Dunn, J. D. G. *The Partings of the Ways* (SCM Press: London/Trinity Press International: Philadelphia, 1991).

Dunn, J. D. G., ed., *Jews and Christians: The Parting of the Ways AD 70 to 135* (WUNT 66, Mohr: Tübingen, 1992).

Edwards, C. *The Politics of Immorality in Ancient Rome* (Cambridge University Press: Cambridge, 1993).

Efroymson, D. 'The Patristic Connection', in Davies, ed., *AntiSemitism*, 98–117.

Egger, B. 'Looking at Chariton's Callirhoe', in J. R. Morgan and R. Stoneman, eds., *Greek Fiction: The Greek Novel in Context* (Routledge: London, 1994) 31–48.

Elliott, J. H. *A Home for the Homeless: A Sociological Exegesis of 1 Peter, Its Situation and Strategy* (SCM Press: London, 1982).

Esler, P. *Community and Gospel in Luke–Acts* (SNTS.MS 57, Cambridge University Press: Cambridge, 1987).

Feldman, L. 'Jewish "Sympathisers" in Classical Literature and Inscriptions', *TAPA* 81 (1950) 200–8.

Feldman, L. *Jew and Gentile in the Ancient World* (Princeton University Press: Princeton, 1993).

Feldmeier, R. 'The "Nation" of Strangers: Social Contempt and Its Theological Interpretation in Ancient Judaism and Early Christianity', in Brett, ed., *Ethnicity and the Bible*, 240–70.

Finley, M. I., ed., *Studies in Ancient Society* (Routledge & Kegan Paul: London, 1974).

Finn, T. 'The Godfearers Reconsidered', *CBQ* 47 (1985) 75–84.

Fitzmyer, J. 'Crucifixion in Ancient Palestine, Qumran Literature and the New Testament', *CBQ* 40 (1978) 493–513.

Foakes Jackson, F. J., ed., *The Parting of the Roads: Studies in the Development of Judaism and Early Christianity* (Arnold: London, 1912).

Fox, R. Lane *Pagans and Christians* (Penguin: Harmondsworth, 1986).

Frend, W. H. C. 'A Note on Tertullian and the Jews', in F. L. Cross, ed., *Studia Patristica X* (*TU* 107, Akademie Verlag: Berlin, 1970) 291–6.

Frend, W. H. C. *Martyrdom and Persecution in the Early Church* (Blackwell: Oxford, 1965).

Frend, W. H. C. *The Rise of Christianity* (Darton, Longman & Todd: London, 1984).

Friedländer, M. *Patristische und Talmudische Studien* (Breitenstein: Wien, 1878).

Gager, J. 'Jews, Gentiles and Synagogues in the Book of Acts', *HTR* 79 (1986) 91–9.

Gese, H. *Essays on Biblical Theology* (ET Augsburg: Minneapolis, 1981).

Gibson, E. *The 'Christians for Christians' Inscriptions of Phrygia* (Harvard Theological Studies 32, Scholars Press: Missoula, 1978).

Goehring, J. 'Libertine or Liberated: Women in the So-Called Libertine Gnostic Communities', in Karen L. King, ed., *Images of the Feminine in Gnosticism* (Studies in Antiquity and Christianity, Fortress Press: Philadelphia, 1988) 329–44.

Goodman, M. 'Jewish Proselytizing in the First Century', in Lieu, North and Rajak, eds., *Jews among Pagans and Christians*, 53–78.

Goodman, M. 'Jews, Greeks, and Romans', in idem, ed., *Jews in a Graeco-Roman World* (Clarendon Press: Oxford, 1998) 3–14.

Goodman, M. 'Nerva, the *Fiscus Iudaicus* and Jewish Identity', *JRS* 79 (1989) 40–4.

Goodman, M. *Mission and Conversion: Proselytizing in the Religious History of the Roman Empire* (Clarendon Press: Oxford, 1994).

Goodman, M. *Who was a Jew?* (Yarnton Trust for Oxford Centre for Postgraduate Hebrew Studies: Oxford, 1989).

Goodspeed, E. *Die ältesten Apologeten* (Vandenhoeck & Ruprecht: Göttingen, 1914).

Goulder, M. 'Silas in Thessalonica', *JSNT* 48 (1992) 87–106.

Goulder, M. 'Σοφία in Corinthians', *NTS* 37 (1991) 516–34.

Goulder, M. 'The Visionaries of Laodicaea', *JSNT* 43 (1991) 15–39.

Goulder, M. *A Tale of Two Missions* (SCM Press: London, 1994).

Grässer, E. 'Die Juden als Teufelssöhne in Johannes 8,37–47', in W. Eckert, N. Levinson and M. Stöhr, eds., *Antijudaismus im Neuen Testament?* (Kaiser: Munich, 1967) 157–70.

Haddad, Y. Y. and Findly, E. B. *Women, Religion and Social Change* (SUNY: Albany, 1985).

Hall, S. *Melito of Sardis On Pascha and Fragments* (OECT, Clarendon Press: Oxford, 1979).

Halperin, D. 'Crucifixion, the Nahum Pesher, and the Rabbinic Penalty of Strangulation', *JJS* 32 (1981) 32–46.

Handler, R. 'Is "Identity" a Useful Cross-cultural Concept?', in J. Gillis, ed., *Commemorations: The Politics of National Identity* (Princeton University Press: Princeton, 1994) 27–40.

Hare, D. *The Theme of Jewish Persecution of Christians in the Gospel according to St. Matthew* (SNTS.MS 6, Cambridge University Press: Cambridge, 1967) 66–79.

Harkins, P. *Saint John Chrysostom. Discourses Against Judaizing Christians* (Fathers of the Church. Catholic University of America: Washington, 1979).

Harris, J. R. *The Apology of Aristides* (Texts and Studies 1.1, Cambridge University Press: Cambridge, 1891).

Hayter, M. *The New Eve in Christ: The Use and Abuse of the Bible in the Debate about Women in the Church* (SPCK: London, 1987).

Heine, S. *Women and Early Christianity* (SCM Press: London, 1987).

Hengel, M. 'Die Synagogeninschrift von Stobi', *ZNW* 57 (1966) 145–83.

Hengel, M. *Crucifixion*, reprinted in *The Cross of the Son of God*, 93–185.

Hengel, M. *The Cross of the Son of God* (SCM Press: London, 1986).

Hengel, M. *The Son of God*, reprinted in *The Cross of the Son of God*, 1–90.

Henrichs, A. 'Pagan Ritual and the Alleged Crimes of the Early Christians', in P. Granfield and J. Jungmann, eds., *Kyriakon: Festschrift J. Quasten* (Aschendorff: Münster, 1970) I, 18–35.

Herford, R. T. *Christianity in Talmud and Midrash* (Williams & Norgate: London, 1903, reprinted KTAV: New York, n.d.).

Hertz, J., ed., *The Pentateuch and the Haftorahs* (Soncino Press: London, 1950).

Himmelfarb, M. 'Judaism and Hellenism in 2 Maccabees', *Poetics Today* 19 (1998) 19–40.

Hobsbawm, E. and Ranger, T., eds., *The Invention of Tradition* (Cambridge University Press: Cambridge, 1983).

Holdheim, S. *Geschichte der Enstehung und Entwicklung der jüdischen Reformgemeinde in Berlin* (Berlin, 1857).

Holfelder, H. 'Εὐσέβεια καὶ φιλοσοφία: Literarische Einheit und politischer Kontext von Justins Apologie', *ZNW* 68 (1977) 48–66; 231–51.

Hommel, H. 'Juden und Christen im kaiserzeitlichen Milet', *Sebasmata* II (WUNT 32, Mohr: Tübingen, 1984) 200–30 (reprinted from *Ist.Mitt.* 25 (1975) 167–95).

Hooker, M. and Wilson, S. G., eds., *Paul and Paulinism: Essays in Honour of C. K. Barrett* (SPCK: London, 1982).

Horbury, W. and Noy, D. *Jewish Inscriptions of Graeco-Roman Egypt* (Cambridge University Press: Cambridge, 1992).

Horbury, W. 'The Benediction of the *Minim* and early Jewish-Christian Controversy', *JTS* 33 (1982) 19–61 (reprinted in *Jews and Christians in Contact and Controversy* (T&T Clark: Edinburgh, 1998) 67–110).

Horgan, M. P. *Pesharim: Qumran Interpretations of Biblical Books* (CBQ.MS 8, Catholic Biblical Association: Washington, 1979).

Horsley, G. *New Documents Illustrating Early Christianity* 4 (1979) (Macquarie University: Sydney, 1987) .

Hruby, K. 'Exégèse Rabbinique et Exégèse Patristique', *RSR* 47 (1973) 341–69.

Hruby, K. *Juden und Judentum bei den Kirchenvätern* (Theologischer Verlag: Zurich, 1971).

Hübner, H. 'Vetus Testamentum und Vetus Testamentum in Novo Receptum. Die Frage nach dem Kanon des Alten Testaments aus neutestamentlicher Sicht', in I. Baldermann et al., eds., *Zum Problem des biblischen Kanons* (JBTh 3, Neukirchener Verlag: Neukirchen-Vluyn, 1988) 147–62.

Ilan, T. 'The Attraction of Aristocratic Women to Pharisaism during the Second Temple Period', *HTR* 88 (1995) 1–33.

Ilan, T. *Jewish Women in Greco-Roman Palestine: An Inquiry into Image and Status* (TSAJ 44, Mohr: Tübingen, 1995).

Juster, S. *Disorderly Women: Sexual Politics and Evangelicalism in Revolutionary New England* (Cornell University Press: Ithaca, 1994).

Karpp, H. 'Christennamen', *RAC* II, 1114–38.

Kilbourne, B. and Richardson, J. T. 'Paradigm Conflict, Types of Conversion and Conversion Theories', *Sociological Analysis* 50 (1988) 1–21.

Kimelman, R. '*Birkat Ha Minim* and the Lack of Evidence for an Anti-Christian Jewish Prayer in Late Antiquity', in E. P. Sanders, A. L. Baumgarten and A. Mendelson, eds., *Jewish and Christian Self-Definition*, II, *Aspects of Judaism in the Graeco-Roman Period* (SCM Press: London, 1981) 226–44.

Kinzig, W. '"Non-Separatists": Closeness and Co-operation between Jews and Christians in the Fourth Century', *VC* 45 (1991) 27–53.

Kippenberg, H. 'Die jüdische Überlieferungen als "patrioi nomoi"', in R. Faber and R. Schlesier, eds., *Die Restauration der Götter: Antike Religion und Neo-Paganismus* (Königshausen & Neumann: Würzburg, 1986) 45–60.

Klijn, A. F. J. and Reinink, G. J. *Patristic Evidence for Jewish Christian Sects* (NT.S 36, Brill: Leiden, 1973).

Kloppenborg, J. 'Egalitarianism in the Myth and Rhetoric of Pauline Churches', in Castelli and Taussig, eds., *Reimagining Christian Origins*, 247–63.

Kloppenborg, J. and Wilson, S. G. *Voluntary Associations in the Graeco-Roman World* (Routledge: London, 1996).

Kraabel, A. T. 'Greeks, Jews and Lutherans in the Middle Half of Acts', in G. Nickelsburg and G. MacRae, eds., *Christians Among Jews and Gentiles: Essays in Honor of Krister Stendahl* (Fortress Press: Philadelphia, 1986) 147–57.

Kraabel, A. T. 'Melito the Bishop and the Synagogue at Sardis: Text and Context', in D. G. Mitten, J. G. Pedley and J. A. Scott, eds., *Studies Presented to George M. A. Hanfmann* (P. von Zabern: Mainz, 1971) 77–85.

Kraabel, A. T. 'Synagoga Caeca: Systematic Distortion in Gentile Interpretations of the Evidence for Judaism in the Early Christian Period', in J. Neusner and E. S. Frerichs, eds., *'To See Ourselves as Others See Us': Christians, Jews, 'Others' in Late Antiquity* (Scholars Press: Chico, 1985) 219–46.

Kraabel, A. T. 'The Disappearance of the "God-fearers"', *Numen* 23 (1981) 113–26.

Kraabel, A. T. 'The Roman Diaspora: Six Questionable Assumptions', *JJS* 33 (1982) 445–64.

Kraemer, R. S. and d'Angelou, M. R., eds., *Women and Christian Origins* (Oxford University Press: New York, 1999).

Kraemer, R. S. 'Jewish Tuna and Christian Fish: Identifying Religious Affiliation in Epigraphic Sources', *HTR* 84 (1991) 141–62.

Kraemer, R. S. 'On the Meaning of the Term "Jew" in Graeco-Roman Inscriptions', *HTR* 82 (1989) 35–52.

Kraemer, R. S. *Her Share of the Blessings: Women's Religions among Pagans, Jews, and Christians in the Greco-Roman World* (Oxford University Press: New York, 1992).

Krauss, S. 'The Jews in the Works of the Church Fathers', *JQR* 5 (1892) 122–57; 6 (1893–4) 82–99, 225–61.

Lacocque, A. 'The "Old Testament" in Protestant Tradition', in L. Boadt, H. Croner and L. Klenicki, eds., *Biblical Studies: Meeting Ground of Jews and Christians* (Studies in Judaism and Christianity, Paulist Press: New York; 1980) 120–42.

Lampe, P. *Die stadtrömischen Christen in den ersten beiden Jahrhunderten* (WUNT 2.18, Mohr: Tübingen, 1989).

Lefort, L.-Th., ed., S. Athanase, *Lettres festales et pastorales en Copte* (CSCO Copt. 19, 20, Dubecq: Louvain, 1955).

Lemer, G. *The Creation of Patriarchy* (Oxford University Press: New York, 1986).

Levenson, J. D. 'The Universal Horizon of Biblical Particularism', in Brett, ed., *Ethnicity and the Bible*, 143–69.

Levenson, J. D. 'Theological Consensus or Historicist Evasion? Jews and Christians in Biblical Studies', in Brooks and Collins, eds., *Hebrew Bible or Old Testament*, 109–45.

Levine, A.-J. 'Second Temple Judaism, Jesus, and Women: *Yeast of Eden*', *Biblical Interpretation* 2 (1994) 8–33 , reprinted in A. Brenner, ed., *A Feminist Companion to the Hebrew Bible in the New Testament* (The Feminist Companion to the Bible 10, Sheffield Academic Press: Sheffield, 1996) 302–31.

Levine, E. *The Aramaic Version of the Bible. Contents and Context* (BZAW 174, de Gruyter: Berlin, 1988).

Lewis, I. *Ecstatic Religion: A Study of Shamanism and Spirit Possession* (Routledge: London, 1989 [1971]).

Lieu, J. M. 'Accusations of Jewish Persecution in Christian Sources', in Stanton and Stroumsa, eds., *Tolerance and Intolerance*, 279–98 = pp. 135–50 above.

Lieu, J. M. 'Anti-Judaism in the Fourth Gospel: Explanation and Hermeneutics' in Bieringer, Pollefeyt and Vandecasteele-Vanneuville, eds., *Anti-Judaism and the Fourth Gospel*, 126–43.

Lieu, J. M. 'Circumcision, Women and Salvation', *NTS* 40 (1994) 358–70 = pp. 101–14 above.

Lieu, J. M. 'Do God-fearers make Good Christians?', in Porter, Joyce and Orton, eds., *Crossing the Boundaries*, 329–45 = pp. 31–47 above.

Lieu, J. M. 'History and Theology in Christian Views of Judaism', in Lieu, North and Rajak, eds., *Jews among Pagans and Christians*, 79–96 = pp. 117–34 above.

Lieu, J. M. 'Reading in Canon and Community: Deut. 21.22–23, A Test Case for Dialogue', in D. Carroll, D. Clines and P. Davies, eds., *The Bible in Human Society: Essays in Honour of J. Rogerson* (JSOT.SS 200, Sheffield Academic Press: Sheffield, 1995) 317–34 = pp. 151–68 above.

Lieu, J. M. 'The Race of the Godfearers', *JTS* 46 (1995) 483–501 = pp. 49–68 above.

Lieu, J. M. *Image and Reality. The Jews in the World of the Christians in the Second Century* (T&T Clark: Edinburgh, 1996).

Lieu, J., North, J. and Rajak, T. *The Jews among Pagans and Christians* (Routledge: London, 1992).

Lindars, B. *New Testament Apologetic* (SCM Press: London, 1961).

Lüderitz, G. *Corpus Jüdischer Zeugnisse aus der Cyrenaika* (B.TAVO, Reichert: Weisbaden, 1983).

Luz, U. 'Kann die Bibel heute noch grudlage für die Kirche sein?' *NTS* 44 (1998) 317–39.

MacDonald, M. *Early Christian Women and Pagan Opinion* (Cambridge University Press: Cambridge, 1996).

MacMullen, R. 'Conversion: A Historian's View', *The Second Century* 5 (1985/6) 67–81.

MacMullen, R. *Christianizing the Roman Empire AD 100–400* (Yale University Press: New Haven, 1984).

Maier, J. *Jesus von Nazareth in der talmudischen Überlieferung* (Wissenschaftliche Buchgesellschaft: Darmstadt, 1978).

Mamorstein, A. 'Judaism and Christianity in the Middle of the Third Century', *HUCA* 10 (1935) 226–63.

Manns, F. *Bibliographie du Judéo-Christianisme* (Fransiscan Print Press: Jerusalem, 1979).

Marcovich, M., ed., *Pseudo-Iustinus: Cohortatio ad Graecos, De Monarchia. Oratio ad Graecos* (PTS 32, de Gruyter: Berlin, 1990).

Marcus, J. 'The Circumcision and the Uncircumcision', *NTS* 35 (1989) 67–81.

Martyn, J. L. *History and Theology in the Fourth Gospel* (2nd edn, Abingdon: Nashville, 1979 [1968]).

Mattingley, H. 'The Origin of the name *Christiani*', *JTS* 9 (1958) 26–37.

Mayer, G. *Die jüdische Frau in der hellenistisch-römischen Antike* (Kohlhammer: Stuttgart, 1987).

Mayes, A. D. *Deuteronomy* (NCB, Marshall, Morgan & Scott: London, 1979).

McLean, B. 'The Agrippinilla Inscription: Religious Associations and Early Church Formation', in B. McLean, ed., *Origins and Method: Towards a New Understanding of Judaism and Christianity: Essays in Honour of John C. Hurd* (JSNT.SS 86, JSOT Press: Sheffield, 1993) 238–70.

Meecham, H. G. *The Epistle to Diognetus: The Greek Text with Introduction, Translation and Notes* (Manchester University Press: Manchester, 1949).

Meeks, W. *The First Urban Christians* (Yale University Press: New Haven, 1983).

Merkelbach, R. 'Der griechische Wortschatz und die Christen', *ZPE* 18 (1975) 101–48.

Meyer, B. 'The Church in Earliest Christianity: Identity and Self-Definition', in *Christus Faber: The Master Builder and the House of God* (Pickwick Publications: Allison Park, Pennsylvania, 1992) 149–69.

Meyer, B. *The Early Christians: Their World Mission and Self-Discovery* (Michael Glazier: Wilmington, Delaware, 1986).

Millar, F. 'Review of Frend, *Martyrdom and Persecution*', *JRS* 56 (1966) 231–6.

Millar, F. 'The Jews of the Graeco-Roman Diaspora between Paganism and Christianity, AD 312–438', in Lieu, North and Rajak, eds., *Jews among Pagans and Christians*, 97–123.

Miller, P. C. *Dreams in Late Antiquity: Studies in the Imaginations of a Culture* (Princeton University Press: Princeton, 1994).

Mitchell, S. *Anatolia: Land, Men and Gods in Asia Minor* (Oxford University Press; Oxford, 1993) .

Momigliano, A. 'Review of M. Hengel, *Judentum und Hellenismus: Studien zu ihrer Begegnung unter besonderer Berüksichtigung Palästinas bis zur Mitte des 2. Jh. v. Chr.*, (J. C. B. Mohr: Tübingen, 1969)', *JTS* 21 (1970) 149–53.

Morgan, J. R. and Stoneman, R., eds., *Greek Fiction: The Greek Novel in Context* (Routledge: London, 1994).

Moxnes, H. '"He saw that the city was full of idols" (Acts 17:16) Visualizing the World of the First Christians', in D. Hellholm, H. Moxnes and T. Karlsen Seim, eds., *Mighty Minorities? Minorities in Early Christianity – Positions and Strategies: Essays in honour of Jacob Jervell on his 70th birthday* (Scandinavia University Press: Oslo, 1995) 107–31.

Muddiman, J. and G. *Women, the Bible and the Priesthood* (MOW: London, 1984).

Müller, M. 'Graeca sive Hebraica Veritas? The Defense of the Septuagint in the Early Church', *SJOT* 1989/1 (1989) 103–24.

Musurillo, H. *The Acts of the Christian Martyrs* (OECT, Clarendon Press: Oxford, 1972).

Neusner, J. *Judaism and Christianity in the Age of Constantine* (University of Chicago Press: Chicago, 1987).

Neusner, J., Green, W. S. and Frerichs, E. S., eds., *Judaisms and their Messiahs at the Turn of the Christian Era* (Cambridge University Press: Cambridge, 1987).

Novak, D. *The Election of Israel: The Idea of the Chosen People* (Cambridge University Press: Cambridge, 1995).

Noy, D. *Jewish Inscriptions of Western Europe, I, Italy, Spain, Gaul* (Cambridge University Press: Cambridge, 1993).

Noy, D. *Jewish Inscriptions of Western Europe, II, Rome* (Cambridge University Press: Cambridge, 1995).

O'Connor, J. Murphy, 'Lots of God-fearers: Theosebeis in the Aphrodisias Inscription', *RevBib* 99 (1992) 418–24.

Osborn, E. *Justin Martyr* (BHTh 47. Mohr: Tübingen, 1973).

Overman, J. A. 'The God-fearers: Some Neglected Features', *JSNT* 32 (1988) 17–26.

Paget, J. Carleton *The Epistle of Barnabas: Outlook and Background* (WUNT 2.64, Mohr: Tübingen, 1994).

Parkes, J. *The Conflict of the Church and the Synagogue* (Soncino Press: London, 1934).

Peritz, I. 'Women in the Ancient Hebrew Cult', *JBL* 17 (1898) 111–48.

Perkins, J. 'The Apocryphal Acts of the Apostles and the Early Christian Martyrdom', *Arethusa* 18 (1985) 211–30.

Perkins, J. *The Suffering Self: Pain and Narrative Representation in the Early Christian Era* (Routledge: London, 1995).

Petzl, G. *Die Inschriften von Smyrna* (Habelt: Bonn, 1982–7).

Philonenko, M. *Joseph et Aséneth: Introduction, Texte Critique, Traduction et Notes* (SPB 13, Brill: Leiden, 1968).

Plaskow, J. 'Bringing a Daughter into the Covenant', in C. Christ and J. Plaskow, eds., *Womanspirit Rising* (Harper & Row: New York, 1979) 179–84.

Portefaix, L. *Sisters Rejoice: Paul's Letter to the Philippians and Luke–Acts as Received by First-Century Philippian Women* (CB.NTSer 20, Almquist & Wiksell: Stockholm, 1988).

Porter, S. 'What Does it Mean to be "Saved by Childbirth?" (1 Timothy 2.15)?', *JSNT* 49 (1993) 87–102.

Porter, S. E., Joyce, P. and Orton, D. E., eds., *Crossing the Boundaries: Essays in Biblical Interpretation in Honour of Michael D. Goulder* (BIS 8, Brill: Leiden, 1994).

Porton, G. *GOYIM: Gentiles and Israelites in Mishnah-Tosefta* (BJS 155, Scholars Press: Atlanta, 1988).

Räisänen, H. *Jesus, Paul and Torah* (ET JSNT.SS 43, Sheffield Academic Press: Sheffield, 1992).

Rajak, T. and Noy, D. 'How to be an *ARCHISYNAGOGOS*', *JRS* 83 (1993) 75–93.

Rajak, T. 'Dying for the Law: The Martyr's Portrait in Jewish-Greek Literature', in M. J. Edwards and S. Swain, eds., *Portraits: Biographical Representation in the Greek and Latin Literature of the Roman Empire* (Clarendon Press: Oxford, 1997) 39–67.

Rajak, T. 'The Jewish Community and its Boundaries', in Lieu, North and Rajak, eds., *Jews among Pagans and Christians*, 9–28.

Reif, S. *Judaism and Hebrew Prayer* (Cambridge University Press: Cambridge, 1993).

Reventlow, H. G. *Problems of Biblical Theology in the Twentieth Century* (ET SCM Press: London, 1986).

Reynolds, J. and Tannenbaum, R. *Jews and Godfearers at Aphrodisias* (Cambridge Philological Society Suppl. 12, Cambridge, 1987).

Richardson, P. *Israel in the Apostolic Church* (SNTS.MS 10, Cambridge University Press: Cambridge, 1969).

Riches, J. 'Cultural Bias in European and North American Biblical Scholarship', in Brett, ed., *Ethnicity and the Bible*, 431–48.

Robert, L. *Hellenica* II (1946); *Hellenica* XI–XII (1960).

Robert, L. *Nouvelles Inscriptions de Sardes* I (Librairie d'Amérique: Paris, 1964).

Robertson, A. *Select Writings and Letters of Athanasius, Bishop of Alexandria* (The Nicene and Post-Nicene Fathers, T&T Clark: Edinburgh, reprinted 1991 [1891]).

Robinson, J. M., ed., *The Nag Hammadi Library in English* (Brill: Leiden, 1977).

Rogerson, J. 'Biblical Criticism', in R. J. Coggins and J. L. Houlden, eds., *A Dictionary of Biblical Interpretation* (SCM Press: London, 1990) 83–86.

Rogerson, J., ed., *Beginning Old Testament Study* (SPCK: London, 1983).

Roueché, C. *Performers and Partisans at Aphrodisias* (Society for the Promotion of Roman Studies: London, 1992).

Ruether, R. R. *Faith and Fratricide* (Seabury: New York, 1974).

Rutgers, L. 'Archaeological Evidence for the Interaction of Jews and non-Jews in Late Antiquity', *AJA* 96 (1992) 101–18.

Salvesen, A. *Symmachus in the Pentateuch* (JSS.M 15, University of Manchester: Manchester, 1991).

Sanders, E. P. *Paul and Palestinian Judaism* (SCM Press: London, 1977).

Sanders, J. A. 'Hebrew Bible *and* Old Testament: Textual Criticism in Service of Biblical Studies', in Brooks and Collins, eds., *Hebrew Bible or Old Testament*, 41–68.

Sawyer, J. F. A. *From Moses to Patmos: New Perspectives in Old Testament Study* (SPCK: London, 1977).

Saxer, V. *Bible et Hagiographie: Textes et thèmes bibliques dans les actes martyres authentiques des premiers siècles* (P. Lang: Berne, 1986).

Schiffman, L. 'The Conversion of the Royal House of Adiabene in Josephus and Rabbinic Sources', in L. Feldman and G. Hata, eds., *Josephus, Judaism and Christianity* (Brill: Leiden, 1987) 293–312.

Schnackenburg, R. *The Gospel according to St. John* (ET Crossroad: New York, 1968–83).

Schneider, A. *Le Premier Livre Ad Nationes de Tertullien* (Inst. Suisse de Rome: Neuchâtel, 1968).

Schoedel, W., ed., *Athenagoras: Legatio and De Resurrectione* (OECT, Clarendon Press: Oxford, 1972).

Scholer, D. M. 'Tertullian on Jewish Persecution of Christians', in E. Livingstone, ed., *Studia Patristica* XVII.2 (Blackwell: Oxford, 1982) 821–8.

Schürer, E. *Geschichte des jüdischen Volkes im Zeitalter Jesu Christi* (Hinrichs: Leipzig, 1901) (ET cf. Vermes, G.).

Schüssler Fiorenza, E. 'Remembering the Past in Creating the Future: Historical-Critical Scholarship and Feminist Biblical Interpretation', in A. Y. Collins, ed., *Feminist Perspectives on Biblical Scholarship* (SBL, Scholars Press: Chico, 1985) 43–63.

Schüssler Fiorenza, E. 'The Ethics of Biblical Interpretation: Decentering Biblical Scholarship', *JBL* 107 (1988) 3–17.

Schüssler Fiorenza, E. *In Memory of Her: A Feminist Theological Reconstruction of Christian Origins* (SCM Press: London, 1983).

Schwartz, R. *The Curse of Cain: The Violent Legacy of Monotheism* (University of Chicago Press: Chicago, 1997)

Seeberg, R. *Die Apologie des Aristides*, in T. Zahn, *Forschungen zur Geschichte des neutestamentlichen Kanons* V (Deichert: Erlangen, 1893) 161–411.

Segal, A. *Paul the Convert* (Yale University Press: New Haven, 1990).

Segal, A. *Rebecca's Children: Judaism and Christianity in the Roman World* (Harvard University Press: Cambridge, Mass., 1986).

Sheppard, A. R. R. 'Jews, Christians and Heretics in Acmonia and Eumeneia', *Anatolian Studies* 29 (1979) 169–80.

Sheppard, A. R. R. 'Pagan Cults of Angels in Roman Asia Minor', *Talanta* 12–13 (1980–81) 77–101.

Sherwin-White, A. N. 'Why were Early Christians Persecuted? An Amendment', reprinted in Finley, *Studies in Ancient Society*, 250–55.

Sherwin-White, A. N. *The Letters of Pliny: A Historical and Social Commentary* (Clarendon Press: Oxford, 1966).

Shotwell, W. *The Biblical Exegesis of Justin Martyr* (SPCK: London, 1963).

Siegert, F. 'Gottesfürchtigen und Sympathisanten', *JSJ* 4 (1973) 107–64.

Simon, M. *Verus Israel* (ET Littman Library, Oxford University Press: Oxford, 1986).

Skarsaune, O. *The Proof from Prophecy: A Study in Justin Martyr's Proof-text Tradition* (NT.S 56, Brill: Leiden, 1987).

Slingerland, H. D. *Claudian Policymaking and Early Repression of Judaism at Rome* (S. Florida Studies in the History of Judaism 160, Scholars Press: Atlanta, 1997).

Slugowski, B. R. and Ginsburg, G. P. 'Ego Identity and Explanatory Speech', in J. Shotter and K. Gergen, eds., *Texts of Identity* (Sage: London, 1989) 36–55.

Smallwood, E. M. 'The Alleged Jewish Tendencies of Poppaea Sabina', *JTS* 10 (1959) 329–35.

Smith, J. Z. 'Fences and Neighbours: Some Contours of Early Judaism', in W. S. Green, ed., *Approaches to Ancient Judaism* II (BJS 9, Scholars Press: Chico, 1980) 1–26.

Stanley, C. *Paul and the Language of Scripture* (SNTS.MS 74, Cambridge University Press: Cambridge, 1992).

Stanton, G. N. 'The Fourfold Gospel', *NTS* 43 (1997) 317–46.

Stanton, G. N. and Stroumsa, G. G., eds., *Tolerance and Intolerance in Early Judaism and Christianity* (Cambridge University Press: Cambridge, 1998).

Stanton, G. N. *The Gospels and Jesus* (Oxford University Press: Oxford, 1989)

Stark, R. *The Rise of Christianity* (Princeton University Press: Princeton, 1996).

Steck, O. *Israel und das gewaltsame Geschick der Propheten: Untersuchungen zur Überlieferung des deuteronomischen Geschichtsbildes im Alten Testamente, Spätjudentum und Urchristentum* (Neukirchener Verlag: Neukirchen-Vluyn, 1967).

Stern, M. *Greek and Latin Authors on Jews and Judaism* (Israel Acad. of Sci. and Hums.: Jerusalem, 1974–84).

Stewart, Z. 'Greek Crowns and Christian Martyrs', in E. Lucchesi and H. D. Saffrey, eds., *Antiquité Païenne et Chrétienne: Mémorial A. J. Festugière* (Cramer: Geneva, 1984) 119–24.

Stockmeier, P. 'Christlicher Glaube und antike Religiosität', *ANRW* 23. 2, 872–909.

Stockmeier, P. *Glaube und Religion in der frühen Kirche* (Herder: Freiburg, 1972).

Stowers, S. K. *Letter Writing in Greco-Roman Antiquity* (Westminster Press: Philadelphia, 1986).

Stuhlmacher, P. *Jesus of Nazareth – Christ of Faith* (ET Hendrikson: Peabody, 1993).

Syme, R. *Tacitus* (Clarendon Press: Oxford, 1958).

Tabbernee, W. *Montanist Inscriptions and Testimonies: Epigraphic Sources Illustrating the History of Montanism* (PMS 16, Mercer: Macon, 1997).

Taylor, M. *Anti-Judaism and Early Christian Identity: A Critique of the Scholarly Consensus* (SPB 46, Brill: Leiden, 1995)

Teubal, S. *Sarah the Priestess: The First Matriarch of Genesis* (Swallow: Athens, Ohio, 1984).

The Torah. The Five Books of Moses: A New Translation of the Holy Scriptures according to the Massoretic Text, First Section (Jewish Publication Society of America: Philadelphia, 1967).

Theissen, G. 'Christology and Social Experience', in *Social Reality*, 187–201.

Theissen, G. 'Some Ideas about a Sociological Theory of Early Christianity', in *Social Reality*, 257–87.

Theissen, G. *Social Reality and the Early Christians* (ET T&T Clark: Edinburgh, 1993).

Theissen, G. *The Social Setting of Pauline Christianity* (ET T&T Clark: Edinburgh, 1982).

Thompson, E. H. 'Beneath the Status Characteristic: Gender Variations in Religiousness', *JSSR* 30 (1991) 381–94.

Thompson, T. L. *The Bible in History: How Writers Create a Past* (J. Cape: London, 1999).

Thrall, M. *The Ordination of Women to the Priesthood: A Study of the Biblical Evidence* (SCM Press: London, 1958).

Tilley, M. 'Scripture as an Element of Social Control: Two Martyr Stories of Christian North Africa', *HTR* 83 (1990) 383–97.

Torjesen, K. J. *When Women Were Priests: Women's Leadership in the Early Church and the Scandal of their Subordination in the Rise of Christianity* (Harper: San Francisco, 1993).

Treu, K. *Die griechische Handschriften des neuen Testaments in der UdSSR* (*TU* 91, Akademie Verlag: Berlin, 1966).

Trevett, C. *Montanism: Gender, Authority and the New Prophecy* (Cambridge University Press: Cambridge, 1996).

van Bremen, R. *The Limits of Participation: Women and Civic Life in the Greek East in the Hellenistic and Roman Periods* (Gieben: Amsterdam, 1996).

van Damme, D. 'Gottesvolk und Gottesreich in der christlichen Antike', *Theologische Berichte III* (Benziger: Zurich, 1974) 157–68.

van Damme, D. 'ΜΑΡΤΥΣ – ΧΡΙΣΤΙΑΝΟΣ Überlegungen zur ursprünglichen Bedeutung des altkirchlichen Märtyretitels', *Freiburger Zeitschrift für Philosophie und Theologie* 23 (1976) 286–303.

van der Horst, P. W. 'A New Altar of a Godfearer?', *JJS* 43 (1992) 32–7.

van der Horst, P. W. *Ancient Jewish Epitaphs* (Pharos: Kampen, 1991).

van der Klaauw, J., ed., 'Diskussion', in J. W. van Henten et al., eds., *Die Enstehung der Jüdischen Martyrologie*, 220–61.

van Henten, J. W. 'Zum Einfluss jüdischer Martyrien auf die Literatur des frühen Christentums, II, Die apostolischen Väter', *ANRW* II, 27. 1, 700–23.

van Henten, J. W. *The Maccabean Martyrs as Saviours of the Jewish People: A Study of 2 and 4 Maccabees* (Leiden: Brill, 1997).

van Henten, J. W., Dehandschutter, B. and van der Klaauw, J., eds., *Die Enstehung der jüdischen Martyrologie* (SPB 38, Brill: Leiden, 1989).

van Minnen, P. 'Drei Bemerkungen zur Geschichte des Judentums in der griechisch-römischen Welt', *ZPE* 100 (1994) 253–8.

van Unnik, W. C. 'Der Fluch der Gekreuzigten: Deuteronomium 21,23 in der Deutung Justinus des Märtyres', in C. Andresen and G. Klein, eds., *Theologia Crucis: Signum Crucis. Festscrift für Erich Dinkler zum 70. Geburtstag* (Mohr: Tübingen, 1979) 483–99.

van Unnik, W. C. 'The Redemption in 1 Peter 1 18–19 and the Problem of the First Epistle of Peter', in *Sparsa Collecta* II (NT.S 30, Brill: Leiden, 1980) 1–82.

Vermes, G. 'Circumcision and Exodus IV. 24–26', in *Scripture and Tradition in Judaism* (SPB 4, Brill: Leiden, 1973) 178–92.

Vermes, G., Millar, F., et al., eds., E. Schürer, *The History of the Jewish People in the Age of Jesus Christ* (T&T Clark: Edinburgh, 1973–87).

von Harnack, A. *The Expansion of Christianity in the First Three Centuries* (ET Williams & Norgate: London, 1904–5).

von Kellenbach, K. *Anti-Judaism in Feminist Religious Writings* (Scholars Press: Atlanta, 1994).

von Rad, G. *Deuteronomy* (ET OTL, SCM Press: London, 1966).

Wagener, U. *Die Ordnung des 'Hauses Gottes': Der Ort von Frauen in der Ekklesiologie und Ethik der Pastoralbriefe* (WUNT 2.65, Mohr: Tübingen, 1994).

Walsh, J. J. 'On Christian Atheism', *VC* 45 (1991) 255–77.

Walzer, R. *Galen on Jews and Christians* (Oxford University Press: London, 1947).

Watson, F. B. *Text, Church and World. Biblical Interpretation in Theological Perspective* (T&T Clark: Edinburgh, 1994).

Wegner, J. R. *Chattel or Person: The Status of Women in the Mishnah* (Oxford University Press: New York, 1988).

Wendebourg, D. 'Die alttestamentlichen Reinheitsgesetze in der frühen Kirche', *ZKG* 95 (1984) 149–70.

White, L. M. 'Shifting Sectarian Boundaries in Early Christianity', *BJRL* 70 (1988) 7–24.

White, L. M. *Building God's House in the Roman World* (Johns Hopkins: Baltimore, 1990).

White, L. M., ed., *Social Networks in the Early Christian Environment: Issues and Methods for Social History* (Semeia 56, Scholars Press: Atlanta, 1992).

Wilcox, M. 'The "Godfearers" in Acts. A Reconsideration', *JSNT* 13 (1981) 102–22.

Wilcox, M. '"Upon the Tree" – Deut 21:22–23 in the New Testament', *JBL* 96 (1977) 85–99.

Wilken, R. 'Christianity as a Burial Society', in *The Christians as the Romans Saw Them* (Yale University Press: New Haven, 1984) 31–47.

Wilken, R. 'Collegia, Philosophical Schools and Theology', in S. Benko and J. J. O'Rourke, eds., *Early Church History: The Roman Empire as the Setting of Primitive Christianity* (Oliphants: London, 1972 [= *The Catacombs and the Colosseum* (1971)]) 268–91.

Wilken, R. *John Chrysostom and the Jews: Rhetoric and Reality in the Late Fourth Century* (University of California Press: Berkeley, 1983).

Wilken, R. *Judaism and the Early Christian Mind* (Yale University Press: New Haven, 1971).

Wilkens, U. 'Statements on the Development of Paul's View of the Law', in Hooker and Wilson, eds., *Paul and Paulinism*, 17–26.

Williams, M. H. 'Θεοσβής γάϱ ἦν: The Jewish Tendencies of Poppaea Sabina', *JTS* 39 (1988) 97–111.

Williams, M. H. 'The Jews and Godfearers Inscription from Aphrodisias – A Case of Patriarchal Interference in Early 3rd Century Caria?', *Historia* 41 (1992) 297–310.

Wills, L. *The Jewish Novel in the Ancient World* (Cornell University Press: Ithaca, 1995).

Wilson, B. *Patterns of Sectarianism* (Heinemann: London, 1967).

Wilson, S. G. 'Gentile Judaisers', *NTS* 38 (1992) 605–16.

Wilson, S. G. *Related Strangers: Jews and Christians 70–170 C.E.* (Fortress Press: Minneapolis, 1995).

Wimbush, V. '"... Not of this World ..." Early Christianities as Rhetorical and Social Formation', in Castelli and Taussig, eds., *Reimagining Christian Origins*, 23–36.

Winter, U. *Frau und Göttin* (Vandenhoeck & Ruprecht: Freiburg, 1983).

Wire, A. Clark *The Corinthian Women Prophets: A Reconstruction through Paul's Rhetoric* (Fortress Press: Minneapolis, 1990).

Wise, M. O. *A Critical Study of the Temple Scroll from Qumran Cave 11* (University of Chicago: Chicago, 1990).

Witherington, B. *Women in the Ministry of Jesus* (SNTS.MS 51, Cambridge University Press: Cambridge, 1984).

Wolfenson, L. B. 'Implications of the Place of the Book of Ruth in Editions, Manuscripts, and Canon of the Old Testament', *HUCA* 1 (1924) 151–78.

Wolter, M. 'Ethos und Identität in Paulinischen Gemeinden', *NTS* 43 (1997) 430–44.

Workman, H. *Persecution in the Early Church* (Epworth: London, 1960 [1906]).

Zahn, T. *Grundiss der Geschichte des neutestamentlichen Kanons* (Deichert: Leipzig, 1904).

Zeegers-Vander Vorst, N. *Les Citations des Poètes Grecs chez les Apologistes Chrétiens du IIe Siecle* (Rec. de Trav. d'Hist. et de Phil. 4.47, Bibliothèque de l'Université: Louvain, 1972).

General Index

Index of Modern Authors